DEFENDING
LEICESTERSHIRE
AND RUTLAND

DEFENDING
LEICESTERSHIRE
AND RUTLAND

MIKE OSBORNE

FONTHILL

Fonthill Media Language Policy

Fonthill Media publishes in the international English language market. One language edition is published worldwide. As there are minor differences in spelling and presentation, especially with regard to American English and British English, a policy is necessary to define which form of English to use. The Fonthill Policy is to use the form of English native to the author. Mike Osborne was born and educated in England; therefore British English has been adopted in this publication.

Fonthill Media Limited
Fonthill Media LLC
www.fonthillmedia.com
office@fonthillmedia.com

First published in the United Kingdom and the United States of America 2017

British Library Cataloguing in Publication Data:
A catalogue record for this book is available from the British Library

Typeset in 10.5pt on 13pt Minion Pro
Printed and bound by CPI Group (UK) Ltd, Croydon, CR0 4YY

Acknowledgements

Thanks are due to the following for information, access to sites, or permission to use photographs or other illustrations: Austin Ruddy; the Charley Heritage Group and Terry Sheppard; Lt-Col. Richard Chesterfield at Kendrew Barracks; Captain James Barringer at the Defence Animal Centre, Melton Mowbray; Ron Dane and Kerry Nimmons; Dr Mike Heyworth, CBA, York; Rachael Humphreys of Beaumanor Hall; Robin Jenkins and the staff at the County Archive Office; Squire de Lisle of Garendon; Rose Mollett of Tolethorpe; Mr Orton of Hinckley; RSM Sue Roberts at St George's Barracks; Dr William Ward; and Helen Wells, Historic Environment Record Officer for Leicestershire and Rutland.

My thanks also go to Alan Sutton, Jay Slater, and Joshua Greenland at Fonthill Media for their enthusiasm and professionalism. As ever, I owe a debt of gratitude to Pam, my wife, for her encouragement and interest, help with research, and technical support.

CONTENTS

List of Abbreviations

AA	anti-aircraft
AA	Automobile Association
AALMG	Anti-aircraft light machine-gun
ACF	Army Cadet Force
ADTTT	Air Defence Tactical Training Theatre (Rapier dome-trainer)
AFV	Armoured Fighting Vehicle
AOP	Air Observation Post (light aircraft for artillery direction)
ARC	Army Reserve Centre (formerly TAC)
ARP	Air Raid Precautions
ASD	Ammunition Supply Depot (army)
ASP	Aircraft Servicing Platform
A/T	anti-tank
ATA	Air Transport Auxiliary (civilian ferry pilots)
ATC	Air Training Corps
ATS	Auxiliary Territorial Service (1938–49, then WRAC)
AWA	Armstrong Whitworth Aircraft
BCF	British Concrete Federation (maker of prefabricated huts)
BEF	British Expeditionary Force (First and Second World Wars)
BHQ	Battle Headquarters
CBA	Council for British Archaeology
CCF	Combined Cadet Force (successor to Junior OTC)
CD	Civil Defence
COD	Central Ordnance Depot
CRO	Civilian Repair Organisation (aircraft repair workshops)
DAC	Defence Animal Centre (Melton Mowbray)
DFW3	War Office Directorate of Fortifications & Works, Dept.3
DL	Defended Locality
(E & R)(S)FTS	(Elementary & Reserve)(Service) Flying Training School
ECM	Electronic Counter-measures
ELOINT	electronic intelligence

FAA	Fleet Air Arm (reformed in 1938)
GCI	Ground Control Interception (radar directing fighter aircraft)
GHQ	General Headquarters (GHQ Line, GHQ Reserve etc.)
GOC	General Officer Commanding
GPO	General Post Office
HAA	Heavy Anti-aircraft
H(G)CU	Heavy (Glider) Conversion Unit (pilot training)
ICBM	Inter-Continental Ballistic Missile (e.g. Polaris, Trident)
IRBM	Intermediate-Range Ballistic Missile (e.g. THOR)
ITC	Infantry Training Centre
LAA	Light Anti-aircraft
LADA	London Air Defence Area (AA scheme First World War into 1930s)
LDV	Local Defence Volunteers, later Home Guard
MAD	Mutually Assured Destruction (nuclear exchange)
MAFF	Ministry of Agriculture, Fisheries & Food (post-Second World War)
MAP	Ministry of Aircraft Production (Second World War)
MOD	Ministry of Defence
MT	Motor Transport
MU	Maintenance Unit (RAF units supplying aircraft & munitions)
NFS	National Fire Service (Second World War)
OCTU	Officer Cadet Training Unit
OCU	Operational Conversion Unit (pilot and aircrew training)
ORP	Operational Readiness Platform
OS	Ordnance Survey
OTC	Officer Training Corps (school or university cadet corps)
OTU	Operational Training Unit (RAF Bomber/Training Commands)
PIAT	Projector Infantry Anti-Tank (bazooka-type weapon)
PBX	Private Branch Exchange (telephones)
pdr	pounder (as in weight of projectile) 1 lb = 454 g
POW	Prisoner of war
RAuxAF	Royal Auxiliary Air Force (until 1957)
RAF	Royal Air Force (from 1 April 1918)
RAFVR	Royal Air Force Volunteer Reserve
RAMC	Royal Army Medical Corps
(R)AOC	(Royal from 1918) Army Ordnance Corps (until 1993)
RAPC	Royal Army Pay Corps (from 1992, Adjutant General's Corps)
(R)ASC	(Royal from 1918) Army Service Corps
RAVC	Royal Army Veterinary Corps
RCAF	Royal Canadian Air Force
REME	Royal Electrical and Mechanical Engineers (formed 1942)
RFA	Royal Field Artillery
RFC	Royal Flying Corps (up to 31 March 1918)
RHA	Royal Horse Artillery

RHQ	Regimental Headquarters
RLC	Royal Logistic Corps (from 1993)
RNAS	Royal Naval Air Service (until 31 March 1918)
(R)OC	(Royal from 1941) Observer Corps
ROF	Royal Ordnance Factory
RSG	Regional Seat of Government
SAA	small arms ammunition
SAC	Strategic Air Command (USAF)
SAGW	Surface to Air Guided Weapon (e.g. Bloodhound)
SIGINT	signals intelligence
SIP	Self-Igniting Phosphorus (grenade)
S/L	searchlight
SMLE	Short Magazine Lee Enfield (.303-inch rifle)
SOE	Special Operations Executive
STS	Special Training School (SOE)
TA	Territorial Army (from 1920–39 and 1947–2014)
TAC	Territorial Army Centre (drill hall 1947–2014, see ARC)
TAFA	Territorial & Auxiliary Forces Association
tb	temporary brick (single brick with buttresses in RAF buildings)
TDS	Training Depot Station
TF	Territorial Force (from 1908–1918)
TNA	The National Archive (Kew)
TTTE	Tri-National Tornado Training Establishment (Cottesmore)
UKWMO	United Kingdom Warning & Monitoring Organisation
UP	un-rotated projectile (as in Z battery, AA rockets)
USAAF	United States Army Air Force (Second World War)
USAF(E)	United States Air Force (Europe) (post-Second World War)
VAD	Voluntary Aid Detachment (First World War)
VCR	Visual Control Room (atop a watch office)
VP	Vulnerable Point
VTC	Volunteer Training Corps (First World War Home Guard)
WAAF	Women's Auxiliary Air Force (later WRAF)
WOYG	War Office 'Y' Group (radio interception)
WRAC	Women's Royal Army Corps (from 1949–92)
W(R)VS	Women's (Royal) Voluntary Service

Introduction

One could be forgiven for thinking that the counties of Leicestershire and Rutland, nestling in the centre of the country, should have been far removed from military activity. In actual fact, Leicestershire's position between two of Roman Britain's primary arteries, Watling Street and Ermine Street, and crossed by the Fosse Way, suited it as a springboard for campaigns of conquest. Leicester was one of the Five Boroughs of the Danelaw; was so much fought over in the Anarchy that two of the principals agreed a Demilitarised Zone; and as a centre of Lancastrian power, it became a focal point in the Wars of the Roses, seeing Richard III set off for Bosworth Field and receiving his battered corpse for anonymous burial. The siege of Leicester towards the very end of the first Civil War was the penultimate act in the drama that saw Charles I defeated at Naseby. Rutland has also enjoyed prominence in military developments. Early in the French wars, troops of volunteer cavalry (the first in Britain) were formed in Oakham and, moreover, provided with their own riding school, the first ever such dedicated building. During the Cold War, THOR nuclear missiles, Bloodhound surface-to-air guided missiles, and bomber aircraft carrying Britain's nuclear deterrent were all based in the county.

During the Defence of Britain Project—the systematic recording of twentieth-century defence-related sites carried out in the 1990s—some surprising activities came to light. The 'Y' Station at Beaumanor Hall, where dozens of ATS listeners supplied enemy radio intercepts to the code-breakers at Bletchley Park, was one. Another is highlighted by a painted map that occupies a whole wall of the estate office at Garendon. This shows the country lanes of much of Leicestershire littered with roadside dumps of bombs, shells, and chemical weapons—the last, fortunately, was never used, but they were all stockpiled as preparation for the operations that accompanied the D-Day landings.

These two counties, therefore, represent a microcosm of our crowded islands. Standing alongside each other are Norman earthworks and grand fortified palaces; airfields and anti-invasion defences; the location of Whittle's jet engine development; and some of the factories that drove Britain's world-beating aviation industry. Almost every category of military site is present. The land-locked nature of our counties may have limited this inventory in one way, but it made possible those activities best-conducted out of an enemy's gaze: the training of soldiers, aircrew, and spies; secret developments such as Whittle's; the hush-hush 'Y' Group intercept operation; and the deployment of nuclear weapons. The wide open spaces of the east Midlands also afforded great armies, whether Vikings, Yorkists, or Royalists, the room to assemble, to manoeuvre, and to settle the affairs of state.

Leicestershire and Rutland enjoy a rich and varied military landscape, which deserves greater recognition. In this book, I have attempted to explore and explain that richness and variety by describing them in their social, historical, architectural, and military contexts.

Mike Osborne
June 2017

1

Leicestershire and Rutland before 1066

Prehistoric Camps, Forts, and Linear Earthworks

In Iron Age times Leicester, though a tribal centre of the territory of the Corieltauvi, was subordinate to Old Sleaford in Lincolnshire. These lands extended northward as far as the River Humber and abutted the lands of the Iceni on the Fen-edge to the east. There are a number of probable and confirmed Iron Age forts or enclosures in our counties but only two of any real significance: Breedon on the Hill and Burrough on the Hill, or Burrough Walls, with only the latter still projecting signs of its former glory. From earlier times, a Neolithic causewayed enclosure has been discovered by geophysical survey at Husbands Bosworth, and a Bronze Age camp at Woodhouse. The causewayed enclosure at Husbands Bosworth consists of two concentric ditches, enclosing an oval area of around 3.75 acres (1.5 hectares), interrupted by the eponymous causeways. A second, slightly larger example, interpreted from aerial photography, has been inferred at Appleby Magna. These monuments are little-understood and were most likely constructed for purposes other than the overtly or specifically defensive. Near Woodhouse, Beacon Hill Camp consists of a single bank and ditch ringing the hill-top, standing 325 feet (100 m) above sea-level. A hoard of Bronze Age material, discovered on the site, may provide clues to its date.

The purpose of Iron Age forts is no clearer than that of forts from earlier eras. They appear to have performed a variety of functions, which included defence against attack by invaders or neighbours; venues for tribal or clan celebrations or other gatherings; secure storage for agricultural surplus; and a focus for seasonally linked ritual or other spiritual activity. Although there is often evidence of hut-circles, it is quite possible that their residential occupation was only intermittent, possibly seasonal, or in times of emergency or perceived danger. Breedon on the Hill at 806 feet (248 m) and Burrough Walls at 690 feet (210 m) above sea-level occupy two of the highest points in the counties, and this both highlights the symbolic nature of such prominence and emphasises those defensive considerations that might influence dominance over the surrounding area. The bulwarks at Breedon on the Hill is a univallate fort dating from the fourth or third century BC, and was occupied through to the Roman period. Due to ongoing quarrying, the bank and ditch survive only on the west side. The entrance lay in the middle of the western side, approached via a zig-zag cobbled track up the hill, passing beneath the southern rampart, then entering the in-turned gate passage. The core of the rampart consisted of rubble behind heaped earth or turf. It was revetted at the front with drystone walling, with timber uprights about 6 feet (1.85 m) apart. At some later date, the rampart has been raised by some 18 inches (0.45 m) of earth and stones, capped by turf. Traces of hut circles and storage pits were excavated in the 1960s. The site was subsequently occupied by a Saxon monastery, now represented only by the remarkable sculptures housed in the entirely later church.

At Burrough Walls, a much better idea of the shape and extent of an Iron Age hillfort may be gained. Occupied from 200 BC into late-Roman times, with a peak of activity between 100 BC and AD 50, the fort, enclosing an area of 12 acres (5 hectares), is perched on a limestone promontory, exploiting a naturally strong defensive position with steep falls on three sides. On the lip of the hill, this natural strength has been enhanced by a single bank of stone and turf, a ditch, and a strongly defended entrance. The neck of the promontory, on the fourth side, has been quarried for stone and this has produced an impressive ditch in front of the entrance. The slope of the hill has been scarped to increase its steepness; the ramparts rise 10 feet (3 m) above the interior of the fort. The ditch on the north has a 16–20-foot (5–6-m) deep counter-scarp. The banks of hillforts are usually composed of the spoil from the surrounding ditch and, at Burrough Walls, excavation has uncovered two different construction methods. On the northern side, layers of beaten earth and rubble were laid over a stone core to form an inward-sloping bank without revetment. On the west, a quite different method was used. Here, although the core was the same, drystone walls were added to both inner and outer faces of the rampart to act as revetments. The presence of different construction methods on the same site for no obvious reason may indicate different building periods or attempts to repair or strengthen the defences. Ramparts were often reinforced with a framework of timber posts and crosspieces forming an interior scaffold, but here there is no evidence for that. The gateway on the south-east is in-turned so that anyone entering what is, in effect, a funnel, extending 150 feet (45 m) into the interior of the fort, will be overlooked on both sides by ramparts still standing over 6 feet (2 m) high, from which missiles could be thrown. This passage was added to an existing simple gateway. The initial modification consisted of banks made of iron-stone rubble contained by dry-stone walls. Subsequently, these inner banks were widened by building lateral ribs of large boulders, then filled with rubble, and finished off with layers of clay to hold the whole structure together with the sides of the entrance passage faced with drystone walling. This passage incorporated a stone-built guard chamber, 15 × 33 feet (5 × 10 m) inside the gate. The excavator suggests that there may be a corresponding one on the opposite side of the passage, as yet unexcavated. Similar examples of this sophisticated arrangement, improving on the usual dog-leg route through the ramparts of a barbican, appear in forts on the Welsh borders and in the Cotswolds. The banks will have been crowned by timber palisades, possibly surmounted by fighting platforms supported on timber posts embedded in the bank, with similar construction techniques being applied to the defences of the gateway where deep postholes suggest that a robust pair of timber gates were hung at the inner end of the gate passage.

The garrison, necessary to effectively defend such an extensive perimeter, would have been impossible to assemble unless the tribe's total manpower resources were

Burrough on the Hill, Burrough Walls hillfort: the ramparts of the in-turned entrance.

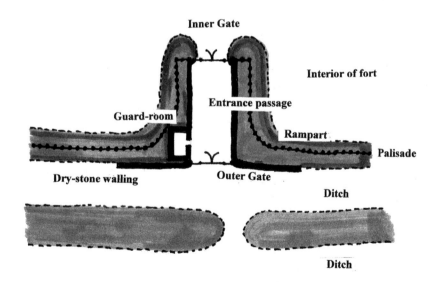

BURROUGH-on-the-HILL Iron Age Fort
Sketch-plan to show the defences of the entrance

Burrough on the Hill, Burrough Walls hillfort: a reconstructed plan of the entrance.

concentrated together at once. This would suggest that it would only have been in times of dire emergency that families and livestock were gathered inside the camp, and every available man mustered for its defence. In the interior of the camp, around 200 storage pits have been located, along with the curving traces of hut-circles. All these discoveries would tend to confirm that the camp was decidedly defensible and was used, at different times, as a storage facility with some residential presence.

Other probable Iron Age sites include Life Hill near Billesdon, Ridlington (R), and Bury Camp at Ratby, where a defensive bank encloses a sub-rectangular area of 7½ acres (3 hectares). On the hill of Robin-a-Tiptoe at Tipton-on-the-Hill is a possibly unfinished hillfort. The medieval churches of both Bringhurst and Market Overton (R) are set within rectangular, pre-historic enclosures: that at Bringhurst being large enough to enclose farmsteads as well, and at Market Overton, set high on the ridge. Scraps of Iron Age pottery from Appleby Magna's triple-ditched enclosure, and finds of a similar age from Belton Moat, a small circular earthwork, all suggest further such sites, and a site south-east of Dunster Barn at Lockington may be yet another.

King Lud's Entrenchments at Croxton Kerrial, although formerly believed to be post-Roman in date, may represent a further monument type from the Bronze Age. Despite a lack of archaeological evidence, this dyke is now considered as part of a system of boundary ditches, here marking the boundaries between Leicestershire and Lincolnshire, and running from Northamptonshire to the River Humber. King Lud, though not in the same ubiquitous league as Cromwell or King Arthur, nevertheless enjoys a significant presence in the landscape. A further possible candidate for dyke status, Anstey Park Pale, probably marks a medieval hunting park.

Roman Forts, Fortified Settlements, and Small Towns

In the early years of the Roman conquest, AD 45–60, the Fosse Way initially formed the western edge of Roman occupation, and then the start-line for further westward expansion up Watling Street. These two Roman roads, along with Ermine Street, which borders our counties on the east, supplied the strings on which forts were threaded like beads. The presence of defences often served as recognition of the importance of a place to the Roman government, particularly if its location was on a strategic road. Small Roman towns generally lay around 10 miles (16 km) apart, and many had originated as forts. A number of such sites meeting these criteria can be found in Leicestershire and Rutland.

At Wigston Parva, on the eastern verge of Watling Street, is a small fort dating from the time that the Romans first arrived in the area. It was of standard design, roughly square with a gate in the middle of each side. The rampart was around 8 feet (2.5 m) high with a regulation military V-shaped ditch in front. The gates were twin portals 20 feet (6 m) wide and were made of timber. Each gate tower was supported on eight posts, evidenced by their postholes. Slots, originally packed with stones, appear to provide evidence of cross-bracing. Oddly, in one of the two gates excavated, one tower stood a little forward of the other.

Other forts on Watling Street included Witherley/Mancetter (Manduessedum); High Cross (Venonae); and Caves Inn/Shawell (Tripontium). At Mancetter, there is evidence for a large military establishment, probably another early fort on the west side of Watling Street but apparently spreading eastwards. High Cross is closer than Wigston Parva to the actual junction of the Fosse Way and Watling Street, long recognised as a Roman site producing building rubble, tesserae, and pottery. Aerial photography has revealed a small, double-ditched enclosure round the road junction. There is evidence of occupation from the late first to the fourth century, but no structures that might be described as specifically military. At the other end of our counties, Great Casterton, very close to Ermine Street, also began life as an auxiliary fort of the Claudian era and was occupied into the AD 80s. Its typical playing-card shape still shows up in the crop-marks to the north-east of the later Roman town. In AD 60–70, its area was reduced and new defences constructed, which included the Southeast Gate. Like that at Wigston Parva, this consisted of two timber towers, evidenced by the two sets of six postholes that held their vertical supports. A rampart walk may have occupied a timber walkway above the twin entrance passageways. It is likely that these gates may have been recessed to create a killing zone in front of them, overlooked by the flanking towers.

Caves Inn/Shawell (Tripontium) stands where Watling Street crosses a stream, and it consists of a defended area of around 3 acres (1.2 hectares), bounded by a ditch 14 feet (4.3 m) wide and 10 feet (2.5 m) deep. It has been dated to the early-fourth century and thus it represents an example of a *burgus*, one of a chain of forts built to safeguard the Empire's most important roads against the encroachments of barbarian raiders. Tripontium, mentioned in the Imperial guidebook, also had an earlier *mansio*, which was a fusion of post office, hotel for official travellers, and town hall. The fort ditch was backfilled soon after it was first dug, but use of the *mansio* continued into the fifth

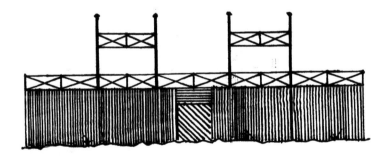

GREAT CASTERTON Roman Fort
Sketch to show the likely configuration of
one of the four gateways of the early fort

Great Casterton: a reconstruction of how the Roman fort's gateway might have looked.

century. Possibly, there were not enough troops available to garrison the fort as they were needed on the vulnerable coasts of the Saxon Shore. A further *burgus* may be represented by the later earthwork enclosure at Mancetter (Manduessudum), which is superimposed over earlier earthworks and contains buildings from the fourth century.

There are other small Roman towns that exhibit less evidence for their origination in forts. Medbourne, on the road from Leicester to Godmanchester and Cambridge, threw up a scatter of coins and traces of a high status building with a tessellated pavement. Ibstock/Ravenstone is aligned along a Roman road that joins Leicester to Ryknild Street somewhere around Walton-on-Trent (Staffordshire). There is both excavated and photographic evidence for a settlement at Thistleton/Market Overton with domestic, industrial, and religious structures. Early references to a defended area with gates and a wall 4-foot (1.3-m) thick point to the existence of either a fort, town defences, or both. Market Harborough may also have had its origins as a defended Roman settlement, but Willoughby-on-the-Wolds (Vernemetum), on the Fosse Way north of Leicester, always remained an undefended roadside settlement. Based on the intervals between Roman military posts, Bardon, on the route between Leicester and Derby via Melbourne (Derbyshire), has been inferred as the probable site of a Roman fort. Sawley 'fort', on the south bank of the Trent (SK478307), has been regarded as Roman or even Civil War in origin, but archaeological investigation has shown it to have been a refuge, located on the only available dry ground in times of flood. There have been no finds of pottery or anything else, given that this has always been only a very temporary refuge.

Roman Town Defences

The foundation of the new Roman town of Leicester (Ratae Corieltauvorum), after AD 43, marked a relocation of the Corieltauvi centre of power from Old Sleaford. Ratae developed as a settlement providing a focus for Roman Government, a base for the Roman Army, and a market for agricultural surplus. As the army moved west and north, by the end of the first century, its military importance had declined. Evidence of industrial activity in the second century, but less in the fourth century, suggests that the town had become less utilitarian and more symbolic of Roman dominance. There are strong reasons for thinking that Ratae functioned as a legionary fortress, even if for only a short while, before the centre of gravity moved to York by around AD 70. The ditch of a fort has been found, but whether this reflects the size and status of a major fortress is as-yet unknown. The town was laid out *c.* AD 100 as an almost square enclosure measuring 600 × 700 yards, with the River Soar as its western side. The area enclosed 105 acres (42 hectares) and was larger than that of Lincoln, for instance, suggesting that more of the poorer areas were also included in the defended area alongside the grander civic and mercantile quarters. The town defences appear to have been built in the late-second to early third century. Some stretches of the bank and wall were apparently contemporaneous as at Great Casterton (R) and elsewhere, but it would seem likely that most of the stone wall would have been inserted into the bank at a later date, as was done at neighbouring towns in Nottinghamshire or at Alcester (Warwickshire). The rampart bank was 20 feet (6 m) wide and composed of a mixture of sand and gravel over a metre in height, topped by a wall of stacked turves. The remains of wooden stakes have been found suggesting that this rampart might have been revetted. Despite a very vague trace, in a single location, of an apron that could have supported a projecting tower, there is no other evidence for bastions. In several places on the line of the walls, building operations have uncovered significant numbers of mortared Charnwood granite blocks. The later town had imposing stone civic buildings and the houses of a wealthy mercantile class on a regular grid of roads, now traceable by the discovery of tessellated floors, dispersed across the walled area. Some of these buildings, set at right-angles to the street, are thought to have been shops. Two surviving structures point to the sophistication of the town: the major upstanding monument, the Jewry Wall, was part of an extensive public baths complex, and the earthworks of the Rawdykes at Aylestone represent traces of a Roman aqueduct.

The town defences of Great Casterton (R) date from the late-second century and consist of substantial earth banks and ditches, with a stone wall, 10–13 feet (2.5–3 m) thick, all constructed at the same time. The site, of around 15 acres (6 hectares), is protected on three sides by the river Gwash and surrounded by a steep-sided ditch, possibly double or even treble in places, on the north-east. Around AD 350, bastions

Great Casterton: the surviving rampart and ditch of the Roman town.

for artillery, probably large *ballistae* or crossbows firing heavy, metre-long bolts, were added. These projecting towers overlapped the ditch, which had to be filled and replaced by a wider, but shallower one. Studies of Romano-British history have revealed a sudden need for defence in the years AD 160–180, often associated with fires in towns and villas. This may be evidence of general unrest provoked by emperors such as Commodus or merely localised conflict. The adjacent villa, built at the same time as the town's defences were strengthened, appears to have been burned down about a generation later

Saxons and Danes

Evidence from one of the three Romano-British sites excavated at Empingham (R) revealed continuous occupation into the seventh century. From the evidence provided by place names and pagan cemeteries, it would appear that the Anglo-Saxons probably reached Leicestershire and Rutland by the early years of the fifth century. They could possibly have arrived during the years of the Roman retreat and the handover to those of the Romano-British, who intended to continue their established lifestyle. Early Anglo-Saxon burials have been found close to the centre of Leicester and elsewhere in the Soar Valley from a date that would suggest that they belonged to mercenary soldiers, engaged while the Romans were still nominally running their Province of Britannia. Finds of military items such as the belt buckles uncovered in Leicester and Kibworth, for instance, may have belonged to those corps of Teutonic mercenaries, referred to as *laeti* or *foederati*, paid to guard the iron-ore deposits of the area and who subsequently stayed on as settlers. Those pagan burials in eastern Rutland are close to Sewstern Lane, the prehistoric track and later Roman road, which branches off Ermine Street, and are associated with a cluster of *ham* place names. This could also provide a similar explanation for the *ham* villages in the west of Leicestershire that may have been deliberately settled by such mercenary bands, tasked with policing Watling Street. While there is no evidence for widespread disorder, it is nevertheless apparent that places such as the hillfort of Burrough Walls were reoccupied at this time, reflecting a move away from the former Roman centres of authority and government. By AD 500, the Angles from Schleswig were becoming established throughout the county, the beginnings of a shift from the Celtic to the Anglo-Saxon, recently confirmed by DNA analysis that showed how dominant the Anglo-Saxons would become in just a few generations. Anglian chiefs built their halls and surrounded them with fences and ditches, as much to protect their livestock from predators as for general security. Despite the growth of a new society based on these chiefs with their war bands, everyday dangers were more likely to come from severe weather events and natural disasters that were impossible either to predict or to defend against. As these isolated homesteads grew into villages, then they might, like Kibworth Harcourt, be surrounded by a ditch, which could have fulfilled a number of roles: practical for defence and drainage or symbolic—to mark the bounds. Pottery scatter would appear to show a shift from dispersed farmsteads to these village communities around the late-ninth century when common-field systems first appear.

Leicestershire lay at the heart of the Anglo-Saxon kingdom of Mercia. Founded by a westward movement from East Anglia in the early years of the sixth century, the kingdom would eventually extend from the Severn valley to the Wash, and from the borders of Northumbria in the Peaks and the Humber estuary down to London. From *c.* AD 650, Christianity was spreading into the kingdom, and by AD 700, Leicester had become the seat of a bishop. He may possibly have sat in a church on the site of the present-day St Nicholas, which largely retains its Anglo-Saxon nave on a structural level and architectural details, including a double-splayed window. There are traces of a porch of the type known from other contemporary churches, and the whole church occupies the site of a Roman building, possibly part of the baths complex. The extent of any continued occupation of the city from the exit of the Romans through the Anglo-Saxon period is, as yet, unknown; however, given that the medieval city walls closely follow the line of their Roman predecessors, it is likely that life would have been confined to this enclosure, and that is where the cathedral would have been built. In the later-eighth century, Leicester was developed by Offa as one of his riverine burhs to resist Danish water-borne raids. He may have repaired or reinforced the old Roman walls, contributing to their later consolidation. At Glen Parva (SP577981) cobbled floors of a mid-Saxon settlement are overlaid by thirteenth-century wall footings within a moated enclosure.

In the last third of the ninth century, the Danes completed the conquest of Mercia. In the years AD 865–868, raids had spilled over from East Anglia into eastern Mercia. In AD 871, the Danes sustained punishing defeats at the hands of Alfred of Wessex, and it may have been the quest for easier pickings that drew them to leave the Thames and settle new bases at Torksey on the Trent and, in AD 873–74, to over-winter the Danish army at Repton (Derbyshire)—an important Mercian royal site. These moves were followed by raids into Leicestershire, and probably at this time, the sacking of the monastic settlement of Breedon on the Hill. Appeals to Wessex for help went unheeded, possibly reflecting the reverse situation before the Battle of Ashdown in AD 871, when Alfred's appeal for Mercian support had been ignored. Resistance to the Danes quickly collapsed and Mercia had been totally overrun by AD 877 when the Danish war bands turned from being conquerors to colonists, parcelling up the lands between themselves, some of these appropriations being reflected in hybrid place names. Later arrivals made do with the marginal land that no one hitherto had wanted, an example being Scraptoft—as undesirable a plot as its name suggests. These settlers, however much they became wedded to the land and took native wives, still owed military service to their jarl or earl, the leader of the army of Leicester, and were required to retain their military identities. Meanwhile in Wessex, Alfred had managed to survive crippling setbacks and had inflicted a heavy defeat on the Danish army at Edington in Wiltshire in AD 878.

Leicester: the Saxon tower of the church of St Nicholas, showing reused Roman tiles.

Leicestershire and the Danelaw

After the submission of the Danish leader Guthrum to Alfred, it would be another six years before a proper treaty could be agreed. This recognised and defined the Danelaw, that area settled and governed by the Danes as being bounded by the rivers Thames, Lea, and Ouse in the south, and by the old Roman road, Watling Street in the west, thus partitioning old Mercia and creating a front-line between two sparring powers. The first Danelaw lasted only a relatively short space of time, but widespread Danish settlement had made a lasting impression on the land. Leicester was chosen as one of the five main towns of the Danelaw, the others being Derby, Lincoln, Stamford, and Nottingham, and there appears to have been a Danish extension to the Roman walled area. On the evidence of street names, which include 'Gates' (from the Norse *gata* meaning 'street'), it would appear that this lay outside the Roman East Gate of the town, where the clock tower now stands, at the junction of Humberstone, Gallowtree, and Haymarket Gates. This would suggest discrete Anglo-Saxon and Danish settlements co-existing side-by-side, and within a short while, each having its own Christian churches. Throughout the later ninth and early tenth centuries, the Five Boroughs maintained their Danish identity through law and commercial practices, early industry appearing to be based on the manufacture of pottery.

Fortunately, Alfred of Wessex and his son-in-law Aethelred, king of the rump of Mercia, realised that only by co-operating and combining their forces could the Danes be held off, particularly after the now peaceful Guthrum had died in AD 890 and his successors intensified their efforts to take over all of England. From his first victory at Tettenhall (Staffordshire) in AD 910, it was to take Edward the Elder and his Mercian allies, under Lady Aethelflaed, several years of slow but steady advances to make significant inroads into the Danelaw. They took Derby in AD 917 and Leicester the following year, putting down continuing local Danish resistance, and according to the *Anglo-Saxon Chronicle*, accepting the peaceful capitulation of the army of Leicester, the majority of whom were submissive. Soon, only the Viking kingdom of York remained in Danish hands.

Burhs and other Fortified Settlements

The *Anglo-Saxon Chronicle* records Leicester as a burh by AD 942, presumably based on the existence of its refurbished Roman and Danish defences. Mercian burhs, like their counterparts in Wessex, were towns defended by local levies, the *fyrd*, or civilian militia. Where stone walls survived from Roman times, these were patched up with gaps being filled by earthen ramparts and timber palisades. There was a formula for assessing the number of men needed to man these defences, based on land tenure. Soldiers were summoned at the rate of one from each hide of land, the area needed to support one family. In good agricultural land such as here in our counties, this would equate to around 60 acres (24 hectares). Four hides of land were reckoned to yield the men to defend 5½ yards (a pole or 5 m) of defensive perimeter. Leicester's Roman walls extended some 3,000 yards, 545 poles, and thus required 2,180 men, each responsible for the defence of 4 linear feet (1.2 m). In size, Leicester is comparable to Winchester, the largest of the *burhs* of Wessex.

Saxon Oakham remains an enigma. The earthworks at Cutts Close, north of the castle, have yielded Saxon pottery and may be reasonably regarded as evidence of *burh* defences. Cartographic evidence, in a map of 1787, shows the northern bank and ditch to have extended westwards, far enough to enclose the church which was a pre-Conquest foundation. It can safely be assumed that the eastern rampart of the castle marks the line of the Saxon earthworks, whilst the present High Street follows their southern limits. It is thus likely that the Saxon *burh* enclosed the church, marketplace, and a manor house. This would have given a perimeter of about 1,100 yards. Oakham formed part of the dowry of Anglo-Saxon queens, including Aelfthryth, the wife of Edgar, and of Emma, married first to Aethelred II and then to Cnut. A large hoard of Anglo-Saxon coins, uncovered in 1749, represents the earliest datable finds from the site. The manor house was most probably represented by a large timber hall, with outbuildings, all within the enclosing bank and ditch. High-status establishments of this importance would also have had a fortified gate built into a tower, the *burh-geat*, or else a freestanding tower of stone or timber within the defended enclosure. This manor may have provided the basis for the post-Conquest motte and bailey castle, which was built inside the burh around 1075.

A Saxon settlement in Ketton (R), occupied from *c.* AD 900 to *c.* 1100, may be representative of many such sites. A timber church, an aisled hall, 40 × 26 feet (12 m × 8 m) with six pairs of aisle posts, and at least two further structures, were separated by a linear ditch from a second hall with a hearth and a separate chamber at one end. The ditch may indicate any number of purposes, but it is likely that, in unsettled times, obstacles against casual raiders would have been seen as necessary. Donington-le-Heath manor house stands on a site previously enclosed within a ditch and palisade, and the evidence of Saxon settlement, revealed by aerial photography, immediately adjacent, may indicate continuity of occupation spanning the Norman Conquest.

By AD 939, the Danes were back invading eastern Mercia, eventually being halted outside Leicester by an army led by Edmund I, who reinstated the old Danelaw boundaries. However, within the next fifty years, the Viking onslaught had become unstoppable, and after the English defeat at Maldon in AD 991, the country was gradually subdued by the Norsemen, culminating in Swein Forkbeard's invasion of 1013. This capitalised on secret alliances with key figures in York and the Five Boroughs, as well as a more obvious alliance sealed by the marriage of his son, Cnut, to Aelfgifu, the daughter of an important family in the Danelaw, who had suffered grievously at the hands of King Aethelred. The pressures exerted on the Anglo-Saxon treasury and military over two decades, culminating in Swein's policy of concerted bribery, blackmail, diplomacy, and ruthlessness, had precipitated the collapse of the Saxon state. Swein then assumed the throne and, following a struggle with Edmund Ironside, who also had regarded the Five Boroughs as a personal powerbase, was succeeded by Cnut.

2

The Early Medieval Period, 1066–1300

In the years following the Conquest, the Normans systematically tightened their grip on the whole of England. Leicester, as an important and well-established centre of trade, administration, and population, was immediately identified as the location for a Norman castle. Oakham was held in 1066 by Edith, Edward the Confessor's widow, but after her death in 1075, it became the property of the king, who is likely to have initiated its refortification. Manors were parcelled out to new Norman lords, many of whom raised their own castles. Many of these essentially ephemeral structures will not have lasted very long, succumbing to natural erosion, neglect, demolition following military action, obsolescence, or redundancy. Probably due to little more than the vagaries of historical boundaries, Leicestershire's twenty-four castles provide a castle density of one in every 34.7 square miles (8,883.2 hectares) and stands in the top third of the national hierarchy. Rutland's seven castles produce a density of one in every 25.3 square miles (6,476.8 hectares), coming seventh in the national list— although it must be remembered that not all of these thirty-one sites would have been in simultaneous occupation. Castles tended to be established in settled, populated areas with social infrastructure in place, building on existing settlements and land holdings. Areas settled in later expansion, as the high boulder-clay wolds of Leicestershire and Rutland, exhibited a lower density of both settlement and castles.

Early Earthwork Castles

Castles served a number of different purposes: residential, administrative, judicial, and military. Differing emphases on these several functions could determine a castle's location and design. In the urban setting of Leicester, the castle was planted on the south-west corner of the Roman walls tucked in against the river. Following a siege, Leicester had been stormed by William's troops and 120 houses demolished for the construction of the castle by Hugh Grandmesnil. Leicester's motte is not mentioned before 1101, but it is assumed to date from the years immediately following the Conquest. The motte and its accompanying bailey overlapped the Roman ditches, thereby creating a new rampart and ditch rather than utilising the existing one, fully to exploit the raised land above the River Soar. As in many such towns, a high motte was built to overlook and hence overawe the townsfolk. In rural settings, a castle could dignify the pre-eminent manor or the centre point of a group of manors held by an important individual. Hallaton was established around 1086 as the administrative centre of an estate not, as has often been reported, during the Anarchy. Geoffrey Alselin's estate included a number of surrounding manors and had been held in 1066 by a Saxon landowner named Toki. Belvoir represented the heart of a group of manors forming a cohesive estate in 1086, assembled by Robert de Todeni from a number of different Saxon landlords subsequent to the Conquest. Creighton suggests that some of these constituent manors would have been given to incoming Normans, or 'Frenchmen', who would be available for the military service that underpinned their tenancies.

As well as the psychological effect of the dominance of a castle mound, a further subliminal message could be imparted by the juxta-positioning of church and castle— the twin symbols of spiritual and temporal power. This is exemplified by Essendine (R), where the church lies within the bailey of the castle, while at Earl Shilton and at Gilmorton, the two structures stand side-by-side. At Essendine, the church may have originated as the castle's chapel, some distance from the associated village. At Earl Shilton, the present churchyard has encroached on the castle's outer defences, and it is not impossible that the church was once contained within them. Castle and church at Whitwick lie very close together, and at Shawell, the church is linked to the adjacent castle by an earthen causeway. This relationship extended also to monastic houses, as at Hinckley where the castle and Benedictine monastery lay together under the protection of the Earl of Leicester. At Belvoir, the priory, later to be home to Roger of Wendover, the chronicler of King John's campaigns, nestled below the castle founded by William the Conqueror's standard-bearer. Another factor could be continuity, and at Oakham, the castle occupied the centre of an established Anglo-Saxon manor, supplying a new focal point for the Norman lordship that was taking over.

The motte and bailey castle at Hallaton lies an unusual distance, some 600 yards, from its settlement. One must assume that this was to take advantage of a defensive site, located on a hilltop at the confluence of two streams and midway between two ancient trackways. Although overlooked on one side, the site allowed the castle to present an impressive profile to travellers. It is interesting to note this apparent trade-off between convenience, impregnability, and image. Hallaton has the classic appearance of a motte and bailey with a Christmas-pudding motte, 118 feet (36 m) high and fully 630 feet (195 m) around its base. It is surrounded by a ditch, 10 feet (3 m) in depth and 25 feet (8 m) across. The semi-circular bailey, 200 × 100 feet (60 × 30 m), and covering an area of 2 acres (0.8 hectares), is surrounded by a bank and ditch. On one side, where motte and bailey meet, is a small rectangular platform, banked and ditched, which has been interpreted as a barbican protecting the base of a flying bridge accessing the motte. An alternative explanation suggests that one or more throwing engines might have been sited here to cover the point at which an enemy assault force could approach the castle's inner defences most closely.

Norman earthwork castles generally took one of two forms: the motte or the ringwork, both of which could have one or more outer courts known as baileys or wards. The motte was an artificial mound of earth surrounded by a ditch and could

Essendine: St Mary's church was built in the outer bailey of the castle—the earthworks of the inner ringwork visible beyond it. The church probably originated as the castle's chapel.

have, as its basis, a natural or earlier artificial feature. The ringwork was a lower platform surrounded by a bank and ditch. Nationally, ringworks and mottes exist in a ratio of 2:7, but there are no ringworks in Leicestershire and only two in Rutland—at Essendine and Woodhead. Sauvey has sometimes been so ascribed but is usually interpreted differently, and an earlier schedule identified Hinckley as a ringwork, but it is now known that there was formerly a motte, levelled and replaced by a house in the eighteenth century. A motte afforded advantages of visibility, dominance, and defensibility over a ringwork, but provided less living space within the more strongly defended area on the motte-top. In some instances, the choice between the two forms could come down to fashion or habit. Hugh Grandmesnil raised a motte at Leicester, so it is unsurprising that he should choose that design for his other castles. The motte at Leicester stood around 50 feet (15.5 m) high but was lowered to make a bowling green in the early years of the nineteenth century. At Shawell, the motte is now only 10–12 feet (3–4 m) high, with a ditch 5 feet (1.5 m) deep. A number of our castles possess mottes that depart from the conical stereotype and are lower and larger in diameter. Gilmorton's motte, once much higher but now a mere 8–10 feet (2.5–3 m) above the surrounding ditch, may have been lowered at a later date.

The motte, of which there were a dozen or so in our counties, could be constructed in a number of ways and from a variety of materials. At Kibworth Harcourt, the Munt,

Hallaton: the motte and bailey castle takes advantage of a lofty position where two streams meet. Its timber tower on the motte would have commanded views over important trackways.

a prehistoric burial mound, was probably the basis. Castle Donington's earthworks, deep double ditches defending a promontory, have been regarded as being Iron Age in origin, as many such castles were, but excavation has challenged this assumption. Its strong position was enhanced by scarping the natural slopes to increase their steepness. At Groby, the motte is made up of granite blocks within a sandy soil and mortared over to provide a flat and stable surface, while Gilmorton's motte has a gravel core. The prominent motte at Hallaton was constructed of alternate layers of boulder clay and gravel, topped with a layer of chalk, all standing on a foundation of compacted organic material. At Oakham, the motte was superimposed over a corner of the earlier, pre-Conquest enclosure. The motte at Burley, only 11 feet (3.4 m) high, was constructed of compacted layers of ironstone rubble, apparently the spoil from the surrounding ditch. A depression on the top was filled to produce a flat area about 25 feet (8 m) across.

There are in England instances of mottes being raised around core structures: stone cellars or towers or simply the posts, which might support a small, timber watchtower, or a more substantial, but still wooden, residential tower. At Groby, the motte encases a stone tower measuring 20 feet (6 m) by 16 (5 m) with walls only 2½–2¾ feet (0.75–0.85 m) thick. It has been suggested that this tower might represent a pre-Conquest structure, later annexed as a readymade keep, but recent excavations by Wessex Archaeology failed to uncover any finds to corroborate this thesis. There being little documentary record, in the absence of hard archaeological evidence, one is thrown back on context and precedent.

Many earthwork castles were insubstantial and short-lived, especially in times of stress (such as the Anarchy of the reign of Stephen). Alstoe Mount at Burley (R) may have been an emergency measure as it was overlaid onto the ridge and furrow of an existing settlement. It has been suggested that a number of motte-like mounds, hypothecated as short-lived products of that conflict, are not what they might seem to be. Some, such as Garthorpe, Desford, Launde, and Melton Mowbray, on the basis of location and place name, may in fact be mill mounds. Others, such as North Luffenham, Gumley, Pilton (R), Shackerstone and Scraptoft are likely to be post-medieval garden features. This does not, however, totally preclude the possibility that any one of them functioned at some time in its life as a castle mound, prior to its adaptation for a new purpose. Damage may also cloud a motte's origins. At Kibworth Harcourt, the earthworks have been comprehensively mutilated over the last 200 years, so only a late-eighteenth-century description, quoted by Michael Wood, points to the castle's appearance. A motte, 20 feet (6 m) in height and 115 feet (35 m) across, was surrounded by a ditch, around 6 feet (2 m) deep and 25 feet (8 m) wide, crossed by a causeway. Further banks and ditches once marked a bailey on the west, and an earlier enclosure ditch surrounded castle and village. The probable builder, Hugh Grandmesnil, was responsible for an almost identical structure, with similar dimensions, at Ingarsby. A further motte, very similar in design, was built by another new Norman tenant at Gilmorton.

Most of these earthwork castles would have had timber buildings: a timber tower on the summit and, if space allowed, a timber palisade with a fighting platform around the lip of the motte. While at Burley (R) there was no trace of a tower on the motte, excavators found timbers in the motte ditch that could have belonged to a palisade. Access was often via a flying bridge over the motte-ditch from the bailey. Halls were generally of timber, as were barns, stables, kitchens, and workshops. Records show that Sauvey was provided with a wooden chapel in 1244, built from locally felled timber and roofed with stone slates from a derelict stable on site.

Water was a significant factor in several of these earthwork castles. Sauvey Castle was built by King John to serve as both the administrative centre of the forest of Rutland and as a royal hunting lodge. Here, curved outer earthworks form a dam, controlling the flow of water and maintaining a shallow lake around the castle. At both Groby and Oakham (R), outer moats were maintained as fishponds, providing a steady supply of food for all the meatless days. Essendine (R) and Woodhead (R) both incorporated fishponds into their defensive moats. At Burley (R), Alstoe Mount has a motte and four baileys, two of which are open on one side, relying for protection on a pond-fed stream that flows down the east side of the site. Mountsorrel was built by the earls of Leicester on a clifftop to the west of the castle borough to whose east was the floodplain of the Soar, necessitating the network of drainage channels that underlie the site.

The prime purpose of several of these early earthwork castles was connected to the administration of the royal forests. Sauvey and Beaumont Chase (R) were built to control access and activity in the royal forests, monitoring poaching and providing bases for legitimate hunting parties. At Beaumont Chase, near Uppingham, a conical motte stands at the apex of a triangular promontory, with semi-circular banks running across the ridge to create the inner and outer baileys. Naturally precipitous slopes were supplemented, where necessary, by scarping. The Earl of Leicester raised mottes at Groby, Earl Shilton, and Sapcote to act as administrative centres for the forest of Hereswood. Until its deforestation in 1235, the Royal Forest of Leicestershire had its headquarters at Oakham and extended from the Welland Valley, northwards along the county border. Flitteris (R), a hunting lodge associated with Oakham Castle on the border of Leicestershire and Rutland, gets its name from being an area of brushwood with disputed ownership. A concern for the aesthetics of the landscape is reflected in the naming of castles, especially the significant use of French terminology for describing topographical features as at Mountsorrel, Belvoir (sometime Belvedere), and Beaumont. Castles were sometimes given ornamental and horticultural landscapes, examples of which include Sauvey's fishponds and Ashby's later 'Wilderness'.

Early Stone Castles

Throughout England, many castles, initially of earthwork and timber, were being upgraded to fortresses of stone by the early years of the twelfth century. It would appear that Belvoir acquired a shell keep: a straight substitution of its motte-top palisade for a wall of stone with lean-to buildings round its inner walls, leaving a circular courtyard in the centre. Belvoir received a royal licence for its refortification in 1203, and a further licence to crenellate granted to Robert de Roos in 1267. If its depiction on a medieval seal is to be believed, then a three-storey tower keep with round-headed windows was built inside Belvoir's shell wall. Leicester's earthwork defences had been slighted some time after 1088 by William Rufus, when its owner misguidedly supported the unsuccessful applicant for the post of successor to the Conqueror; the castle changed hands again in 1101, when its former owner was fined for rebelling against Henry I. Around 1118, the castle's defences, probably the curtain walls and gatehouse, were rebuilt in stone by Robert le Bossu, son and heir of Robert de Beaumont, Earl of Leicester. Only traces remain, but excavations found a collapsed section fronted by a 40-foot-wide (12-m-wide) ditch. Castle Donington had stone curtain walls and at least five towers when it was destroyed in 1215. The royal castle of Mountsorrel occupied a naturally strong position, dominating the important road that was to become the A6, and possessed stone defences at the time of its demolition in 1217. Sauvey was built by King John in 1211, possibly on an already occupied site, and although there were timber structures such as the chapel, it appears to have had stone curtain walls, a gatehouse, and possibly a keep, while a barbican outside the main gate may have had only a timber palisade. By the late 1200s, stone and other materials and fittings were being removed from the site, which, having no civil or military value, had fallen into disrepair. An overnight stop by King John, *en route* from Mountsorrel to Rockingham in 1209, in a house called 'Trencheland', could refer to Sauvey's predecessor building or it might refer to Allexton, near Uppingham, where John also stayed on occasion; later on, there was a prison serving the Forest of Rutland. At Sapcote, excavated in 1958, a stone-lined well was found, filled with building rubble that included architectural fragments such as a carved stone capital. Pottery sherds of fourteenth- and fifteenth-century date were found, so the site was either occupied for a long time or it was of later build.

Oakham Castle was walled in stone around the beginning of the thirteenth century, possibly by Walkelin de Ferrers. The motte at the south-east corner was partly cut away, the remnant being revetted in stone. A gateway—still visible under its later restoration—and several mural towers were built (probably by Richard, Earl of Cornwall, brother to Henry III) soon after 1252. Barber suggests sites for eight towers, which include a pair flanking the gatehouse, but can only cite strong evidence for two on the west and a third halfway along the east wall. From observation of the footings, these towers were round rather than square. Superimposed on an earlier ringwork on a prominent rise, Woodhead Castle (R), is now represented only by its earthworks measuring 90 × 75 yards. Its ground plan suggests a quadrangular moated stone castle typical of the late thirteenth century. Now, any surviving masonry is obscured by grass, but it has been suggested that the gateway may have been flanked by towers and that would make the presence of corner towers likely. Foundations of internal buildings ranged around the curtain walls are also visible. As at neighbouring Essendine, there appears to have been a small rectangular bailey attached to the ringwork. It was presumably in a finished state before 1290, when Edward I visited.

Oakham: the gateway, added to earlier curtain walls around 1250, may have had flanking towers. It was rebuilt in the seventeenth century, matching two gateways at Burley on the Hill.

Castle Halls

Following the tradition of the timber aisled halls of the Anglo-Saxon period, evoked so vividly by the Beowulf story, several of our castles boasted versions in stone by the mid-1100s, providing two of England's finest examples. Leicester's was probably completed by Robert de Beaumont, second Earl of Leicester, who died in 1168, while at Oakham, Walkelin de Ferrers had built his new hall *c.* 1180. This may have been a direct replacement in stone of the Anglo-Saxon hall, which must have undergone a great deal of patching over the preceding three centuries. It measures 65 feet (19.8 m) by 44 feet (13.4 m). The capitals on the columns of the arcade are so close stylistically to those in the choir of Canterbury Cathedral that it is likely they came from the same masons, with a date somewhere between 1175 and 1184. The south wall contains a doorway, previously at the east end but now centrally placed, and four pairs of windows. This hall represents one of the earliest examples of the development of architecturally ambitious stone-aisled halls, and the advent of the screens passage next to the main entrance for accessing the service rooms. The buttressed east wall has two blocked doorways that originally led to the buttery and pantry, whose footings were excavated in the 1950s, with, between them and accessed by another blocked door, a passage leading to the kitchen, detached in the interests of safety.

Leicester's great hall, measuring 84 feet (25.6 m) by 58 feet (17.7 m), has been adjudged the oldest surviving aisled hall in Europe, but it has lost its interior layout to its conversion into law courts in 1821, when the arcade posts were removed. One remaining timber capital is carved from timber felled after 1152. The renewal of the roof timbers has been dated, by dendrochronology, to 1697. Norman features survive in the south gable wall in the form of a door and windows. The mid-twelfth-century timber arcades of the aisled hall, showing high-quality craftsmanship, survive in only fragmentary form. A possible twelfth-century chamber, above an undercroft, is axially aligned to the hall—a rare example of what may have been a fairly common juxta-positioning of these two elements.

The manor of Ashby-de-la-Zouch was acquired by the Beaumont Earls of Leicester around 1100. Soon after 1150, the timber hall had been rebuilt in stone with a solar block at the north-west end, later converted to the buttery. Both these buildings appear to have been of two storeys, reached by the same external staircase. This stone building would have been supplemented by a detached kitchen, barns, and outhouses (all of timber), and surrounded by a timber palisade and gate tower, never intended as serious defences. A further freestanding stone or timber hall was built at Donington-le-Heath manor house before the end of the thirteenth century, but it has not survived. The remaining two-storey structure, dated to 1273–1308, was most probably a chamber block with a first-floor residential apartment over an undercroft. There is an internal stair in one of the two wings, which stand at right-angles to the main block, and a later external stair as well. A medieval barn stands nearby, and both buildings are on a moated platform that may have been walled or fenced. Substantial stone-built houses, which may have been regarded as having defensive features, continue to surface. On a site adjacent to Garthorpe church, a high-status building, with associated stone-revetted terracing, all dating from the thirteenth century, was partially excavated in 1998.

Oakham Castle: the hall of *c*. 1180, possibly replacing a timber Anglo-Saxon hall, was built inside the ringwork that may also have been Anglo-Saxon in origin.

Ashby-de-la-Zouch Castle: the two buildings adjoining the Kitchen Tower on the left were built in stone in 1150 to replace the original timber hall. They were later remodelled by Lord Hastings as a buttery, solar, and great hall, but both retain Norman masonry.

Town Defences

Leicester largely developed on the 130 acres (52 hectares) enclosed by the Roman walls that remained the basis for the medieval town defences. In 1173, the town was besieged and captured. A contemporary account by the monk, Matthew Paris, describes how the wall was undermined and supported by timber props, which were then set alight, bringing down a section of wall. Excavations at Westbridge Wharf have uncovered the granite footings of the wall and have exposed evidence of burning. The walls were razed, but murage grants—enabling the burghers to raise funds by tolls on trade to pay to rebuild their walls—were made in 1286, 1293, and 1316. However, as early as 1291, townsmen were being prosecuted for robbing stone from the town walls, and it is possible that their real significance came from constituting a customs barrier, with the gates (possibly kept in better shape than the walls) acting as toll bars. The speed map of around 1610, shows twin-towered gatehouses at the cardinal points, which probably date from the early 1300s.

Ecclesiastical Defences

Beaumont Leys was a grange granted to the Knights Templar by Simon de Montfort, Earl of Leicester, in 1252. It consisted of a rectangular enclosure measuring 200 yards by 150 yards, surrounded by a bank and ditch and containing ranges of buildings around a central courtyard. This complex probably resembled that of the Templar preceptory at South Witham in Lincolnshire, which was surrounded by a stone wall with a gatehouse, also possessing what the excavators there described as a strong tower or small stone keep. These defences reflected the nature of the Templars as a military order. When they were suppressed in 1308, the crown transferred their properties to the Knights Hospitaller. The Templar preceptory at Rothley was established in 1231 on land granted to them in 1203, and passed to the Hospitallers in 1312. An almost freestanding thirteenth-century chapel has an attached vaulted porch, which was originally the lower part of a tower. The hall was later incorporated into the north wing of an H-shaped house (*c.* 1600), then rebuilt and incorporated into the nineteenth-century Rothley Court (now a hotel). Rothley preceptory originally comprised the hall, tower, and chapel; a dormitory; kitchen and attached buttery, bakery, and brew house; stables; and storehouses for produce and supplies. A market charter was granted in 1285. In the cellar of the much later manor house at Heather are said to be traces of the medieval Commandery of the Knights Hospitaller, whose chapel became the parish church, much restored in 1846. Another Templar preceptory at Great Dalby, established by 1206, absorbed the properties of Heather, Rothley, and Swinford under the Hospitallers. The names of Temple Hall Farm, Temple Mill Farm, and Temple Farm at Wellsborough, west of Market Bosworth, suggest extensive Templar properties in that area. The manor house of the bishops of Lincoln at Lyddington was only licensed in 1336, but it is known that its predecessor had stood within a moat from the twelfth century, so the licence to crenellate may have been granted retrospectively.

Monastic precincts were usually walled to ensure that comings and goings could be monitored by a porter in a gatehouse. At both Bradley and Charley Priories, there are

Rothley: the chapel of this Templar preceptory. Behind the shield, the vaulted porch represents the stump of a tower.

earthworks that define the line of those precinct walls. The Augustinian Abbey of St Mary's in Leicester was founded in the twelfth century outside the town walls. It would appear that the core of the Great Gate and the precinct walls, later incorporated into the mainly brick walls, all originated from this original foundation.

The Castle in War

Although the military dimension was long seen as important in castle design, serious testing of a castle's defences was rare. Liddiard records only eleven attacks on the twenty-four castles in Leicestershire, and none on the six in Rutland, but some of those attacks that did take place would prove devastating to both defenders and fortresses.

The Anarchy 1135–1154

Following the death of Henry I, his niece, Mathilda (or Maud), widow of the Holy Roman Emperor and hence referred to as the 'Empress', was his designated successor. This was challenged by her cousin, Stephen, who assumed the crown, forcing England into a civil war, referred to as 'The Anarchy', which lasted for nineteen years. With the nobility split between the two protagonists and a general breakdown of royal authority, the way was clear for any petty robber-baron or armed gang to throw up an earth and timber fortress and terrorise its hinterland. It is quite likely that some of those unauthenticated mottes may have served this purpose for a few seasons, subsequently gaining legitimacy as mill-mounds or landscape features. Alstoe Mount at Burley (R) is superimposed on the earthworks of a deserted village and its attendant field system, suggesting that it may have been raised during this period of upheaval. Although dating has placed it no more precisely than being earlier than the mid-twelfth century, this still places it within the relevant timeframe.

It was not unknown for nobles to transfer their allegiance from one party to the other depending what could be gained at the time, but it is quite remarkable that the Earls of Chester and Leicester should come to an understanding, while very definitely supporting different parties. In 1148, they agreed to create a demilitarised zone in which a strict moratorium on castle-building would be enforced. The zone extended over a square with sides of roughly 30 miles (48 km), with Castle Donington and Belvoir marking its northern corners; Coventry and Rockingham its southern ones; and Leicester at the centre. Neither earl could build in that square except by mutual

**Earthwork castles in Leicestershire & Rutland
and the Demilitarized Zone around Leicester**

Sketch map to show earthwork castles and the demilitarised zone of the Anarchy.

consent; both were responsible for the demolition of castles built by third parties; the Earl of Chester passed Mountsorrel to the earl of Leicester to hold, and Whitwick and the neighbouring Ravenstone, whose location is still a matter of debate, on the boundary between the earls' spheres of influence, could only be fortified at all if both earls agreed. The treaty held for five years. When Henry II, son of the Empress, came to the throne in 1154, he ordered the destruction of some of those castles that had been raised inappropriately.

Henry II and his Sons

Queen Eleanor supported the rebellion of their sons, Young Henry, Richard (the Lionheart), and Geoffrey against her husband, Henry II, with de Beaumont, Earl of Leicester, as her principal adviser. With Leicester under siege by Richard de Lucy (the king's justiciar), the Earl brought a force of Flemish mercenaries to England, intending to take the Midlands and raise the siege, but was defeated in battle near Bury St Edmunds. Leicester eventually fell to de Lucy and, as a punishment for rebellion, the king ordered Leicester's town walls to be razed to the ground. The Earl, along with his countess, was captured and imprisoned by Humphrey de Bohun, the constable of England, only finally being released when those of his knights holding the castles of Leicester, Mountsorrel, and Groby surrendered. Leicester Castle itself was then slighted, as may have been the Earl's castle at Hinckley, while Mountsorrel passed into royal ownership. Excavations at Groby demonstrated that the motte had been deliberately thrown down at about that date (*c.* 1176). It is likely that any structure that might have stood on Leicester's motte would not have been replaced.

The Barons' War 1215–1216

After the signing of Magna Carta in the spring of 1215, King John petitioned the Pope for its annulment and turned on his barons. William d'Albini was imprisoned in Corfe Castle (Dorset), but his loyal household held Belvoir Castle for him against the king. John's threats that their lord would be starved to death brought their surrender and John promptly installed Poiteven mercenaries in the castle. In 1215, the royal castle of Mountsorrel had been put into good order by John, who erected timber hoards, or fighting platforms, on the walls. However, he had then been forced to put it into the hands of Saher de Quincy, Earl of Winchester, who had been given the lands of the Earldom of Leicester. Castle Donington, a stronghold of John de Lacy, another of the rebel barons, had agreed to surrender once it was known that John's army was closing in. In May 1216, those barons who were in rebellion invited Prince Louis of France to come to England with an army to aid the rebellion. In June, John died campaigning in Norfolk and Lincolnshire, and the task of reasserting legitimate royal authority passed to the boy-king Henry III and his regent William Marshall. By early 1217, Marshall, aided by Ranulph, Earl of Chester, had begun the reduction of the remaining rebel fortresses. Ranulph brought up siege engines and commenced operations against de Quincy's garrison in Mountsorrel. At de Quincy's urging, Prince Louis split his forces and despatched de Quincy with seventy French knights from his own siege operations at Farnham, Surrey. Joined by extra troops, drawn mainly from the garrison of London, this force marched to relieve the hard-pressed Mountsorrel garrison, which consisted of ten knights and some sergeants under Henry de Braybrooke. Threatened by the approach of so considerable a force, Ranulph destroyed his siege machines and withdrew his troops to Nottingham, while the rebels, mainly French knights and soldiers, having relieved Mountsorrel, made for Lincoln, ravaging the Vale of Belvoir on the way. They then reinforced the rebel army besieging Lincoln Castle. Marshall and the Earl of Chester unexpectedly approached Lincoln from the north and routed the rebel army. The garrison of Mountsorrel fled, and Chester destroyed the castle, which, with the arrival of a peace settlement, was withheld from de Quincy. It has been suggested that the decision of Louis to divide his army in order to mount the expedition to raise the siege of Mountsorrel was the turning point in the struggle. After this, the Regent and the young king were able to gain ultimate victory. However, Henry III's troubles were not completely behind him. The leftovers of John's misrule included mercenaries such as the notorious Fawkes de Breaute, who is said to have been in possession of Oakham in 1220. Henry III was showing himself in the region in 1223 and Sauvey capitulated to him, along with Rockingham in Northamptonshire. De Breaute, alternately sheriff of seven Midlands counties and the most wanted criminal in England, contrived to avoid a violent end on the scaffold and died of food poisoning in France by 1226, long after Henry had granted Oakham to his royal brother Richard, Earl of Cornwall. In 1223, there was more baronial opposition to the king, led by the Earl of Chester. They gathered at Leicester for their Christmas 'court', but, realising they were in a minority, soon backed down and recognised the king's authority.

More Rebellion and Unrest

In 1264, barons under Simon de Montfort, Earl of Leicester, raised an army to oppose Henry III, and after defeating him at Lewes (Sussex), he went on to repel a French invasion. Many Leicestershire lords and their retinues were called to fight in de Montfort's army. This conflict involving the king and the barons often spilled over into local feuds, fuelled by loyalty to one party or the other on the national stage, exacerbated by a general lawlessness. De Montfort's vain attempt to establish a constitutional monarchy in England petered out, ending with his defeat and death at Evesham, Worcestershire. After this, de Montfort's sons were disinherited and the Earldom of Leicester went to the king's brother, Edmund of Lancaster, who became the first of a sequence of Lancastrian lords to establish a powerbase in the region.

3

The Late Middle Ages and the Tudor Period, 1300–1600

A Time of Plague and Rebellion

In the first half of the fourteenth century, our counties had a population of around 50,000 people, roughly double that recorded in the Domesday Book in 1086. Leicester had recovered from its destruction of 1173, but would shortly go into decline as a result of the switch from the manufacture of cloth to the Flanders wool trade. A more devastating event, however, was the Great Plague, or Black Death, of 1349. While the average death toll across the country was around a third, with 2,000 of Leicester's 6,000 population succumbing; 37 per cent of the counties' clergy perished, owing to their position on well-travelled routes, with many villages suffering up to 70 per cent mortality.

Fortunately, population levels quickly recovered, but the authorities' intransigence over wage levels and the free movement of labour, coupled with increased levels of taxation and, specifically, the hated Poll Tax, led to rebellion. In 1381, the Peasants' or Great Revolt broke out in the south-eastern counties of Essex and Kent. The militant leaders of the movement, having entered London and ostensibly extracted generous concessions from Richard II, then spread out into East Anglia and sought to raise the whole country against those who, to them, represented injustice: the hangers-on of the royal court, the landlords, tax collectors, JPs, and lawyers. A force of armed rebels was despatched northwards where towns awaited their arrival with enthusiasm or apprehension. In Leicester, 1,200 armed citizens waited to oppose them. Near Market Harborough—having received news that their leaders were dead and that the revolt back in London had collapsed—the rebel force quietly dispersed. Among those suffering collateral damage was the religious radical John Wycliffe, whose preaching had alienated lords spiritual and temporal alike. While denying a political dimension to his quest for the spiritual empowerment of the common people, he was nevertheless forced to withdraw from public life, losing the support of his patrons such as John of Gaunt. He retired to Lutterworth where he died in 1384.

One of the rebels' objections to increased taxes concerned the way so much of the money was being wasted on pointless military expeditions. The Hundred Years' War against France, typified in the popular mind by such debacles as that of John of Gaunt in 1378, created ever greater demands for taxes from those who saw no benefit in this aristocratic gallivanting. Gaunt, son of Edward III, acquired the vast duchy of Lancaster through marriage and inheritance and had his base in Leicester. During the rebels' assault on London, his magnificent Savoy Palace had been looted and burned by the mob. Gaunt was away campaigning on the Scottish borders, but his officers may well have received his orders to mobilise the citizens of Leicester against the rebellion. In 1371, he had married the Infanta of Castile, and his costly but ineffectual campaign of 1386 to secure her throne was seen as one more drain on England's treasury. Gaunt died in his castle of Leicester in 1399, shortly before his son usurped the throne as Henry IV, displacing Richard II.

Castles and Fortified Manor Houses

It was against this backdrop of social upheaval, political chaos, and rampant militarism that the building of private strongholds must be examined. Many of the earlier earthwork castles had disappeared by the early 1300s. Ingarsby, for instance, had become a grange of Leicester Abbey and the village consciously depopulated by the Abbot. Those castles that had never been rebuilt in stone, such as Hallaton or Beaumont Chase, had become grassy humps and bumps in the landscape. Mountorrel and Castle Donington had been destroyed in the reign of John, and Sauvey had fallen into disrepair. Subsequent periods of relative peace had encouraged the minor nobility to go for comfort over defensive utility. Although Ashby is described as a strong house or fortified manor, by the mid-fourteenth century, the Zouch family had created a seigneurial landscape around it, comprising parklands, a warren, dovecote, fishponds, and gardens, covering some 60 acres (24 hectares). A few castles continued to play a role, however. A survey of Oakham (*c.* 1340) described a castle 'well walled', entered over a 'drawbridge with iron chains', and comprising a hall with a two-storied solar block containing four chambers attached to its west end; the buttery and pantry attached to the hall's east end with the detached kitchen; two stables and a hay-barn; a prison; and a chamber for the porter. In the immediate surroundings of the castle were fish stews, mills, pastures, woodlands, and meadow.

Although the defences on the motte had been slighted in 1173, Leicester Castle clearly found its heyday in the fourteenth century, when the domestic buildings of the bailey came into their own. This was especially so in the second half of the century, when the castle became the centre of the newly aggrandised and enlarged Duchy of Lancaster. Here, the Great Hall remained the castle's centre of gravity, with a block of private apartments to the north and the kitchen complex with its cellarage for the storage of foodstuffs and wine at the other end. Successive earls maintained a sumptuous household for both their retainers and for visiting royalty and nobility. Additionally, the castle represented the administrative centre of their estates. Since St Mary de Castro, although contained within the enclosure of the castle, also functioned as a parish church, a private chapel for the sole use of the lord and his family was incorporated into the solar block. Belvoir, seat of the de Roos family and Woodhead, owned by Hugh Browe in 1373, also remained in continuous occupation. Belvoir was granted to William Lord Hastings in 1461 after de Roos had been executed.

Hastings looted lead and other materials for his own building projects and rebuilding only began in 1526. If there ever had been a motte at Melton Mowbray, it was long vanished by this time. King Street was the traditional site of the fortified manor of the Mowbrays, known as the Old Mansion House. It was demolished in 1780 and ultimately replaced by Lord Melbourne's Manor House, adjoining the bowling green later occupied by the picture house. Still in Melton Mowbray, road widening in the 1820s necessitated the demolition of 'The Ramparts' at Spittle End and Chapel Close, reported by Brownlow with the comment that nothing is now (1980) known of their age or nature. They may or may not have represented a defensive bank, which could have had medieval or Civil War origins.

Early in the fourteenth century, a number of licences to crenellate were granted in Leicestershire: to Robert de Holand at Bagworth in 1318; to Henry de Beaumont at Whitwick in 1321; and to Bishop Henry of Lincoln at Lyddington in 1336. There has been much discussion of that licensing process in recent years. Current consensus appears to agree that a licence to crenellate was more than the medieval equivalent of planning permission. A licence implied royal approval of the licensee and would be flaunted as such among the successful applicants' peers and neighbours. From the other point of view, it could be seen as a way in which an insecure monarch, such as Edward II, might exercise patronage and canvass support. That it was still considered desirable to give one's residence the appearance of a fortress is a comment on those troubled times. Hugh Despenser and his son became the most hated men in England by administering Edward's unpopular regime, and they were eventually hanged prior to their master's reported murder. In 1311, Despenser was granted a blanket licence to crenellate all his properties across the land. In 1323, concerted attacks were carried out on his Leicestershire manors, five local knights being indicted for these assaults. Sir Thomas de Erdyngton's manor of Barrow on Soar was attacked by his neighbour, Sir Hugh de Shirleye, in 1394. Shirleye led a force of '200 men-at-arms, unknown, arrayed for war with hauberks and helmets of iron, bows, arrows, swords, staves and shields'.

By the early fifteenth century, a new wave of building was under way. At Leicester, an extension to the walled area south of the castle had been built in around 1330 to accommodate first some new alms-houses and then, in 1354, a collegiate foundation with church and priests' houses. In 1410, the Magazine Gate, a solid, two-storey gatehouse was built to secure access to this new work, the Newarke. While most of the fenestration is Victorian, features such as the domed cap on the staircase turret, the bartizans, and the archway, with its separate pedestrian and vehicle entrances, are original. New gatehouses were added to the castle in the 1440s. The Turret Gate was originally of three-storeys, with guardrooms each side of the entrance passage and a portcullis chamber above. Much of it was destroyed in election riots in 1832. The castle's other gate was rebuilt in 1446 as a timber-framed structure with an upper chamber over the gate passage, all now integrated with the adjoining house (*c.* 1590).

In the turmoil created by the Wars of the Roses, two local families, both Yorkist supporters of Edward IV, sought to underline their new importance by building impressive monuments employing the language of military architecture. William, Lord Hastings, received licences to crenellate Ashby-de-la-Zouch, Bagworth, and

Above left: Leicester Castle: the exterior of the magazine gate of 1410.

Above right: Leicester Castle: the turret gate, connecting the original castle to the Newarke.

Left: Leicester Castle: the inner gatehouse of 1446 and porter's lodge adjoining Castle House.

Kirby Muxloe in 1474. Edward IV's step-son, Thomas Grey, created marquis of Dorset, developed the Grey mansion at Groby, and then moved on to build Bradgate House from scratch. Little is known of Bagworth, an established fortified manor that appears to have received little attention from Hastings, but Ashby and Kirby Muxloe represent important, if anachronistic, elements in English military architecture.

Ashby, or rather the adaptation of the existing strong house, could have been begun any time after its acquisition in 1464, as Hastings need not have waited for his licence to commence building, but it was most likely begun in 1472. Hastings rearranged the domestic buildings and created a new chapel, but his principal addition was the massive great tower. Such towers appeared to echo the great Norman keeps of the late eleventh and early twelfth centuries, and they shared some functions, but also introduced new ones. Fifteenth-century great towers figure at a number of sites: in brick at Tattershall and Gainsborough (Lincolnshire), Buckden (Cambridgeshire), and Farnham (Surrey); and at South Wingfield (Derbyshire) and Raglan (Gwent) in stone. While the square keeps of the Normans held great halls and kitchens, as well as audience chambers, chapels, and private apartments, these later towers were generally not part of the castle's communal or public space. At Ralph Cromwell's Tattershall, for instance, the tower contained an audience chamber with strictly controlled access. At Raglan, there are five floors containing mainly private chambers for the Herbert family, with a similar arrangement at Ralph Cromwell's 72-foot (22-m) high tower at South Wingfield. The Hastings Tower at Ashby has more in common with these latter two. The main body, square in plan, has four floors, while a rectangular annexe has seven storeys, all accessed by a single spiral stair. The ground floor is mainly storage, the next a kitchen, then a bed-chamber, and, on the top floor, a private camera, its fireplace adorned with Edward IV's sunburst emblem, just in case the family might forget to whom they owed everything. What all these towers have in common is explicitly military motifs: machicolations, battlements, and turrets, and an ambition to dominate their surroundings. They deliver a very clear message about their owners' wealth, power, influence, and enjoyment of royal favour. Most of these castles also had parallel communal accommodation. At Ashby, a second dominant tower held the kitchen, the old hall was remodelled, while the original Norman solar block became the buttery and a new chapel was built. Despite the luxury of these great towers, it would appear that most of the lords actually lived day-to-day in the more spacious accommodation at ground level. There is an argument that the tower might have represented a family bolt-hole in the event of mercenary retainers being suborned by political opponents or jealous neighbours, but there is no real historical evidence for this. Ashby already had gardens in 1467 and Hastings retained this feature, additionally receiving a licence to impark significant expanses of land around the castle.

Whereas at Ashby, Hastings was building on an established structure, at Kirby Muxloe, only an insubstantial manor house existed, affording him the opportunities of a greenfield site. If it was originally intended that the old hall, with its kitchen, pantry, and buttery block at one end and the solar block at the other, were to be retained as elements in the new build, as at Ashby, then it would appear that there was a change of plan. The

Ashby-de-la-Zouch Castle: the Great Tower, which was raised by Lord Hastings soon after 1474. It has lost its top 10 feet (3 m) of parapet and angle turrets, but still rises over 80 feet (25 m) above the surrounding courtyard.

old gatehouse was demolished and a new building platform was laid out within a more extensive moat, allowing for a substantial tower at each corner, and a projection in the middle of each of three sides. A new hall was planned between the off-centre turret in the south wall and the east tower, and other buildings would be ranged around three sides of the quadrangle. The fourth side held the three-storey gatehouse, rectangular with four octagonal corner turrets. Its ground floor consisted of two guardrooms flanking the gate passage with its drawbridge pit, portcullis, and two pairs of gates. The two interior turrets were entered from the courtyard and contained spiral stairs. These are mirror images in that the western stair turns clockwise, while the eastern stair, unusually, rises anticlockwise. The first floor was a residential space that could be divided into two, each half with its own fireplace. The second floor was never built. A dwarf wall was to be built around the lip of the moat with the curtain wall proper rising behind this. A major difference between here and Ashby is that Kirby Muxloe was built in brick and by one of the country's foremost builders in brick, John Cowper. He had built for Henry VI at Eton College, for Bishop Wayneflete at Farnham, and for Lord Cromwell at Tattershall, thus placing Hastings in the patrons' premier league. Work had commenced in earnest at Kirby Muxloe in 1481, but in June 1483, Hastings was executed by Richard of Gloucester and work slowly ground to a halt. Only the moated platform, the outline of the curtains, two floors of the gatehouse, and the west tower had been completed. Despite its unfinished condition, enough was completed to permit an assessment of its effectiveness as a fortification. Beyond the conventional drawbridge, portcullis, battlements, and rampart walk are the gun ports. These are liberally distributed around the base of the gatehouse where there are ten, and the west tower with six. A further gun port in the north-east face of the tower commands the rampart walk leading to the gatehouse. However, the two in each of the forward turrets of the gatehouse actually sit below the water level of the moat and had to be blocked up by the masons. Despite it being well over a century since gun ports had first become regular features of serious fortifications, those installed at Kirby Muxloe were not the most sophisticated of their kind. Not only were they not well sited, but the design of their internal splay made very little traverse possible, so the castle's cannon could only hit targets directly in front of them. Peers points out that this would have meant hitting other parts of the castle at point-blank range. John Kenyon quotes an unpublished note by O'Neil, the acknowledged expert in 1947, which ascribes 30 degrees of traverse to Kirby Muxloe's cannons, giving them the ability to cover every flank and angle. This is clearly debatable, and Kenyon himself thinks that the point is academic. He regards Kirby Muxloe's gun ports as of psychological value, deterring attackers by suggesting the possibility of comprehensive gunfire. It should be noted that the Wars of the Roses did not generally involve assaults on castles, but that the use of cannon on battlefields had great moral force. Had Kirby Muxloe been completed it would have projected an intimidating presence with its cannon-rich façade.

Following the accession of Henry VII, the marquis of Dorset was building at Groby in 1488. A stone-built manor-house with an open hall had been built here before 1446, possibly by the Ferrers family whose heiress married Dorset's maternal grandfather. There may have been a solar block as a cross wing, but no trace remains. The new works from 1488 included a gatehouse, two towers at the front of the house, and several ranges. All this was in brick, and most of it remained unfinished as Dorset was diverted to an entirely new build at Bradgate. Over the next century, Groby was finished with two three-storey ranges and a stair tower, by Dorset junior, possibly in classic Tudor symmetry with a central gatehouse and corner towers. Alterations and additions have been continued up to the present, obscuring earlier work. At some stage, the motte to the rear became a garden feature. Of Dorset's early work, one of his two towers remains to its full height of four-storeys, wearing a pyramid cap on its top, while the other, affected by building alterations in the early twentieth century, survives only as a stump.

Bradgate was begun *c.* 1490 by Dorset, switching his focus from Groby. Although the house was regarded as finished by the time of Dorset's death in 1501, much of what remains will have been built over the next 200 years. Bradgate was a palace rather than a castle, but perpetuated the language of medieval strongholds. A rectangular base court had polygonal brick turrets at the corners and a rectangular four-storey stair turret in the middle of one side. Three of the four corner turrets and the stair tower remain upstanding. The layout conformed to the traditional ideas of the later medieval castle. An outer court, lined with ranges of lodgings for guests or retainers, leads to a porch that accesses the imposing great hall, 110 feet (30 m) long, rebuilt in later years, but probably to its original dimensions. Adjoining the hall at one end are the family's private quarters, consisting of parlour, bedchambers, and dining room, all liberally provided with fireplaces. The chapel has been reroofed and partly restored. The south-facing winter parlour constituted a luxury at this time. At the other end of the hall, through the screens passage, were the pantry, buttery, kitchen, bakery, and brewery, all standing over cellars. The house, deliberately burned out in the late 1600s, stands in its original parkland and was the home of Lady Jane Grey.

Kirby Muxloe: the gatehouse was completed before 1483, when work was abandoned after Richard III ordered the execution of Lord Hastings.

Kirby Muxloe: the interior of the gatehouse and the west tower seen across the unfinished quadrangular courtyard and the moated platform.

Above left: Kirby Muxloe: a gun port in the gatehouse.

Above right: Groby Old Hall: one of the two towers built in the 1480s by Thomas Grey before work here was abandoned in favour of Bradgate House.

Moats and other Defensible Sites

Moats usually enclosed rectangular platforms accessed by narrow causeways or timber bridges, and there are many explanations for their existence. Some were dug around manor houses, farmsteads, or monastic granges, while others protected valuable sources of cash crops such as orchards. They kept domestic animals in and wild animals out. On occasion, they kept marauding robber bands or discharged soldiers at bay. They were often perceived as signs of social standing, so keeping up with the Greys may have provided the motivation for aspiring yeomen or gentry. Moats also provided fishponds to supply food for the 100-plus meatless days in each year, or drainage in low-lying land. Leicestershire's boulder clay provided the most common building material in to the eighteenth century, and puddled clay was the best foundation for holding water in a moat. Consequently there are a significant number of recorded moats in the county. Rutland, with its entirely different geology, though admittedly much smaller in area, still has proportionately many fewer moats. Mitchell's 1975 list in the Transactions of the Leicestershire Archaeological and Historical Society, which excludes obvious castle sites, runs to exactly 100, six of which lie in Rutland. The Council for British Archaeology Research Report 17, of 1978, claimed 120 for Leicestershire and six for Rutland. Of Leicestershire's 120 moats, twenty-seven are scheduled ancient monuments and four (Humberstone, South Croxton, Donington le Heath, and Sapcote) have been excavated. In Rutland, four are scheduled. Many moats, especially some of those which held grand houses on their platforms, have lost their reason for being. North Luffenham's was destroyed in the Civil War, while Osgathorpe's was demolished only in the 1960s.

Two fairly typical moated sites are located within the boundaries of the city of Leicester. The 'Birds Nest' in Battersbee Road lies at the former centre of Frith Park, established for hunting by 1300, with the earliest mention of a lodge in the 1360–70s. Here, the moat is 28 feet (8.6 m) wide and 8 feet (2.4 m) deep with a perimeter of 360 yards. The moat was crossed by a triple-arched bridge, with an inbuilt drawbridge reported as measuring 39 by 12 feet (12 by 3.7 m). There were stone buildings roofed in Swithland slate, which included a three-bay hall, and other buildings of eight bays on the west, nine on the north, seven on the south, and three on the east. Family feuds between the Greys and the Hastings caused Lord John Grey to refortify the Birds Nest as late as 1526. Next to Evington church, Piggy's Hollow is the site of a late thirteenth-century or early fourteenth-century stone manor house owned by the Greys of Codnor, occupying a moated platform measuring 210 by 81 feet (65 by 25 m), from which the buildings had disappeared by the sixteenth century. Along with the moat, the remains of a dam and fishponds can be seen.

The buildings at some significant fortified houses have totally disappeared, as at Bagworth, which Leland reported as ruinous in 1540. Others have been swallowed up in later work, as at Nevill Holt and Staunton Harold, but in some places, important elements remain. The idyllically picturesque Moat House at Appleby Magna was a medieval manor house with a hall and a chapel, but now only a two-storey stone gatehouse survives, linked to a timber-framed Tudor house, all within a moat. Hall Farm at Knaptoft was a manor of the Turpins, now represented only by two ranges of diapered brick, forming a T-shape, one of which is pierced by a gate passage with a stone, four-centred arch. Tolethorpe Hall (R) was built by Sir Nicholas Burton around 1316 and rebuilt in the fifteenth and sixteenth centuries. Here, an altered medieval gatehouse survives, with separate carriage and pedestrian archways, similar both in date and design to those at Northborough Manor and the palace of the bishops of Peterborough, in neighbouring Cambridgeshire. Oliver Cromwell's Castle at Owston, with a moat larger than that at the Birds Nest, appears to have had a gatehouse and stone buildings, now represented only by mounds. Like many other such moats, it had fishponds around it and the whole complex was fed by a stream.

Ecclesiastical Defences

Many of the recipients of licences to crenellate were prelates and abbots, for most medieval monasteries were surrounded by walls and many had quite elaborate entrances. St Mary's, Leicester's Augustinian abbey, retains medieval precinct walls built and rebuilt over the years, whose foundations may be of the thirteenth century. There are polygonal turrets at the angles with rectangular interval ones, some of which contain arrow loops. These are probably original but may have been re-set in later refurbishments. Cavendish House was built out of the fabric of the monastic buildings adjoining the old gatehouse, and came to the first Earl of Devonshire in 1613. It was ruined after Charles I had spent several nights there during the Royalist siege and in the run-up to his defeat at Naseby. Fragments of the Abbey's original inner gatehouse

Tolethorpe: the gatehouse built around 1316 by Sir Nicholas Burton. It is of similar design to others of that date in the locality.

Leicester, St Mary's Abbey: a bastion on the precinct wall, containing two arrow-slits.

are embedded in the ruins of the house. The gatehouse itself was an imposing structure consisting of a rectangular block with corner turrets, built from the middle of the Fourteenth Century around an earlier, simpler gateway. Chambers either side of the entrance passage accommodated the porter's lodge, whilst the upstairs may have held luxurious guestrooms or even the Abbot's own lodging. At Owston Abbey, a late medieval gatehouse, demolished in the eighteenth century, formerly adjoined the south-west corner of the nave. Not all monasteries were rich enough to incorporate secure storage, so in 1371, the Abbot of Croxton Kerrial chose to deposit the valuables of his remote abbey in a strong room in Grantham.

Bishop Henry of Lincoln was granted a licence to crenellate his palace, probably a development of an earlier building, at Lyddington (R) in 1336. The Bede House now standing appears to represent one range of Bishop Henry's new palace, which would have consisted of a quadrangle of stone buildings surrounded by the moat, revealed by excavation. Successive alterations culminated in its conversion to alms-houses by Lord Burghley after 1602.

Lancastrian Leicester and National Events

Leicester lay at the heart of the Lancastrians' lands, having been granted to Edmund, Earl of Lancaster, by his father Henry III. Henry of Grosmont, Earl of Lancaster and Leicester, had an unusually amicable relationship with the burghers of Leicester and was awarded a civic dinner on his return from campaigning in Aquitaine in 1346. Leicester was one of a small number of English towns entitled to stage tournaments, one being held there in 1344. John of Gaunt entertained Richard II in the castle, and after his death there, in 1399, his son, Henry Bolingbroke, returned from exile to seize the throne, receiving a warm welcome from the people of Leicester. The unfortunate Richard II was imprisoned in Leicester prior to his final journey to Pontefract, where he is thought to have been starved to death. The new king, Henry IV, held his first parliament in the great hall of the castle, and his wife, Joan of Navarre, was buried in Leicester. Henry V brought James I of Scotland to Leicester as his prisoner in 1421, and Henry's wife, Katherine of Valois, was installed there prior to her giving birth to the future Henry VI. He was only nine months old when his father died on campaign in France in 1422 and, as a teenager, he was knighted while staying in Leicester Castle. At times of insecurity in London, he held parliaments in Leicester, dissolving the Parliament of 1450, before returning south to confront Jack Cade and his army. In 1455, Henry VI was again holding a parliament in Leicester, but his exclusion of the Yorkists led to armed conflict with defeat for the Lancastrians at St Albans and his capture. Later on, the Queen, in an attempt to restore royal authority by providing a focus for Lancastrian support, moved the court to her Leicestershire heartlands. Here she was surrounded by stalwarts such as Viscount Beaumont, former Constable and Great Chamberlain of England, killed at the battle of Northampton in 1460, and then by his son, born in 1438 and knighted at Northampton.

The Rise and Fall of Lord Hastings

The Hastings family had inherited the manor of Kirby Muxloe through marriage in the mid-1300s, but it was Sir William Hastings, closely associated with Richard, Duke of York, father of Edward IV, who would achieve wealth and power in the next century, if only temporarily. After the decisive Yorkist victory at Towton in 1461, Hastings was rewarded for his loyalty to father and son with the post of Lord Chamberlain to the Royal Household. He was also granted two important properties: Ashby-de-la-Zouch, whose previous owner, the Lancastrian James Butler, Earl of Ormond, had been beheaded after the battle; and Belvoir, formerly held by Thomas, Lord Roos, hanged by Edward IV after the battle of Hexham in 1464. Hastings was probably with Edward at the Battle of Empingham, also known as Loosecoat Field, in 1470, which saw the treacherous Earl of Warwick routed, having been prevented from linking up with a supporting force from Lincolnshire. Three local families fought on Edward's side at Empingham: the Browes of Woodhead, the Burtons of Tolethorpe, and the Mackworths of Empingham. However, when the Yorkist fortunes took an unexpected nose dive, Hastings loyally accompanied Edward into precipitate exile in Friesland. Their return, in the following spring, was quickly followed by two victories over the Lancastrian armies at Barnet and Tewkesbury.

At the Battle of Barnet, on 14 April 1471, Hastings was in command of the left wing of the Yorkist army. Bearing the brunt of the Lancastrian right's initial pressure, his troops fled, hotly pursued by the Earl of Oxford's men. Fortunately for Edward, this disaster was shielded by fog, and the rest of the Yorkist army stood its ground. Oxford managed to recall some of his men to rejoin the fray, but they were first mistaken for the enemy by their own side and then presumed to have changed sides and wiped out. Edward was then able to defeat the weakened army, and the death of Warwick, to whose sister, Katherine Neville, Hastings was married, caused the remaining Lancastrians to break and run. At Tewkesbury, a month later, Hastings was on the king's right. This decisive battle shattered the Lancastrians and saw their heir to the throne and all their leadership killed on the field or executed later. He was then made Lieutenant of Calais, with the task of stabilising the garrison previously loyal to Warwick. This post gave Sir William the opportunity to amass great wealth in the form of pensions—a polite name for bribes—paid out first by Burgundy and then France.

In 1474, William Lord Hastings was granted licences to crenellate his castles of Ashby-de-la-Zouch, Kirby Muxloe, and Bagworth, part of a wider package that included the grant of two fairs and permission to enlarge his three deer parks—all manifestations of his importance and power. Hastings started building at Ashby soon after 1461; at Belvoir, he stripped off lead roofs for use at Kirby where he started work in 1480; and Bagworth was never greatly developed. One of Hastings' affiliation, Sir John Pilkington, another committed Yorkist, became joint Chamberlain of the Exchequer with Hastings in 1477, and he was also granted a licence to crenellate four houses, a further sign of royal approval.

Rivalry between Hastings and the Queen's Woodville brother, Earl Rivers, in 1482, developed into a serious feud between two factions at court. Hastings had been a committed Yorkist all his life, and Rivers was seen as a parvenu who had benefited from his sister's hold over the king. After Edward's death in 1483, Hastings attempted to ensure that the Woodvilles were excluded from the court and that Edward's elder son would assume the throne as Edward V, under the temporary protection of his uncle, Richard of Gloucester. In spite of his record of total loyalty to the house of York and his antipathy to the Woodville faction supporting the young king's mother, Hastings was, without warning, accused by Gloucester of plotting against him. Dragged from a Council meeting, he was beheaded on the spot with no pretence of legal process. This pre-emptive strike was a clear acknowledgement by Gloucester—proclaiming himself king as Richard III—that Hastings would never countenance his seizure of the throne while Edward's heirs were still alive.

The Grey Family of Groby

Sir Edward Grey married Elizabeth Ferrers, a kinswoman of the Earls of Leicester, and entered the service of Henry VI in 1445. In 1452, their son, Sir John (born 1432), married Elizabeth Woodville, producing two sons, Thomas (born 1457) and Richard. Sir John was killed leading the Lancastrian cavalry at the second battle of St Albans in 1461. His widow then married Edward IV, the man responsible for her husband's death. Her sons were favoured under the Yorkist regime and their step-father created Thomas the Earl of Huntingdon, then Marquis of Dorset. In 1475, he began to build a new semi-fortified house at Groby, but probably never finished it, transferring his efforts to the more picturesquely situated Bradgate in 1490. In 1484, Dorset had defected to Henry Tudor's camp and been placed on a list of traitors by Richard III, but within a few months, his name had been removed and it appeared that Dorset might return to the Yorkist fold. In the end, Dorset remained in France as a surety for a large loan made to Henry Tudor by the French, citing his membership of the Garter as his chivalric guarantee. He thus missed the battle and lived until 1501. His brother, Sir Richard Grey, had been seized by the king and despatched to Pontefract Castle where he, along with others found equally traitorous, was summarily executed. This fate would also befall the daughter of the third Marquess of Dorset, Lady Jane Grey, who, named as heir to the throne by Edward VI, was beheaded after a nine-day reign.

Richard III and the Battle of Bosworth

Richard III's forces had assembled at Leicester to counter the revolt of the Duke of Buckingham in 1483. After Buckingham's death, many of his estates in the east Midlands were passed to men, such as Marmaduke Constable and Gervase Clifton, who were entirely dependent on Richard for their advancement. Henry, Lord Grey of Codnor, received Buckingham's Rutland estates. Constable was entrusted with raising the Midlands in the event of an expected invasion by Henry Tudor, an exercise to be funded by loans, raised by another of Richard's appointments from outside, the courtier Walter Grant.

In August 1485, as Henry Tudor advanced from Wales, the various contingents joining Richard's army converged on Leicester. Richard himself with the bulk of the army had marched from Nottingham in a defensive formation with cavalry on the flanks and the baggage and treasure embedded in the ranks of marching troops. On arrival in Leicester, Richard may have stayed at the White Boar Inn. The final night before the battle was spent under canvas at Sutton Cheney, surrounded by his army of up to 15,000 men, while Henry Tudor's army, less than half that number, was encamped in Fenny Drayton and other villages around Atherstone. The Stanleys' force, ostensibly blocking a possible advance by Henry down Watling Street towards London, had not, as yet, joined up with the king's army. As these three discrete forces manoeuvred around the area seeking to coalesce, there were inevitable frictions. In one such action, members of Hastings' affinity, who continued to serve Richard, were killed. They included Richard Boughton, sheriff of Leicestershire, and John Kebell of Rearsby, a JP, both of them Commissioners of Array, responsible for mobilising Richard's troops. Who finally fought in whose army, or who was even present at the battle, remains a source of confusion, as the contemporary chroniclers were themselves uncertain. Similar ambiguities surround the actual site of the battle long remembered as Bosworth Field. Recent excavations uncovering cannon-shot and other artefacts have shifted the likely battleground some distance from Ambion Hill, traditionally held to have been the centre of operations, to a more likely location nearer to Dadlington and Stoke Golding.

The actual course of the battle is slightly clearer. At first, Richard's superior numbers and the moral force of his artillery, created enormous pressure on the Tudor army. Its nucleus of Breton mercenaries, supplemented by local support gathered on the way from Pembroke, together still amounted to only a single formation. Richard, with many more men at his disposal, had drawn on his own experience as well as a working knowledge of the military textbooks to make his dispositions. He spread his large, tightly packed army across the field, with the cannon and archers on the wings, the vanguard under Norfolk in front, and a rear-guard under Northumberland behind. Since many of his troops were untrained levies, he placed most of them, under veteran leadership, behind the cannon and crossbowmen. A reconstruction of the course of the inevitably confused battle can only be speculative, but a plausible scenario has been posited. After initial exchanges of fire, battle was joined. Henry advanced, Norfolk responded, and hand-to-hand fighting quickly ensued. As Oxford pressed hard against Richard's right, destroying Norfolk's vanguard, a flying wedge attacked Richard's left. The breakdown in morale caused by these twin assaults saw whole bodies of Richard's army either melting away or changing sides, while simultaneously creating a corridor between the two melees. At this critical moment, Richard and a small group of his personal bodyguard attempted a knockout blow and made a desperate attack, aiming for Henry Tudor himself. Ever the opportunist, Sir William Stanley led his 3,000 men, hitherto spectators, in a headlong charge down the hill to smash into Richard's troops, unhorsing and killing the king, so effectively ending the battle.

Richard's body was casually thrown over a horse and carried into Leicester, to be displayed for four days, probably in the Church of St Mary or the Annunciation in the Newarke, containing the tombs of illustrious Lancastrians ancestors. This exhibition was intended to prevent the later appearance of potential pretenders. Henry and his army then spent two days in Leicester. Prior to starting out on his triumphal progress to London, Henry made a royal proclamation announcing the death of Richard and many of his faction, forbidding any further unsanctioned violence. Many of the wounded from the battle were treated in the town, which later received an annuity in recognition of the expense. The king's corpse was then interred, entirely without dignity or ceremony, in the church of the Grey Friars, a proper tomb only being provided at the behest of Henry VII some ten years later. Over 500 years on, the king's skeleton has been excavated, and its identification confirmed by the analysis of mitochondrial DNA from two descendants and the physical evidence of his scoliotic spine. Amid unnecessarily costly lawsuits and claims that Richard should be reinterred in York Minster, his battered body finally came to rest in a magnificent tomb in Leicester Cathedral in 2015.

Henry intended to demonstrate magnanimity in victory by limiting retribution and by being generous to those who had helped or at least did not hinder his venture. William Catesby, who had ensured the execution of Lord Hastings and then seized his estates, was taken alive on the battlefield, brought back to Leicester, and beheaded in the marketplace. Many of those who had changed sides or opted out were rewarded. Piers Curteys, for instance, Richard's Master of the Wardrobe, who had taken himself off into sanctuary before the Bosworth campaign, was reconfirmed in his office by Henry and rewarded with the lordship of Leicester. Robert Throckmorton became sheriff of Leicestershire. Sir Ralph Hastings, younger brother of Lord William, served Henry VII and lived until 1495. Henry was ensuring that any authority he chose to delegate remained in the hands of men who owed everything to him.

The Militia in Tudor Leicestershire and Rutland

Periodically, the government attempted to assess the country's capacity to defend itself against foreign invasion through the local militia, the descendants of the Anglo-Saxon *fyrd*. This force was to be raised by the lords-lieutenant of each county on the orders of the government, and was based on a ballot system, each hundred being given the required quota of men to be raised. The survey of Rutland of 1522 assessed the county's military resources, and it is one of the most complete surviving records in the country. Ostensibly an attempt to gauge the manpower and weaponry available for the defence of the realm, the survey effectively doubled as a wealth assessment for tax-gathering purposes. However, it does give useful and interesting insights into the training and equipment of those inhabitants liable to be mustered in time of war. Able-bodied men aged from sixteen to sixty were listed as either bowmen or bill men. The Statute of Winchester of 1285 required men to equip themselves with harness, armour, or protective clothing and weaponry according to their means as measured by income.

Landowners tended to accumulate kit with which to equip their households or tenants as the nucleus of the militia. This survey appeared to reveal that generations of peace had diluted the enthusiasm for fulfilling these military obligations. Thus, even where a man was listed as an archer, it was, in fact, most unlikely that he would possess the requisite bow and arrows that he might be expected to provide at any imminent muster.

The Rutland survey records the number of eligible men apparently available for military service with a note of their means. A large number of those listed, some 17 per cent of the total, are recorded as 'young men and pore', thus not being expected to provide arms or armour. These are shown as landless, but this is not necessarily a disqualification from being identified as a bill man or an archer, either for labourers or for those listed as servants who would be equipped by their households. In one group of fourteen young, landless men in Lyddington, for instance, six are designated as archers and a further five as bill men. Similarly, ten such labourers in Barrowden are all listed as archers or bill men. In all, some 219 men are listed as archers and a further 418 as bill men. The archers would essentially resemble those who fought at Agincourt, and the bill men would have carried the standard infantry weapon, consisting of a spear with an axe-blade pointing one way and a short spike the other. Both would have been lightly armoured, wearing a coat of leather or thick canvas with small metal plates riveted or sewn in. This was known as a 'jack' or 'jestorn'. Another very similar form of upper body protection was the brigandine, which came in two halves that were laced together front and back, and thus referred to as a 'pair'. Sometimes, a shirt or apron of chain mail might be worn, and the throat might be protected by a 'gorget', the elbows by 'splints', and the head by a steel cap called a 'sallet' or a 'bonnet'. The full set of sallet, jack, gorget, and splints was known as a 'harness'. This survey revealed a glaring deficit in this essential equipment. In the case of weaponry, only eleven bows and fifty-three bills were declared, plus a sword and buckler held by the village of Ayston. One hundred sets of harness were held by named individuals, with a further five sets held communally by the villages of North Luffenham, Edith Weston, Church Stoke, Tinwell, and Ryall. Forty of these sets were held between just five individuals, all Esquires: David Cecil of Tinwell, servant to the King, with twenty sets; John Harrington of Exton with ten sets; Francis Brown of Little Casterton with six sets; and Richard Flower of Whitwell and Edward Sapcote of Burley, both of whom supplied horses as well, with six and four sets respectively. A group of five individuals in Oakham, tenants of the king, had a further ten sets of harness and a horse between them, while six tenants of Sir Thomas Lovell of Ryall had seven sets of harness plus bows and arrows for three archers. A gentleman, Richard Willoughby of Ketton, listed as an archer retained by Sir John Zouch, possessed a horse and a set of harness for himself and for one other, and had three neighbours, one a tenant of Edward Sapcote and listed as another archer, who also boasted their own harness. In addition to the balance of three dozen or so full sets of harness, individual items of armour were owned by a further seventy-odd villagers. This equipment included thirty-eight steel bonnets or sallets, twenty-eight jakes or jestorns, three pairs of brigandines or corslets, two mail shirts or aprons, nine pairs of splints, and four gorgets. All this reveals that only a small proportion of the total muster could be properly equipped for war. More worryingly still was that barely a quarter of the designated, and possibly trained, archers and bill men could be appropriately turned out for military action.

In 1539, Melton Mowbray, at a time when Henry VIII was anticipating trouble with France and Spain, raised sixty-one archers and bill men, with the rest of the Hundred producing up to 500 more—the Hundred of Goscote was required to raise 552 men. Each town held a communal supply of weaponry for issue when the militia was called out. Brownlow describes how in Melton Mowbray, towards the end of the sixteenth century, 'armour, muskets, swords, daggers, pikes, curates, pouldrons etc were stored in the kitchen of the inn in the market-place, and accounted for by the Town Meeting'. The militia were called out at times of national emergency. After royal troops, including the militia, had quelled the Lincolnshire Rising of 1536, John Hussey of Woodhead Castle (R) was executed.

Beacons, the traditional way of alerting the authorities to an invasion, went back to Saxon times. There are examples across the counties, commemorated in place names, generally in hilltop locations. Beacon Hill, near Woodhouse Eaves in Charnwood Forest (SK510147), is an example.

4

Stuart and Georgian Leicestershire and Rutland, 1600–1815

This period encompasses a civil war and a world war. Those living in our counties were affected by the first, which brought actual warfare to their doorsteps, and by the second, which took men off to faraway lands, possibly to die in battle, but, more likely, from poorly treated wounds or disease.

The Civil War

Although Leicester was faced with increasingly unreasonable demands for the royal tax known as Ship Money and the county's MP Sir Arthur Haselrig was one of the five members whom Charles ordered arrested in 1641, there were many citizens who remained wedded to the monarchist cause. Overall, however, the majority of the populace, like those of many other shires, would really have preferred neutrality. The county polarised between the royalist Henry Hastings in the north, based in Ashby-de-la-Zouch, and the parliamentarian south, which included Leicester, under Lord Grey of Groby, son of Henry Grey, Earl of Stamford. These two premier families were well into their second century of feuding and jockeying for dominance in the area. By order of Parliament, Grey was appointed Lord Lieutenant in place of Henry Hastings, but musters were initiated by both sides. Warning the mayor of Leicester not to read the King's Commission of Array, Lord Willoughby of Parham, who had been appointed to command Parliament's troops in the region, proclaimed the Militia Ordinance instead, thereby embodying the trained bands. Hastings responded by mobilising local miners from the family pits, equipping them with arms from Ashby Castle and Garendon Abbey, and marching on Leicester in an unsuccessful attempt to secure the town for the King. His father, the Earl of Huntingdon, sensibly opted out of the conflict, repairing to Castle Donington, where he died in November 1643.

Garrisons

The dividing line, drawn across the middle of the county, was marked by garrisons. Henry Hastings who had been made Colonel-General of the King's forces in

Leicestershire and the surrounding counties, established his family seat of Ashby-de-la-Zouch as the centre of royalist military operations. He patched up the remaining fabric of the fifteenth-century tower house, constructed new earthwork defences and built a detached work to protect the eastern approach. This was the triangular, stone-built Mount House, joined to the castle's Kitchen Tower by a tunnel. Hastings also absorbed into his defensive scheme neighbouring buildings, such as the old grammar school (on the present vicarage site). The garrison was charged with maintaining contact with the vital royalist stronghold of Newark upon Trent, which kept open the route between the royalist headquarters in Oxford, York, and the ports of the north-east—vital for the importation of cannon and other munitions. Ashby represented a secure and convenient staging-post on journeys made between these royalist centres. The Queen stopped at Ashby, in July 1643, while conducting cannon from the port of Bridlington to her husband in Oxford. Again, in March 1644, Ashby was one of the safe stopping points on the march of the royalist army, which had left Shrewsbury to march to the relief of Newark upon Trent. From 1642, other royalist outposts were Hemington Hall, surrounded by earthwork defences, and the fortified house of the Nowell (or Noel) family at North Luffenham, dangerously isolated, deep inside parliamentarian territory. Despite the presence of a 200-man garrison, in early 1643, the house was surprised and quickly surrounded by Grey with a force of 1,200 men. After a bombardment, the hall surrendered, to be plundered and fired. Only the moat remains, but an ancient mound, nearby in Morcott Spinney and possibly once a motte, is said to have been where the parliamentarians mounted their cannon to bombard the hall from the slopes of the valley to the south. The royalists had lost one stronghold, but they compensated for the loss. Belvoir Castle was owned by the Earl of Rutland, a supporter of Parliament. On 28 January 1643, however, one of his gentlemen, Colonel Lucas with eight others, threw a rope over a balcony, climbed in, and opened the gates to royalist troops. Belvoir was then garrisoned for the king, a well-placed addition to the screen of outposts protecting Newark upon Trent.

To counter these royalist forces carrying out continual raids on the contested border-zone, several houses were fortified to accommodate parliamentarian garrisons. These included Bagworth, Kirby Bellars, Coleorton, and Burley on the Hill. The palatial Bradgate House, built by the Greys in the late 1400s, had been fortified by the Earl of Stamford who had secured the contents of Leicester's magazine there to prevent it being taken by Hastings. In August 1642, it was attacked by Prince Rupert, and virtually destroyed and abandoned for the duration.

These garrisons could in no way be described as fortresses, but they incorporated many features that rendered them defensible. Most had a solid medieval house as a core, often surrounded by a moat. Although previously impregnable medieval castles had been degraded by the development of gunpowder, most of the mobile forces of the Civil War, which might threaten a garrison, travelled unencumbered by artillery. Where possible, as at Ashby and Belvoir, outworks of earth and timber would be constructed to add an extra layer of protection and keep the enemy at a distance from the inner core. The further away you kept him, the less damage he could cause by bombardment or mining, and the more

Above: Ashby-de-la-Zouch,
The Mount: a triangular
detached fort of the Civil
War period, connected to the
castle proper by a tunnel.

Right: Bradgate House: the
palatial, fifteenth-century,
semi-fortified house
of the Grey family.

casualties he would sustain in attempting an assault. The effective range of a demi-cannon, used to shatter and shake masonry, was less than 1,000 yards, while that of a demi-culverin, which chopped out individual chunks of stone, was only a little longer. Point-blank bombardment from a range of around 400 yards would clearly do more damage, and much more quickly. Stone or brick walls might be bolstered with earth ramparts against both inner and outer faces to absorb shot. Such ramparts might be realistically beyond the scope of most garrisons for it took a thickness of 15 feet (4.5 m) of earth to stop the 27-pound (12.25 kg) shot fired by a demi-cannon, but a mere 30 inches (75 cm) of earth could stop a musket ball. However, it must be remembered that moving artillery was an enormous undertaking. Even the relatively small saker, which fired a 5-lb (2-kg) shot up to 2,000 yards, weighed in at 2,500 pounds (1,136 kg) and required a team of two dozen men and five horses to move it, so a garrison would count itself unlucky if faced with an artillery bombardment.

To prepare a house as a garrison, the buildings themselves might require only minimal modification. Loopholes and gun ports would be knocked through the walls; windows might be blocked up; thatched roofs of outbuildings removed; and gates narrowed and barricaded. Food and fodder would be stockpiled; powder and shot stored somewhere dry; and a water supply secured. The garrison was primarily a base for raiding enemy territory, intercepting the enemy's troop movements, disrupting his supply arrangements, or defining a line of demarcation. Assault by an army with a siege train was unlikely, but if it could resist capture, it would tie up enemy resources and buy time for a field army to manoeuvre.

The maintenance of garrisons was an expensive business, and Hastings' men quickly gained a reputation for terrorising the locality and seizing livestock and grain, as well as cash. Hastings sent warrants to surrounding villages ordering them to send provisions to his garrisons or risk being 'exposed to the plunder of the hungry soldier'. The Dutch mercenary engineer Jan Dalbier was quartered on Kibworth for a time with an unruly regiment of parliamentarian cavalry who stripped the village of food supplies. Those villages unfortunate enough to be located within the orbit of both sides often found themselves being taxed twice over. The tiny garrison of Burley on the Hill still cost Colonel Waite, its commander, between £100 and £200 per week in pay and provisions, and the total cost of

A Saker: one of the guns most likely to have been used at the siege of Leicester. It could fire a ball weighing a little over 5 lb (2.4 kg) to a maximum range of 3,000 yards. This replica was photographed at Ayr Citadel.

Leicestershire's complement of 1,500 garrison troops amounted to a yearly cost of £97,000. Neither Parliament nor King offered prompt payment of expenses, but disagreements were not limited to money. During 1644, Hastings, now Lord Loughborough, the royalist commander of Ashby, complained of the insubordinate behaviour of Lucas, his opposite number at Belvoir, who disputed both the legitimacy of Loughborough's command, and the limits of the territory from which he might extract supplies.

Skirmishes

Constant raiding and counter-raiding took their toll on both towns and manor houses. Melton Mowbray's parliamentarian garrison was first attacked by Colonel Lucas from Belvoir. In one particularly effective action in November 1643, having been tipped off that the Worshipful Committee from Leicester was visiting the town to enact forfeits on royalist townsfolk, he attacked the town with 300 dragoons. The garrison, although outnumbering their attackers, was taken completely by surprise and quickly made prisoner, suffering only one casualty. Lucas carried away 300 of the garrison as well as the officials from Leicester as prisoners. Burley on the Hill built by the Duke of Buckingham in the 1620s changed hands several times. Like Kirby Bellars and Coleorton, it was abandoned by its parliamentarian garrison after the fall of Leicester in May 1645, and a royalist force slighted the outer defences. Parliament later finished the job and it was only rebuilt at the end of the century.

In March 1644, an attempt to prevent the King's army from Oxford linking up with Rupert's cavalry to relieve the siege of Newark upon Trent resulted in a skirmish outside Loughborough. A royalist raiding party had attacked Leicester, seeking to neutralise its garrison while the royalist army passed through the area, but on its return, the party ran into a parliamentarian force at Cotes where the River Soar was crossed by a succession of six bridges. The two parliamentarian commanders, Sir Edward Hartopp and Colonel Thornhaugh, missed a golden opportunity to rout the royalist force that, having driven off an initial, half-hearted attack, was able to fortify the bridges. It took a bombardment by two cannon, brought up from Leicester, to force the royalists to abandon their position. Attempting to regain the sanctuary of Ashby, their fleeing cavalry then suffered further casualties when the pursuit caught up with them through Loughborough.

By the middle of 1644, the local parliamentarian commanders, Gell in Derbyshire and Grey in Leicestershire, took joint action to curb the depredations of the raiding parties based on Ashby and Belvoir, frustrating Lord Loughborough's efforts to capture parliamentarian supply trains. A force of royalist cavalry was intercepted near Hinckley on 1 July, and an attempt to seize ammunition wagons in Leicester was foiled by a pre-emptive strike by Grey's troops. Successive setbacks soon forced Hastings to quit the town and withdraw into the castle in Ashby. In September, his troops failed in an attack on another parliamentarian convoy between Leicester and Nottingham. They then attacked the empty wagons on their return, but were trounced outside Costock by the escorting troops who killed the royalist captain and captured many of his men with their

Cotes Bridge, outside Loughborough, was the scene of an important skirmish in March 1644.

horses and plunder. Another royalist tactic was to abduct puritan clerics. An attempt at Loughborough was foiled by the townswomen, but three men were taken back to Ashby from the church at Mountsorrel (or Rothley in one account). Gell and Grey combined forces again in November 1644 to besiege Ashby making Lord Beaumont's adjacent Tudor mansion at Coleorton the strongly fortified nucleus of a tight blockade. Three separate expeditions from Ashby to collect fodder, to attack a house near Leicester, and to carry out a surprise attack on the troops in Coleorton were foiled, with significant royalist loss for no gain. The depleted force at Ashby then became subject to a closer investment.

The Belvoir garrison continued to hold out but also saw increasing curbs on its freedom to raid, with a parliamentarian garrison being installed at Stonesby near Waltham on the Wolds. In October 1644, an attempt was made to relieve the siege of Crowland (Lincolnshire) by a force from Belvoir, but parliamentarian troops at Bourne intercepted a royalist courier and were able to ambush the royalists, killing sixty and capturing over 300. The sole royalist success in the county during this time was a devastating raid on Market Harborough which plundered the town from the 'sign of the Ram all along to the Crown'.

By the start of 1645, the parliamentarian forces under Grey and Gell appeared to be in the ascendancy, but there was little room for complacency. Pitched battles had, up until now, been rare in the county, but in February 1645, a force of about 3,000 royalist cavalry under Sir Marmaduke Langdale had been despatched by the king to provide aid to the Newark garrison. Proceeding from Market Harborough, they came up against a similar number of parliamentarian horse under Colonel Rossiter, outside Melton Mowbray. The royalists manoeuvred to gain favourable ground, but Rossiter's men played into their hands by surging forward from what had been a strong defensive position. The royalists deployed their baggage train along each flank as protection, thus both blunting the enemy's charge and preserving the wagons from pillage. After three attempts to break the royalist line, the parliamentarians were routed, leaving over 100 dead on the field and as many prisoners, with a similar number of casualties on the royalist side. A royalist officer described the action as leaving neither side able to claim victory, but it was nevertheless a symbol of a royalist resurgence. Nineteenth-century building operations, north of Melton's cattle market, uncovered numbers of skeletons assumed to be casualties of the battle.

In April, the Self-Denying Ordinance was enacted. This forced those officers who also served as MPs to resign their commissions, so both Lord Grey and Sir Arthur Haselrig, representing respectively the City and County of Leicester passed their commands to colleagues. Haselrig had commanded the Leicestershire regiment of 'lobsters', heavy cavalry, similar to Cromwell's Ironsides. In May, the king moved eastwards via Ashby and Loughborough to threaten Leicester as a way of heading off the parliamentarian threat to take Oxford, his capital. On 29 May, the King and Prince Rupert arrayed an army of over 6,000 men before Leicester's Newarke; two cannon were fired to attract the attention of the townsfolk; and a trumpeter relayed the king's command to surrender. This was rejected by Colonel Sir Robert Pye who commanded the garrison, and Rupert immediately began a bombardment.

The Siege of Leicester

The Roman and medieval defences of Leicester were much decayed by the early seventeenth-century, although Grey, who had his headquarters in the castle, might have initiated some minor work on the defences. However, the question of how unprepared for a siege the city was caused much acrimonious debate after its capture, so it is likely that few improvements had been carried out. The castle occupied the south-west corner of the town, with the fifteenth-century Newarke lying to the south of the earlier medieval core. Its main gate, used in the seventeenth century as a store for the town's munitions, is still known as the Magazine Gate. Correspondence passing between Lord Grey and the Corporation appear to highlight at least two significant weaknesses in the defences. One related to allegations that certain persons of means were ensuring that their houses within the Newarke were being strengthened, at the expense of the bulk of the citizenry, the defences of whose homes being thereby neglected. The second involved the refusal by the Clerk to the Corporation to allow new works to be constructed on his land, a potential weak spot at the junction of the Newarke wall with the southern defences. After the siege, it was felt that had the town walls, particularly those surrounding the Newarke, been backed by an earthen bank and fronted by a thick earthen rampart, as was the current practice, they would have offered much more resistance to Rupert's cannonade. The leadership was also accused of a lack of professionalism in that they should have shortened the defensive perimeter and demolished many more houses in order to do so. In this case, the inhabitants might have questioned what was actually being defended. Grey must take the blame here for failing to appoint a more experienced governor with a less parochial, if brutal perspective.

In the time available, only a limited amount of improvement was possible. The walls of the Newarke and those of St Mary's churchyard were loopholed for standing and kneeling musketeers, and some gun loops were also cut. A bank and ditch around the medieval town as far as the stream that runs into the Soar north of the town was constructed. Where this line crossed roads, flankers were incorporated, and there would appear to have been a large bastion at Horse Fair Leys, which acted as a platform for most of the town's artillery. South of the Newarke, Grange Farm was ordered to be demolished to improve the defenders' fields of fire. Later, other properties on the outskirts of the defensive perimeter, particularly those harbouring royalist troops who first had to be dislodged, were also cleared away. The defenders numbered just over 2,000 men, with possibly as few as nine guns, the number reported captured after the capitulation. Three cannon, despatched from the Tower of London armouries earlier in the month, almost certainly never arrived in time. Around 250 regular cavalry were reinforced at the last minute by 100 horse from the garrison at Kirby Bellars, and by 200 dragoons *en route* to Nottingham. Fewer than 500 regular infantry were supported by 900 untrained townsmen, and a further 150 men recruited from surrounding villages. This force would prove totally inadequate in numbers to man a circuit of defences that measured more than 3 miles around.

Rupert's textbook bombardment of the Newarke with six heavy guns, possibly emplaced on the Roman aqueduct known as the Rawdykes, quickly opened a breach in the wall at Grange Lane. That night, an assault was made here and, more tellingly—in that the defenders were forced to respond to multiple simultaneous assaults—at points on the northern and south-eastern defences. The defenders built a retrenchment behind the breach out of woolsacks and debris, but the attackers kept up the pressure. In other places, ceramic hand grenades were used to clear the defenders from the gates; ladders were used to cross the ditch; and infiltrators were able to cut the drawbridge chains allowing royalist cavalry to enter the town. Gradually, as royalist troops stormed the defences on all sides of the town, fierce hand-to-hand fighting took place around High Cross and St Martin's church, forcing the defenders to retreat down High Cross Street into the Newarke. Despite a sally by the defenders' cavalry, Rupert's men captured the town battery in the bastion at Horse Fair Leys, and the other assault parties converged on the Newarke where the exhausted defenders were finally forced to surrender after three days without respite.

The Composition (terms of surrender) were, on the face of it, very generous. The personal safety of defender and the non-combatant alike was guaranteed, and the town was to be preserved from plunder. However, the reality was very different, though possibly not as bad as some commentators claimed. On the pretext of mopping up pockets of continuing resistance, royalist troops murdered defenceless men and women and lynched a puritan preacher. The royalist chronicler Clarendon admits that the troops ran amok:

[They pursued] their advantage with the usual license of rapine and plunder, and miserably sacked the whole town without any distinction of person or places, churches and hospitals as well as other houses being made a prey to the enraged and greedy soldier.

Above: Leicester: the walls of the Newarke were loopholed for muskets during the first siege of 1645.

Right: Sketch map to show the defences of Leicester during the siege of 1645. The Roman and medieval walls were supplemented by an earthwork rampart and ditch on the east and south, with hornworks where the main roads left the city. At Horsefair Leys stood a bastion. The walls of Newarke were loopholed for musketeers. Siege batteries were thrown up on the south to bombard the Newarke.

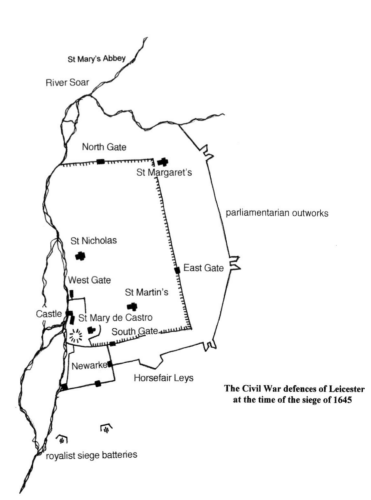

St Mary's Abbey

River Soar

North Gate

St Margaret's

parliamentarian outworks

St Nicholas

East Gate

West Gate

St Martin's

Castle

St Mary de Castro

South Gate

Newarke

Horsefair Leys

The Civil War defences of Leicester at the time of the siege of 1645

royalist siege batteries

Charles I is credited with mixed feelings, on the one hand regretting that some of the victims might actually have been his loyal subjects, riding through the street calling for restraint, while on the other, being accused at his trial of encouraging the eradication of his enemies. If the commanders of a town had been given the opportunity to surrender without bloodshed, but had refused as had Leicester's, then the conventions of war allowed for violent retribution. It could be argued that, given the smallness of the garrison, the lack of ordnance, the length of the defensive perimeter, and the weakness of the defences, only a token defence should have been offered. The royalist troops were enraged because they had unnecessarily suffered possibly three times as many casualties (including some thirty officers) in the assault than had the defenders. How many of the defenders and townsfolk were killed after the surrender will never be known, but the total of fatalities on both sides exceeded 700—a number probably doubled by those subsequently dying of wounds since even minor injuries would often become gangrenous. The amount of plunder carted away, which included the town's civic regalia, is clearer, as 140 wagon-loads were removed to Newark upon Trent. A final imposition on the townsfolk was an additional fine of £2,000. The king, having achieved his objective of removing the threat to his capital, returned to Oxford, leaving behind a garrison of 1,200 men under Lord Loughborough to repair the fortifications. Unaccountably, unless it was seen to be obstructing the defences, the soldiers burned down Cavendish House, built around 1600 out of the ruins of the abbey.

Archaeological excavation has uncovered remains of spherical, ceramic hand grenades, and clusters of spent cannon balls in a number of locations including the Newarke and Horsefair Leys. A number of musket and gun loops can still be seen in the walls of the Newarke.

Defeat for the King

Having succeeded in his object of luring the parliamentarian General Fairfax away from his investment of Oxford, and forcing their garrisons into a precipitate withdrawal from parliamentarian Coleorton, Burley, and Bagworth, Charles could not have anticipated the events of the next two weeks. While he manoeuvred around south Leicestershire, Fairfax was intent on forcing an encounter in the field. The royalist army had been depleted by its losses in the fighting and the installation of a garrison at Leicester. The king had marched to Market Harborough, intending to return to Leicester and thence to the relative safety of Newark upon Trent, but soon learned that Fairfax might be threatening Buckingham. He therefore marched toward Northampton, being joined by Rupert's cavalry from Great Glen. Fairfax, with an army of 14,000 men, roughly twice the number of the royalists, brought the king to battle at Naseby on 14 June 1645, winning a crushing victory. With only a brief stop at Wistow Hall to exchange his accoutrements for something less conspicuously regal, the king was conducted to Ashby. Most of his surviving infantry surrendered on the field, but many of his horse were cut down in flight, some almost gaining Leicester. Many of the wounded were carried from the field of battle to the church in Market Harborough. Within two days of his victory, Fairfax and Cromwell had returned to Leicester's already battered walls.

Strongholds Regained

The parliamentarian cavalry surrounded the town and, using cannon captured at Naseby, immediately commenced a bombardment of the very walls so easily breached a fortnight previously and now tumbling once more. Having learned discretion from such recent experience, Lord Loughborough gratefully accepted terms. Captives were released and Parliament gained, in addition to all the royalist cannon and munitions, all those lost in the first siege. The town was compensated for its losses from the proceeds of sequestrated royalist estates. In 1646, the garrison slighted the remaining fortifications and left the town.

Asby-de-la-Zouch was next to be invested, but the defences proved too strong for a frontal assault, so the parliamentarian force settled down to a long siege. It was only after nearly six months that the defenders, weakened by an ever-diminishing diet, succumbed to an outbreak of plague and were forced to surrender on 2 March 1646. As a condition of surrender, Lord Loughborough and his brother not only gained safe conducts to leave the country, but also secured their estates from sequestration. A further condition of these more than generous terms was that the castle's strong defences, notably the great tower, should be slighted. However, this was not effected until 1649, after a report to Parliament drew attention to its status as both habitable and defensible.

In October 1645, it was the turn of Belvoir Castle to face the prospect of a prolonged siege, and on 5 October, Sir Gervase Lucas, the governor, took in a reinforcement of 300 horse under Gerrard. By 4 November, the castle was still not fully invested as the King stopped by on his way north. Within two weeks, Poyntz and Rossiter set up camp at Bottesford prior to cutting off Belvoir from the outside world, and strengthening the blockade of Newark. On 22 November, the outworks were stormed and the water-supply cut off, forcing the defenders to retire behind the inner defences on top of the enormous motte. The Duke of Rutland allowed Belvoir village to be burned to clear the approaches to the castle, and a mortar, supervised by a Mr Garner, was brought up. Contemporary accounts speak of the parliamentarian officers driving their troops on at sword point, and rewarding them with £40 worth of strong drink, after the successful assault in early February 1646. Lucas was given terms that allowed him to take his garrison to Lichfield, with arms and colours. As at Ashby, the castle was slighted in 1649. Leicester's walls gradually eroded as the town expanded, but only in 1773 were the gates finally demolished as a hindrance to traffic.

The Army in the Eighteenth Century

After the Restoration of Charles II in 1660, the regular, or New Model Army established in 1645, was swiftly reduced in numbers, but some of the existing regiments were reformed as the basis for a new standing army under Captain-General Monck. Wars against the Dutch and Monmouth's rebellion of 1685 prompted the establishment of further regiments.

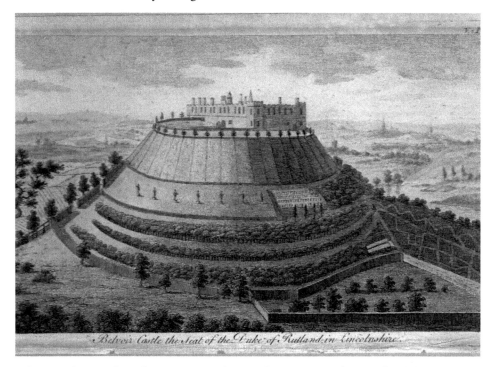

Belvoir Castle: an eighteenth-century print showing the Norman castle mound and the later house of 1655–68. The embattled angle-towers are survivors of the fifteenth-century rebuild by the de Ros family. They had regained a ruinous building following the execution of Lord Hastings, who had robbed building materials for his castles of Ashby and Kirby Muxloe. (*Author's collection*)

The 17th Foot or Leicestershire Regiment

The regiment was first formed in 1688 and served in most of the wars of the next century both in Europe and in North America. Until the end of the eighteenth century, regular regiments spent the majority of their time abroad as the notion of a standing army at home was anathema to most Britons. In 1782, however, infantry regiments of the line were instructed to foster local ties with a view to better developing recruiting bases. The 17th Foot was allocated Leicestershire, reflecting this link in its new title. During the French Wars (1793–1815), the two battalions of the Leicestershire Regiment, after participating in a failed expedition in the Low Countries, reverted to a single battalion establishment, which was posted to India. It remained there until 1823, fighting in a number of taxing campaigns, being rewarded with the 'Hindoostan' badge and gaining its 'Tigers' nickname.

The Militia

Leicester and Rutland were both recorded as having militias in 1648, partly funded by the sale of materials salvaged from slighted fortifications such as Ashby-de-la-Zouch. The high cost of raising and maintaining cavalry was noted especially. As a result of economies, the Rutland militia cavalry was reduced to eighty troopers in 1655. In 1697, there were 175 troopers organised into three troops of horse under Colonel Ross and 609 infantrymen in six companies of foot under Colonel Lister. The start of the Seven Years' War in 1756 saw a revival of a New Militia and a total reorganisation under the Lords Lieutenant, who were now responsible for raising county regiments of Militia. In 1760, the Leicestershire Regiment of Militia was formed but many counties had not completed the task until 1778, by which time a new conflict had developed in the American colonies. Leicestershire was assessed at 560 men, with Rutland providing a further 120. These units were generally composed of long-serving, and thus trained, substitutes who would be subject to the same discipline as the regulars, but would only operate in the British Isles, usually out of their home county to avoid conflicts of interest if employed on internal security duties. A reassessment in 1802 (the 42nd Act of Parliament during the reign of George III) gave comparative militia strengths of 643 for Leicestershire and eighty-three for Rutland. The 26th or Leicestershire Regiment of Militia served in Ireland in 1798, and at other times during the wars, under the command of the Duke of Rutland, were stationed at the heart of the invasion coast in Dover. By this time, the wars had caused so many of the militiamen to transfer into the regular army that it became necessary to recruit a whole new Local Militia purely for home defence.

Volunteer Corps

Alongside the Militia, volunteer companies of infantry and cavalry were raised, usually on the initiative and under the command of a member of the establishment, often from the local aristocracy. The original impetus for such bodies originated in fears of foreign invasion, particularly at the time of the 1745 Jacobite Rebellion with its accompanying threat of French support, and further threats from France during the Seven Years' War. However, it could be argued that a stronger motivation for the creation of a volunteer force derived from fears of the potential impact the events of 1789 in France might be having on the English working man. Many local defence associations were raised unashamedly to protect the property of the middling and upper classes with little pretence of patriotic endeavour. By 1794, there were over thirty volunteer Yeomanry cavalry corps in existence, with seventy-two corps of volunteer infantry or artillery nationwide, and these numbers would steadily increase throughout the period. Many were stood down after the Peace of Amiens in 1802, but would be re-embodied the next year when hostilities resumed. By the end of 1803, some 3,500 men had come forward to serve in the several corps that had been raised in Leicestershire and Rutland.

Volunteer Yeomanry Cavalry

By one of those strange quirks of history, the very first such unit in the country was formed, ironically, in the smallest county, and one which could not be much further from an invasion coast. What is stranger is that two volunteer cavalry regiments were formed in Rutland. The Earl of Winchilsea, Lord Lieutenant of Rutland, forwarded to the government a proposal for a 'mounted corps of Gentlemen and Yeomanry' in March 1794. The idea gained substance at a meeting at Oakham Castle and recruiting began, attracting over 150 suitable gentlemen and yeomen under the earl's leadership. It is claimed as the first Yeomanry regiment based on the government's recently publicised regulations. Presented with their colours at Uppingham in October 1795, the initial three troops of fifty expanded to four of seventy-three, before stabilising with an establishment of around 170 men. They served continuously throughout the wars, and even survived well into the nineteenth century.

The Rutland Fencible Cavalry was the inspiration, also in 1794, of Gerald Noel Edwards MP of Catmose House, Oakham, and formerly an officer in the Militia. What made Mr Edwards's undertaking even more remarkable was his provision of a dedicated riding school, stables, and limited domestic accommodation for the Fencibles, and this at a time when barracks for the regulars were still a rarity. The domestic part, now known as Catmose Cottage and occupied by the Registry Office, and the riding school and stables, now the Rutland County Museum, still stand on Catmos Street in Oakham. This perfectly preserved complex represents the national prototype for the class of building later known as drill halls. The Fencibles served in Scotland; offered to serve in Ireland but were rebuffed; and were disbanded in 1800. It is likely that the Lord Lieutenant's regiment would have enjoyed more of a draw and that there was really no room for two such outfits in such a small place.

A meeting at the Three Crowns in Leicester was called in April 1794 to advance the proposed formation of a regiment of Leicestershire Yeomanry cavalry to consist of six troops, each of fifty men. On 4 July, the full complement, as projected, paraded on the racecourse and was named the Loyal Leicestershire Volunteer Cavalry. Their officers provided temporary accommodation for them in a converted workhouse. Within a short time, further troops had been raised at Ashby-de-la-Zouch and Lutterworth. Although these units were dissolved in 1802, they were speedily resurrected a year later, after the breakdown of the Peace of Amiens, as it became clear that the need for them had intensified and they were to remain in being after the peace of 1815.

The Volunteer Infantry

The meetings held at Leicester's Three Crowns in 1794 also produced the Loyal Corps of Leicestershire Volunteer Infantry of one company of 100 men, soon increased to two companies. In December of that year, sixty citizens of Melton Mowbray enrolled in the Melton Loyal Volunteer, under the command of a respected local solicitor, Mr Parkes. In recognition of the apparently parlous state of the nation's defences, they agreed to extend their commitment by accepting deployment to anywhere in the British Isles, much like the Militia's terms of service. By 1798, similar corps of volunteer infantry had sprung up in Ashby and Hinckley. All this activity ran alongside the expansion of the Local Militia, and in 1797, Melton Mowbray hosted a training camp for the 4th Battalion of

Oakham: the Riding School of the Rutland Fencible Cavalry.

Oakham: Catmos Cottage was the domestic element of the Fencibles' HQ and Riding School.

the Leicestershire Local Militia, whose members were complimented on their behaviour toward the townsfolk. In 1798, Mr Edwards of Oakham, having inherited the estates of the Earl of Gainsborough and now assuming the Noel family name, formed the Rutland Volunteer Infantry. Along with the other such units that went into suspended animation in 1802, they reformed in 1803, but with a smaller establishment of three companies, each of eighty men. This must have been some compensation for his failed fencibles.

The renewal of the war against Napoleon prompted the raising of new units. The Duke of Rutland found 1,000 volunteers for the Belvoir Volunteers. Unlike Mr Parkes the solicitor, not all officers enjoyed the confidence of their men. The Duke of Rutland appointed the Prince Regent's foppish friend, Captain 'Beau' Brummell, to command his new Belvoir Volunteers. During his time as a serving officer, Brummell avoided postings to unfashionable places, but now greatly enjoyed designing uniforms for his new command. Sadly, he missed their inspection by the Commander-in-Chief as he fell off his horse on the way to the parade. Lack of confidence in officers who were unable to deliver the correct commands caused a mutiny in Melton Mowbray in 1804, and the local volunteer unit was summarily disbanded. Some units based their conduct on principles that were democratic and egalitarian rather than military, and obedience to orders was not always given immediate priority with predictable results.

Other infantry corps included the 500-plus-strong West Leicestershire Regiment of Loyal Volunteers, the Loyal Leicester Volunteers (with an increased establishment of 480), and smaller corps at Loughborough, at Shepshed and Garendon, and at Ashby-de-la-Zouch. These all generally maintained sufficient discipline to get by, but had their difficulties, with expulsions, forced resignations, misunderstandings, disagreements, rivalries, and resentments. Five years later, most of these had ceased to exist as residual enthusiasm waned and the danger of invasion receded. Resignations and absenteeism forced the demise of many, but those that had managed to last longer were still mainly disbanded, like the Rutland Volunteer Infantry in 1810. Unlike most of its fellow corps, the Earl of Winchilsea's 'Sharpshooters', a corps of riflemen, which he had raised to support the Yeomanry, analogous to the light infantry skirmishers or 'Greenjackets', survived until 1813. After 1804, Ashby-de-la-Zouch hosted French officers, on parole as prisoners of war. Having given their word of honour not to attempt escape, they would not have troubled the town's militiamen.

Local tradition records that Loughborough's Devonshire Square commemorates the use of the space as a parade ground by a regiment of Devon men. Colonel Hay's 1908 history of the Constitutional Force, or Militia, confirms that, in 1812, the Devon Militia was posted to the East Midlands in response to the activities of the Luddites. It was customary to bring in unfamiliar troops from distant parts of the country in order to avoid local militiamen from being subverted by relatives or acquaintances.

Logistics: The Grand Junction and Grand Union Canals

In March 1795, some local fencibles attempted to detain two deserters who were given sanctuary by navvies working on the Grand Union Canal at Kibworth. When the altercation became violent, and they were attacked by the navvies, the fencibles summoned reinforcements from Leicester. A troop of the Loyal Leicestershire Volunteer Cavalry was despatched, and, as the action moved closer to Leicester, a JP read the Riot Act at Oadby, with volunteer and regular infantry both arriving on the scene to restore order. Four trouble-makers were identified by the fencibles, arrested, and sent for trial to Leicester, and a further nine navvies were arrested. All were eventually acquitted, and the deserters were never found. This action in support of the Civil Power was a foretaste of what was to come later, particularly for the Yeomanry, who would increasingly find themselves dealing with industrial unrest.

The canals proved useful in moving troops around quickly in time of war. In 1798, the 1,285 men of the Leicestershire Militia were sent to Ireland to quell nationalist unrest. They were marched to Nuneaton for onward transportation to Liverpool via the Coventry, Trent and Mersey, and Bridgwater Canals, in boats each holding 100 men and weighing 12 tons.

Throughout the Napoleonic Wars, there was a perceived threat of a French invasion, and despite an expectation that the Royal Navy would prevent an enemy landing, it was still deemed advisable to have contingency plans. As late as 1811, long after the threat should have evaporated, detailed plans were drawn up for the southward transference of the militia regiments concentrated in Staffordshire in the event of an invasion. They would join the force known as Thames Army. Based on a census of canal boats, these troops would either join the Coventry Canal from Lichfield or the Birmingham Canal to be transported through Braunston onto the Grand Junction Canal and thence down to London. Baggage from Lichfield was to be carried by wagon through Hinckley, Lutterworth, and Market Harborough and on down the present A6 to London. In 1812, a great improvement was made to the canal system when the Grand Union was connected from Norton Junction east of Braunston, via the newly constructed Foxton Locks, to the Soar Navigation, which ran past Leicester and Loughborough and on up to the Trent at Trentlock, between Burton and Nottingham.

Foxton Locks, opened in 1812, connected the Grand Union Canal to the River Trent, easing the transportation of troops and munitions until the coming of the railways.

5

The Victorian Period, 1815–1914

The conclusion of the French wars brought economic depression right across England. In our counties, as in many others, the mechanisation of industrial processes, particularly in the hosiery and lace industries, prompted violent reactions. A state of peace at home coexisted with a whole sequence of wars abroad. These ranged from small-scale colonial punitive expeditions; through defence against violent attacks on British imperialism with the subsequent savage reprisals; and to confrontations and armed conflict between the great powers. To accommodate the conflicting demands on the nation's military resources, large-scale and radical reorganisations of the army were gradually planned and eventually implemented. The Victorian army consisted of several elements that would all come together by the start of the First World War. The Regular Army already existed, but would undergo radical change; the Yeomanry and Militia would each evolve very differently from their beginnings; and the Volunteers would be developed as a parallel force to the regulars.

The Reorganisation of the Regular Army

Since the orders of George III in 1782 to cultivate local connections, the 17th Foot may have been recruiting from the city and county, but they spent most of the nineteenth century abroad, for the most part in Asia: India, Aden, Afghanistan, and Burma, with a single excursion to the Crimea in 1854–56. The Regiment's 2nd Battalion was raised in 1858, and after a spell in Canada it, too, was sent to India. In 1881, the government reforms led by Edward Cardwell formally tied regiments to specific localities, generally counties, and required them to establish permanent regimental depots, usually in the county town. The 17th Foot officially became the Leicestershire Regiment with a depot at Glen Parva, centre of the 17th Military District. The 58th Foot, hitherto loosely linked with Rutland, was joined with the 48th Foot to form a new Northamptonshire Regiment. With the outbreak of war in South Africa in 1899, the Leicesters' 1st Battalion was posted from India to Natal, engaging in close-run actions and enduring the four-month siege of Ladysmith. Back home, training attempted to build on the lessons of the previous conflict. Summer camps were held across the area: Edale in 1906, Whitwick in 1911, and, in 1909, the 1st Battalion got the chance to shoot on the state-of-the-art ranges at Lydd in Kent.

Prince Albert's Own Leicestershire Yeomanry Cavalry

Most yeomanry regiments were disbanded in 1815 or, at best, granted a stay of execution until about 1832, after which time they were generally needed less often for riot-control. It would not be until the end of the century that many would be re-embodied for service in South Africa. However, the Leicestershire Yeomanry Cavalry was one of those few units to boast unbroken service, gaining the attribution of 'Prince Albert's Own' in 1844. The Leicestershire Yeomanry were essentially amateur soldiers who drilled in their ten troops, scattered across the counties, only coming together as a complete regiment once a year. This assembly took place during Leicester's Race Week, held every September on Victoria Park racecourse, but after 1859, their annual exercises were brought forward to a week in May. Despite limited opportunities to drill together, their annual inspections reported favourably. An experienced officer from the 3rd Light Dragoons was appointed as adjutant in 1834 and served until 1863. He was succeeded by another professional cavalry officer from the 17th Lancers. There was a regular staff-sergeant for each troop, but the regiment had to pay a Regimental Sergeant-Major from private funds. A sign of the 600-plus troopers' commitment and status was the fact that, in 1856, over 90 per cent of them were owner riders. The regiment was seen as part of the community, a source of local pride, and able to draw on local support. In the 1880s, Henry Clarke, with a shop at 371–2 Gallowtree Gate, Leicester, was their armourer.

The officers came from the upper echelons of local society and included members of the aristocracy and MPs. Such connections permeated the regiment's activities. In 1898, the annual camp was held at Garendon Park, whose owner, Major E. M. P. de Lisle, commanded 'C' Squadron from 1902–06. Other venues for annual camps included Croxton Park and Aston-on-Trent, Staffordshire, where joint exercises were held with the Staffordshire and Derbyshire Yeomanries. Shooting practice was carried out on the range at Syston. The fashionable hunting scene, centred on Melton Mowbray widened the regiment's connections still further. In 1884, for instance, Craven Lodge was bought by Colonel Baldock who later commanded the 3rd (County of London) Imperial Yeomanry, nicknamed the 'Sharpshooters', formed in 1901 from veterans of the South African wars. The Leicestershire Yeomanry formed a company of the Imperial Yeomanry for service in South Africa, fighting the Boers. This 7th Company, consisting of five officers and 132 troopers, joined with similar companies from other yeomanry regiments to form the 4th Battalion Imperial Yeomanry. They fought throughout 1900–01, being joined in late 1900 by a second company, the 65th raised in Leicestershire. Both companies returned home in autumn 1901, having lost several killed and many more the victims of disease.

The Militia

After the end of the French wars, the militia was allowed to stagnate. A new order of precedence was established by William IV in 1833, and a War Office circular of 1845 set out a new basis of voluntary recruitment. Henceforth, there would only be resort to the ballot in an emergency. Finally, in 1852, all this was formalised in a new Militia Act. The Militia had long been eligible for service anywhere in the British Isles and, consequently, a detachment of fourteen officers and 324 other ranks from the 26th Leicestershire Regiment of Militia was sent to Ireland in 1856 on internal security duties. This was so that regular troops, on garrison duty in Ireland, could be released for service in the Crimea or in India at the time of the Mutiny. As with the Yeomanry, Militia officers were men of prominence in the county. The Duke of Rutland commanded the Leicestershire Militia, with his son, the Marquis of Granby, as second-in-command. Some of the officers had previous military experience: one in the 7th Hussars, another as commandant of a fort in West Africa, and the adjutant who had served for twenty-two years as an officer in the 19th Foot, later the Green Howards. In 1881, Cardwell's reorganisation brought the Militias into the regimental fold. The 26th Leicestershire Regiment of Militia became the Leicestershire Regiment's 3rd Battalion and moved into the regimental depot. Similarly, the Rutlandshire Militia, along with the Northamptonshire Militia, was taken into the 48th Regimental District in Northampton. While in the past, a militiaman who signed up for the regulars could be charged with desertion, the Militia was now to be seen as a legitimate source of recruits for the regiment's two regular battalions, and an instrument for running the depot and training recruits. Militiamen were eligible to serve abroad if they chose to volunteer. In early 1902, twenty-five officers and 584 other ranks of the Leicesters' 3rd (Militia) Battalion embarked for South Africa. The British strategy was to constrain the movements of the Boer commandos by constructing lines of blockhouses, linked by wire fences and served by the railways. The Militia constructed and garrisoned these blockhouses, and patrolled the railway lines, releasing regular troops to the field army. They returned home at the end of the year, having lost ten men to enemy action, extremes of weather, and disease.

The Rifle Volunteers

The 'Scares' of the 1860s were caused by general fears attached to the accession of Napoleon III in France and his family's long-held ambitions, and specific concerns generated by his revolutionary armoured warship, *La Gloire*. This was to operate from the newly built French naval base at Cherbourg, and perceived as lying too close to Portsmouth for comfort. These anxieties resulted in a massive and expensive construction programme to defend the British naval bases: Portsmouth, Chatham, Portland, Plymouth, and Milford Haven. These enormous fortresses would soon come to be known as 'Palmerston's Follies'. After the Crimean War and the Indian Mutiny a few years previously, there had been a feeling that the standard of the nation's musketry would benefit from improvement.

All these perceptions of vulnerability prompted, in 1859, the formation of a national rifle association, and this, in turn, led to a call for the creation of a volunteer movement to be organised on military lines but at the local level. Mayor Biggs of Leicester was one of those who pointed out that, under the rules of war, armed civilians would be hanged as *francs tireurs* if caught by an enemy, and that a uniformed corps would pose fewer risks. Consequently, Leicester was among the first cohort of Rifle Volunteers Corps to form. The 1st Leicestershire Rifle Corps was among the earliest in the country, becoming No. 31 in the official Order of Precedence. It formed on 31 August 1859, three months before the first volunteer officer was commissioned in London, and on the same day as Edinburgh's first ten corps. It assembled at the Old Cricket Ground on 3 November 1859 for the loyal oath to be administered by the mayor. Beginning with the Belvoir corps in February 1860, this year saw the formation of three more Leicester corps and others in Melton Mowbray, Loughborough, Lutterworth, Hinckley, and Ashby-de-la-Zouch. In July 1860, these ten corps formed the 1st Administrative Battalion of Leicestershire Rifle Volunteers. Although the 3rd Melton Corps maintained a company in Oakham, Rutland men otherwise had to join neighbouring corps as individuals.

Having opposed from the start the whole notion of an armed volunteer movement, the War Office quickly realised that it needed to assume some form of control. Each corps had adopted its own uniforms, often meeting the costs out of their own pockets, paying entry fees and annual subscriptions; had elected their own officers; and had made their own rules. Once the administrative battalions had been formed, the War Office insisted on some consistency of discipline and training, introducing the idea of efficiency. Riflemen were required to attend around thirty drills each year, to make use of regular opportunities for shooting practice in order to gain proficiency, and to be turned out smartly. The Leicestershire volunteers wore grey uniforms until 1877, when they changed to the scarlet of the regular soldier. Towns with volunteer units took pride in them and gave them prominence in local events. In 1888, the band of the rifle volunteers, for instance, led a Salvation Army march through Melton Mowbray, and the citizens of Market Harborough turned out to welcome home their victorious shooting team, fresh from another triumph. Still having to raise funds, the volunteers ran fetes and dances, theatrical performances, and put on displays of martial skills. The original membership had been drawn largely from the middling sort of people, but, as the commitments to military training were increased, many of those employed in demanding professional or commercial occupations were forced to resign. The young men from the working- or artisan-classes who took their place were attracted by the camaraderie, the chance to show off to the girls in their smart uniforms, and the frequent opportunities to win cash prizes in shooting matches or athletic sports. The lives of senior officers tended to revolve around the volunteers. The sixtieth birthday of Colonel Halford, a prominent leader of the volunteers for nearly thirty years, was marked by the presentation of a Maxim gun, paid for by his fellow officers. It may have been just what he always wanted, but no place could be found for it at his home and he duly presented it to the battalion.

In 1880, the 1st Leicestershire Administrative Battalion was consolidated with eleven companies, ordered 'A' to 'L'. Lutterworth's 7th Corps, in a town with a declining population, was disbanded after thirteen years' service, but a new corps, in Market Harborough, would shortly be added. Three years later, the Leicestershire Rifle Volunteers became the 1st Volunteer Battalion of the Leicestershire Regiment, and in 1900, two more companies were raised in Leicester and one each in Wigston and Mountsorrel, thereby creating a battalion of sixteen companies, or twice the normal establishment. The Leicestershire Regiment, part of the 27th Brigade, now consisted of two regular battalions, one militia battalion, and the volunteer double-battalion.

The Territorial Force

With the exception of Prince Albert, who thought of everything, no one had really considered the purpose of the volunteers and their relationship to the regulars. By the early 1900s, soldiers, politicians, and opinionated newspaper proprietors were beginning to question Britain's supposed invulnerability and the ability of the Royal Navy to defend the nation's shores against invasion. They called for compulsory military service through conscription and an increase in the Regular Army's strength. Although, after 1906, the Liberal Government was more concerned with welfare reforms than national defence, their Secretary of State for War, Richard Haldane, proposed a reserve army to be known as the Territorial Force (TF). It would be resourced entirely by the government, but administered by local, generally county-based Territorial Associations. It would be available to plug the gaps left by a regular army, which was always of inadequate size for the global demands being made on it. If a European war should break out, for instance, the regulars would not be able to meet all its imperial commitments and fight on the Continent, so these reserves would be needed. In the end, the TF was only sanctioned as a home defence force, leaving its members free to volunteer for overseas service but with no compulsion.

From 1908, the TF was organised in fourteen self-contained regional divisions, consisting of artillery, cavalry, infantry, engineer, service corps, and medical support. Units based in Leicestershire and Rutland belonged to the North Midland Division, with HQ in Lichfield (Staffordshire), under Northern Command in York. The Leicestershire Yeomanry were part of the North Midland Mounted Brigade along with the Lincolnshire and the Staffordshire Yeomanries, supported by the newly raised Leicestershire Royal Horse Artillery (RHA), whose HQ was at No. 1 Magazine Square in Leicester together with its accompanying ammunition column. The Mounted Brigade HQ was at No. 7 Magazine Square. The two volunteer battalions of the Leicestershire Regiment now became the Regiment's 4th and 5th Battalions, belonging, together with the two equivalent battalions of the Lincolnshire Regiment, to the Lincolnshire and Leicestershire Infantry Brigade with its HQ in Grantham. The 4th Battalion was made up of the Leicester companies based on the Magazine, plus the Wigston company, for whom the most likely base was the Institute in Long Street. The 5th Battalion was spread across the county with its HQ at Loughborough. The divisional artillery and engineer units were all stationed in the other north Midland counties, but the 2nd North Midland Divisional Field Ambulance was based in Oxford Street, Leicester. The 5th

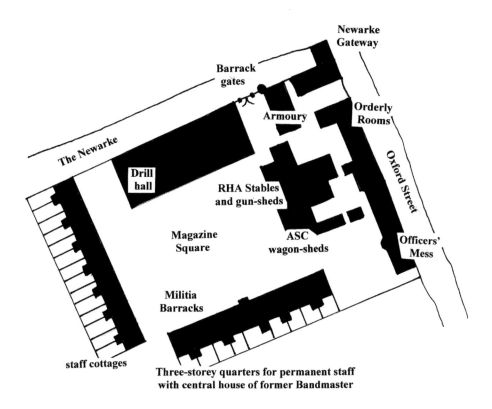

Leicester: a reconstruction of the Magazine Square showing the possible building uses, *c.* 1908.

Leicester: the administration block of the 5th Northern General Hospital RAMC (TF) in the old Leicestershire County Asylum, now the Fielding Johnson Building of the University.

Northern General Hospital, RAMC, TF, was in the old Leicestershire County Asylum, now the Fielding Johnson Building of the University. The North Midland Divisional Transport and Supply Company, ASC, TF had its HQ at No. 7, while the Lincoln and Leicester Infantry Brigade's ASC Company was based at No. 11 Magazine Square. The Leicestershire Territorial Association was responsible for the recruitment, day-to-day administration, and discipline of all these units.

Barracks

Until the end of the eighteenth century, troops tended to camp temporarily under canvas or to be billeted in inns or private houses. In the 1790s, fears that troops on internal security duties would be subverted by the communities in which they lodged, coupled with the general dislike of the billeting process on the part of those who had to accommodate rough soldiery, led to a review of the situation. Cavalry barracks were built in several industrial cities in order that regular troops might be available to aid the civil power. Coventry, Northampton, and Nottingham were among the three dozen towns and cities in which cavalry barracks were actually built. Although Leicester was scheduled for a cavalry barracks in 1794, as was Lincoln, neither were ever built. In 1840, the threat posed by Chartism, especially in industrial communities, prompted a further wave of barrack construction and a cavalry barracks was built in Loughborough. It was in Sparrow Hill, now Nottingham Street, on a site occupied by the Royal Mail sorting office and bounded on the east by Barrack Row. The existing hosiery factory on Duke Street was built against the north wall of the barracks, which subsequently became a foundry. Such barracks usually consisted of a parade ground, surrounded by stables with quarters for the troopers in rooms above. One end would be a smart mansion for the officers, while other buildings such as haybarn, cookhouse, armoury, forge, and guardhouse would line the perimeter walls.

With the reinvigoration of the Militia in the 1850s, there came a need for barrack accommodation. In Leicester, the traditional town magazine was the obvious location, and this once more became, in effect, Leicester's armoury in 1859. The gatehouse was extended to provide some quarters for permanent staff, probably in the angle formed by the south side of The Newarke and the east side of Oxford Street. Barrack blocks, demolished in 1967 for road improvements, may have been built at that time to house the Militia until 1881, when it became the Leicestershire Regiment's 3rd (Militia) Battalion and moved into the new regimental depot.

Leicester was not to be provided with a proper barracks until 1881, when the depot of the Leicestershire Regiment was built at Glen Parva. This was built to a design that was the standard for all the new localised infantry depots. The central feature was the armoury, which was built in the form of a three-storey medieval keep with two diagonally opposite turrets and battlements. Some of these, such as those in Yorkshire, were built in stone, but Leicester's, as were many others, was of brick. The interior consisted of mass-concrete slabs supported on rolled wrought-iron I-beams sitting on cylindrical, cast-iron columns. This fireproof construction was vital as large amounts of munitions

Leicester: interior view of the Magazine Gateway that became the armoury and nucleus of the Militia barracks.

Glen Parva Barracks: a barrack block dating from *c.* 1880, at the regimental depot of the Leicestershire Regiment.

Glen Parva Barracks: the officers' mess of *c*. 1880 is still in use as an active Army Reserve Centre.

were stacked in the lower floor magazines, with racks of rifles and uniforms above—enough to equip up to 3,000 men. The programme, which included thirty-odd new builds as well as twice as many adaptations of existing buildings, was overseen by Major Seddon at the War Office, who supervised the work of local engineer officers. Leicester's keep has gone but examples can still be seen at Lincoln and Lichfield. The keep usually stood next to an arched gateway and guardroom, set in a perimeter wall, loopholed for musketry, and with flanking bastions at the corners. Several two-storey barrack blocks contained multiples of twenty-four-bed dormitories, ablutions, and NCOs' quarters. An officers' mess, often recognisable by its half-hexagonal bay window, officers' stables, drill shed, canteen, hospital, workshops, married quarters, and storerooms, completed the standard layout. At Glen Parva, the officers' mess, hospital, guardroom, and a single barrack block remain alongside the prison, which occupies much of the site. In 1902, the War Office acquired a stud farm that had been established at Melton Mowbray with a Victorian stable block (dated 1895). It became an Army Remount Depot, and it now forms the basis of the Defence Animal Centre.

Drill Halls

One of the War Office's stipulations regarding the efficiency of the new Rifle Volunteer corps in 1860 was that secure storage for arms and ammunition must be provided. As the bureaucratic demands on the volunteer units increased, then an orderly room became desirable. While many COs were solicitors or suchlike, then they might provide office space in their homes or places of work, but permanent solutions were needed. A third accommodation need was for covered spaces in which to drill on cold winter's evenings. Every evening in 1872, Leicester's 5th Corps drilled at the Corn Exchange which had been completed by 1855, while the 1st Corps used the Abbey Meadow, and occasional whole battalion drills took place in the Market Place. Further additions to the Militia Barracks anchored on the Magazine Gateway included, in 1894, a drill hall, for the use of the two volunteer battalions of the Leicestershire Regiment. By this time, the Militia battalion would have moved into Glen Parva. Magazine Square was completed around this time, housing the offices of various volunteer units, with a parade square in the centre. When the TF was established in 1908, a number of constituent units and formation HQs were listed as occupying addresses in Magazine Square. It would appear that some of the premises of the square fronted onto Oxford Street, which is listed, in 1914, as the base of the Leicestershire Regiment's 4th Battalion and of the North Midland Divisional Field Ambulance.

Outside Leicester there appear to have been few, if any dedicated premises in which the volunteers could train. The Yeomanry with their particular requirements for space and the attention of farriers, tended to use the country mansions that often produced their officers. Where most of the Yeomanry brought their own mounts, there was less need for the stabling and tack rooms, which brought yeomanry units in many other counties to use rural hostelries or urban horse repositories as venues for their drill nights. The Rifle Volunteers must have used a wide range of premises: chapels and public halls, village schools and inns, and even industrial premises. There appears little evidence that dedicated drill halls were built until after the 1881 reorganisation, from which time, the drill hall in Loughborough's Granby Street, demolished in the 1990s, appears to date. In at least two cases, existing buildings were taken over as drill halls probably around the establishment of the Territorial Force. In 1892, a boarding house, for Market Harborough's relocated grammar school, was built in Coventry Road, but had become the town's drill hall by 1909. The Mountsorrel drill hall was originally built in 1901 for its own use by the Mountsorrel Granite Company. Its chairman was William Francis Martin who was the Yeomanry's adjutant, and he probably oversaw its acquisition by the TF. The drill hall at Ashby-de-la-Zouch, with its drill station at Coalville, both appear to have been in military occupation from sometime after 1908 but before 1914.

A trio of drill halls that opened in 1914 stand at Oakham's Penn Street, King Street in Shepshed, and Asfordby Road in Melton Mowbray. Although they share a modified Renaissance style found in drill halls across England at this date, they are so similar that they must have come from the drawing board of the same architect. Their sash windows, rusticated quoins, keystones, and door surrounds, with carved crested date stones over the doors, bring some architectural distinction to what were often utilitarian buildings lacking features. At each site, a two-storey front block has a large hall behind. Melton has later garaging on each flank, whereas Shepshed has an adjoining two-storey block in similar style. At Oakham, the staff house is tacked on at the back. These three drill halls, HQs for three companies of the Leicesters' 5th Battalion, were ready just in time for the run-up to the First World War.

Left: Leicester Corn Exchange, completed by 1855, was the venue for Leicester's 5th Corps of Rifle Volunteers on their regular drill nights.

Below: Mountsorrel: the building put up in 1901 by the Mountsorrel Granite Co. and taken over as a drill hall by the Leicestershire Yeomanry and the Leicestershire Regiment.

Coalville: the drill hall that in 1914 was a drill station for 'A' Company, 5th Battalion, Leicestershire Regiment, and for the Army Service Corps Transport and Supply column of the North Midland Mounted Brigade.

Shepshed: the 1914 drill hall of 'G' Company, 5th Battalion, Leicestershire Regiment.

Oakham: the drill hall in Penn Street, dating from around 1914, built for 'A' Squadron, Leicestershire Yeomanry, and 'B' Company, 5th Battalion, Leicestershire Regiment.

All these drill halls, while displaying quite marked differences of design and origin, still exhibited the same principal elements. One block, usually at the front, contained the orderly room, where the administrative functions were discharged; quarter-master's stores, where uniforms and equipment were stored and issued; a mess room for the officers; and a canteen for other ranks, often with recreational facilities ranging from billiards to magazines and newspapers. In line with this block was the actual hall, often sufficiently large to drill a whole company. Extrapolating from the 1911 OS 6-inch map of Leicester, the drill hall there would appear to measure around 120 by 30 feet (35 by 9 m), though not as large as Lancashire's whole battalion halls—nevertheless, it was a generous footprint. Generally, behind the hall stood a secure armoury for the storage of arms and ammunition, and down the side was an indoor 25-yard rifle-range. While most shooting, by choice, took place on outdoor 500-yard ranges such as Sixhills, the Morris Tube, inserted into the muzzle of the standard rifle, allowed it to fire a smaller-calibre bullet, making possible local indoor practice on cold winter nights. The complex was completed by accommodation for the caretaker or a permanent staff instructor. This could be a two-storey house attached to the side or the rear of the hall, or a flat, built into the administrative block. Notwithstanding the ideal layout, reality dictated what was possible on the ground. Loughborough's drill hall was, of necessity, a series of elements in line, occupying the long, narrow envelope of a site sandwiched between the cattle market and Queens Park.

Although the 4th Battalion was concentrated on Leicester with an eighth company in Wigston and detachments in Anstey and Syston, rural counties like Leicestershire and Rutland tended to spread their volunteers across wide areas, making towns such as Ashby-de-la-Zouch, Market Harborough, and Loughborough nodal points of a network of drill stations. The 5th Battalion operated in twenty different drill stations, while the Yeomanry, with its squadrons based in Leicester, Loughborough, Lutterworth, and Melton Mowbray, used a further dozen locations as drill stations, from Uppingham and Oakham to Ibstock and Hinckley. An annotated extract from a 1913 return listing the TF units in Northern Command (TNA WO114/55) appears to solve the problem of the 5th Battalion's 'G' Company, based at Shepshed, having satellite drill stations, according to several records, at Barrowden, Bisbrooke, and Ketton, assigning these three locations, a little more humanely, to Oakham, along with Cottesmore, Whissendine, and Uppingham. Even the keenest rifle volunteer might baulk at a 60-mile roundtrip to attend a company drill, even on a bicycle.

Local information is that there was no building in Uppingham dedicated to use by the Rifle Volunteers who were formed at the School, only in 1889. Although schools including Eton and Harrow had started cadet corps in 1860, Uppingham's previous Headmaster, Thring, had hitherto resisted the formation of such a corps. The old gymnasium, opened in 1905 as a Memorial Hall, now the Uppingham Theatre, with the current CCF Armoury built onto its side, has been suggested as an indoor venue. The present 1930s Town Hall, built as the Southwell Church Rooms, strongly resembles a drill hall and was requisitioned by the Army during the Second World War.

Annual Camps for the Volunteers

From the inaugural meetings of his Melton corps, Colonel Turner had sought every opportunity to promote the notion that each corps was but a part of something bigger and needed to learn to manoeuvre in larger bodies. However, it was only in 1879 that the first annual camp for the Leicestershire Rifle Volunteers was organised. It was held under canvas at Willesley Park near Ashby-de-la-Zouch, but constant torrential rain and a 5.30 a.m. reveille must have dampened the enthusiasm of all but the most dedicated. The Yeomanry followed suit some time later.

Cadet Units

With the setting up of the TF, provision for cadets in an Officers Training Corps (OTC) was included. The Senior OTC was based on the country's twenty-two universities, while the Junior OTC consisted of contingents in 163 of the nation's public and grammar schools. Uppingham required all its pupils to pass a shooting test and maintained a 500-yard outdoor rifle range on Wardley Hill outside the town. The school corps consisted of three companies. Oakham, too, had a corps of one company, with an outdoor range on Brooke Road, where the concrete firing positions remain. The two schools joined up with Oundle (Northamptonshire), Rugby (Warwickshire), and the Oratory and King Edward's, both from Birmingham, for combined field days. Oakham's armoury was in the old gaol, now the school's arts centre. At Uppingham, the armoury adjoins the memorial hall, built in 1905 and used as a gymnasium, prior to its conversion to a theatre in 1970.

Oakham, Kilburn Road: the former Armoury of the School OTC was originally the old Gaol and Ancaster hunting stables; the school CCF now occupies a purpose-built Cadet Centre nearby.

Transport: The Grand Junction & Grand Union Canals

Troop movements continued along these established routes during the decades after the end of the French wars. In 1820, a squadron of the 9th Lancers travelled from Nottingham along the Loughborough and Leicester Canals to join the main Grand Union at Norton Junction for onward travel to London. The opening of Foxton Locks and the Blisworth Tunnel did not provide a complete solution since, while journey time might be shortened, in times of drought, there was insufficient water for the canals to operate.

In 1832, the Board of Ordnance agreed a new three-year contract with Pickfords, the carriers. Costs worked out at around a penny per person per mile. Although railway charges were comparable, the train was generally more direct, so more economical. In the years 1830–35, Pickfords carried discharged soldiers and their families totalling nearly 1,100 fares, only forty-five of which were for Leicestershire destinations: Leicester, Loughborough, and Hinckley. The trip from Paddington Basin to Leicester took three days and cost the Ordnance Board £2.10s for officers and their wives, and 10s for NCOs, soldiers, and their wives. Despite being limited officially to London to Liverpool journeys, Pickfords diverted boats to carry soldiers to Leicester as late as 1841, but troop movements by canal gradually tailed off and ceased altogether in 1844 as the railways took over entirely.

Aid to the Civil Power

The conjunction of unemployment caused by the economic depression, consequent low wages, and the introduction of machinery into labour-intensive industries all contributed to widespread social and political unrest. Attacks on factories, such as that in Loughborough in 1816, public executions of Luddites the next year, and expected demonstrations in the wake of the Peterloo Massacre in Manchester caused fearful magistrates to put the Yeomanry on standby. Not until the Reform Bill disturbances of 1831–32, however, were the Yeomanry called out in force. The Leicestershire Yeomanry were commanded by Lt-Col. Keck, the local Tory MP. He led his four troops of cavalry in containing disturbances in Loughborough and also in Derby. They maintained patrols, day and night, for a week until calm was restored. Over the next twenty years, there were intermittent riots and the activities of the Chartists caused alarm among the middle classes. A request from the burghers of Loughborough to form an Armed Association to protect their interests was turned down. Although Leicestershire, in 1839, was one of the first counties to inaugurate a full-time constabulary, the problems attached to recruiting and deploying special constables meant that heavy reliance continued to be placed on the Yeomanry to act in violent confrontations. Fortunately, there were few serious casualties on either side.

6

The First World War, 1914–18

The outbreak of war in August 1914 saw the immediate deployment of the British Expeditionary Force (BEF) to France and Belgium, and the mobilisation of the TF. The local TF units were part of the 46th (North Midland) Division, the first volunteer unit to be posted to the Western Front. At home, strenuous efforts went into recruiting both second-line TF units and Kitchener's 'New Armies', and to putting the economy on a war footing by converting industry to the production of munitions and ensuring that agriculture provided maximum yields. Mercifully spared the horrors of aerial bombardment to a large extent, our counties were, nevertheless, involved in air-raid precautions and training for air warfare.

The Deployment of Local Units: Regulars and TF

The Leicestershire Regiment started the war with its five battalions, but by the end, the Regiment had twenty-two. The 1st Battalion, stationed at Fermoy in Ireland, was sent to France with the BEF's 6th Division, and spent the entire war on the Western Front, fighting in the bloodiest of battles, winning countless medals (including a VC), and suffering crippling casualties. They were joined at the end of 1914 by the 2nd Battalion arriving from India, who stayed until early 1916, also winning a VC, before being posted to the Middle East. The 1/4th and 1/5th Battalions mobilised at their respective drill halls in Leicester and Loughborough prior to joining up with the rest of the 46th Division in an area centred on Luton. The division was then posted to France, staying there for the duration, and winning another VC. In the meantime, the 3rd Battalion deployed to Portsmouth Garrison, being joined there by the newly raised 10th (Reserve) Battalion before a move in spring 1915 to Humber Garrison where they stayed. Second-line TF battalions, the 2/4th and 2/5th, were recruited in Leicester and Loughborough and sent to join the 59th (2nd North Midland) Division in St Albans as part of Third Army, with its HQ at Luton Hoo. This constituted Central Force, formed for home defence in July 1914, which included second-line TF infantry and artillery, with yeomanry as cyclists. Both battalions served in Ireland and then, in 1917, in France. The 3/4th and 3/5th Battalions joined the North Midland Reserve Brigade and were stationed mainly in Lincolnshire, training replacements and drafts for the first-line battalions, while carrying out home defence duties. Members of the TF could not be forced to serve overseas, and those who chose to exercise this prerogative would be regrouped in 'Provisional' battalions.

From August 1914, Kitchener commenced recruitment of his 'New Armies', complete battalions, brigades, and divisions composed entirely of basically raw recruits, with barely a leavening of experienced officers and NCOs. The 6th (K1), 7th (K2), and 8th and 9th Battalions (K3) all formed at Glen Parva Barracks prior to being sent to training camps in Aldershot and Tidworth before their moves to the Western Front.

The 6th Battalion received a baptism of mud at Bourley Camp off the Fleet road in Aldershot. It was so bad that the camp was shut and the men moved to the vacated barrack blocks of Badajos Barracks, and were then sent to billets in nearby Liphook (Hampshire). Other battalions spent time in billets in Andover, Folkstone, and New Romney prior to sailing across the Channel from Southampton to Le Havre, and thence by train to Flanders. Kitchener was not the only active recruiting agent. In October 1915, the Mayor of Leicester raised the 11th Battalion, which was accepted by the War Office and went to France as a pioneer battalion alongside the 13th (Labour) and the 14th (Service) Battalions. The 12th (Reserve) Battalion formed in Leicester in 1916 and went to Newcastle in the 19th Reserve Brigade on coast defence duties, as the possibility of a German invasion never fully disappeared. Similarly, a 1st (Home Service) Garrison Battalion was formed at Easington (Northumberland) becoming the 9th Battalion of the National Defence Corps. By 1917, conscripts who were still too young to be posted to the Front were formed into training battalions and distributed among the massive Nottinghamshire training camps of Welbeck and Clipstone, under the aegis of 69th (Home Defence) Division. The 51st (Graduated) Battalion, formed in Ipswich, the 52nd (Graduated) Battalion, formed in Witham (Essex), and the 53rd (Young Soldier) Battalion formed in October 1917 in Cannock Chase (Staffordshire) then sent to Clipstone were badged as battalions of the Leicesters. The history, composition, and deployments of these twenty-two battalions of the Leicestershire Regiment neatly illustrate the make-up of the British infantry throughout the war.

Prince Albert's Own Leicestershire Yeomanry mobilised in Leicester as part of the North Midland Mounted Brigade, but travelled to France in November 1914 to join the 3rd Cavalry Division, serving until March 1918. It was withdrawn for conversion to a cyclist unit but a change of plan brought it briefly into the Machine-Gun Corps teamed with the Somerset Yeomanry. Once the German offensive had been repulsed, it regained its horses and returned to the 3rd Cavalry Brigade. The 2/1st Leicestershire Yeomanry was formed in 1914 and alternated between horses and bicycles as home defence troops in Kent and Norfolk. The 3/1st Leicestershire Yeomanry formed in 1915 and was absorbed into a succession of reserve cavalry regiments in Aldershot. The stables of Wicklow Lodge in Melton Mowbray had been requisitioned by the Leicestershire Yeomanry in 1914.

The 1/1st Leicestershire RHA (TF) mobilised and went into billets in Hazel Street School, using the Filbert Street recreation ground for training. They were to spend the first two years of the war in the North Midland Mounted Brigade stationed mainly in

Melton Mowbray, Wicklow Lodge: the stables were first requisitioned by the Yeomanry, and then the house itself became a war hospital

Norfolk, where training was centred on Diss. At this time, a young officer, William Bragg, was posted to the RHA. A fellow of Trinity College, Cambridge, and already the recipient of a Nobel Prize, the twenty-five-year-old scientist found it difficult to fit in with his fellow officers, whose interests centred around horses and hunting. After an uncomfortable year, he was moved out to France where he invented the sound-ranging techniques that allowed the positions of enemy artillery to be pinpointed accurately. Like the Leicestershire Yeomanry, replaced in the brigade by the Welsh Horse among others, the other constituent units had also been detached. In 1916, the Leicestershire RHA joined with the Somerset RHA as 3rd Brigade RHA and was shipped out to Egypt. A further change came in 1917, when it joined with the Hampshire and Berkshire RHA as 20th Brigade RHA, continuing to serve in Egypt and Palestine. The 2/1st Leicestershire RHA (TF) served in the UK, supplying drafts and carrying out home defence duties until 1916. It then combined with a Kent-based Howitzer brigade to become the 223rd Home Counties Brigade, RFA, and spent two years in France.

The CLXXVI/176 (Leicester) RFA (Howitzer) Brigade was a New Armies artillery unit for whom 800 recruits were being sought. Its HQ, depot and stores were at the Leicester Tigers' clubhouse on Welford Road, with offices in the adjacent Nurses Institution. The unit went to France in January 1916, but was broken up that August, its members being redistributed—130 men going to CLX/160 (Wearside) Brigade RFA and the remainder to CLII/152 (Nottingham) Brigade RFA.

Recruitment and Conscription

Right through the first few months of the war, men flocked to Leicester's recruiting offices—in Humberstone Gate, on the corner of New Street and Peacock Lane, and at the Town Hall—to sign on. Similar events were taking place across the counties in other recruiting offices such as the drill hall in Melton Mowbray. The Royal Navy had a recruiting office in Market Street from spring 1915. In the first three months of war, almost 5,000 men had enlisted in the 17th Recruitment area centred on the Glen Parva barracks. Many of those men would make their debut on the battlefield of the Somme in July 1916, long before which time the supply of manpower was already drying up and new solutions were being sought. An earlier campaign to introduce conscription, led by Field Marshal Lord Roberts of Kandahar and Alfred Harmsworth, Lord Northcliffe, proprietor of the *Mail* and the *Mirror* newspapers, had failed, but was about to be resuscitated. Although the government was very much against the idea of compulsory military service, it could see no real alternative. In summer 1915, large numbers of volunteers across the country had carried out a census to meet the requirements of the National Registration Act, passed, somewhat reluctantly, by Parliament to establish the size of the pool of untapped manpower, eligible and available for military service. This would then permit the Derby Scheme of attestation to commence. Men could enrol immediately or else continue in their employment, deferring their call-up. Despite large numbers of men attesting their availability, there were still not enough, so the Military Service Act was passed; by April 1916, universal conscription of men between eighteen and forty-one was begun.

A further way of preparing the way for first volunteering and then conscription was to recruit teenagers into Cadet Battalions. Early in the war, Tom Crumbie, secretary of Leicester Tigers rugby club for nearly thirty-five years, organised a Junior Training Corps that quickly attracted 1,800 members. He built a Junior Training Hall on Aylestone Road next to the Tigers' ground and, when it proved inadequate, he took over the Empress skating-rink as an extension. This complex, containing two underground rifle ranges and a swimming pool, later became the Granby Halls—only demolished in 2001. In 1915, the 1st Cadet Battalion, affiliated to the Leicestershire Regiment's 4th Battalion, was formed with 850 cadets from Leicestershire's schools. Wyggeston provided the whole of 'A' Company, while the other three companies each drew from four or five schools in a locality. For example, 'C' Company drew from the grammar schools of Ashby-de-la-Zouch, Coalville, Hinckley, and Market Bosworth. In 1916, a summer camp for 170 cadets was held at Burton Lazars on Burton Flats Racecourse, using the stands for dormitories and with an officers' mess in the luncheon room. Rutland's 1st Cadet Battalion, from 1917 affiliated to the 5th Battalion of the Leicestershire Regiment was disbanded in 1920. From before the war, the Church Lads' Brigade had been a paramilitary organisation, its members learning to drill and shoot with obsolete Martini-Henry rifles. Between them, these several organisations prepared thousands of youngsters for military service, laying the foundations for their formal training. The effects of these policies were, of course, very noticeable. Many of

Above left: Leicester Town Hall served as a recruiting office throughout the First World War.

Above right: Melton Mowbray's drill hall in Asfordby Road was a mobilisation centre for serving TF personnel, and a recruiting office for both second- and third-line TF units and Kitchener's New Armies.

those who became infantry subalterns commanding front-line platoons confirmed the fateful statistic, which gave them a life-expectancy of just six weeks. Some 447 former pupils of Uppingham School, for example, gave their lives during the war.

The Leicester Volunteer Training Corps (The Leicestershire Volunteer Regiment)

Late in 1914, Leicester was one of the many towns and cities that recruited its citizens into a volunteer organisation to support the war effort. The Leicester Citizens Volunteer Training Corps (VTC) (or Volunteer League) was raised by the mayor to 'defend the hearth and home if need arise'. Simultaneously, other such organisations were forming, and early in 1915, the War Office, ever hostile to civilian initiatives, somewhat grudgingly suggested a national scheme. This Central Association of VTCs encouraged the affiliation of local groups, and a meeting in Leicester, chaired by the Duke of Rutland, brought the counties' disparate groups together under the banner of the Leicestershire Volunteer Regiment. Nationally, by 1915, the VTC consisted of perhaps 2,000 corps with up to 600,000 members. In Leicester, at least 3,000 men took part in regular daily training sessions at the Magazine, the County Cricket Ground and the Empress skating rink, involving drill, physical jerks, and shooting. In the early days of the war, Boy Scouts had carried out guard duties on infrastructure considered vulnerable to sabotage, such as telegraph lines, rail bridges, and tunnels. The VTC would henceforth take on such duties as carrying out night patrols, standing sentry at railway stations and other such vital communications points, and making random spot-checks on sensitive utilities such as waterworks, guided by a schedule of such vulnerable points drawn up by the local military. Interest was sustained and morale maintained in a variety of ways: members were issued with a uniform and had access to rifles from the early days, contrary to War Office policy of only issuing armbands and forbidding weapons, which only changed in autumn 1915; there were groups that specialised in first aid or motor transport; there were cyclist and mounted sections; parades, inspections, and competitions heightened members' motivation to improve their turnout and skills; and youngsters were given the opportunity to acquire military skills and habits prior to joining up. Some physical activities were given a fun context. In 1915, a walking contest was held between the Mountsorrel and Quorn companies, along a route that, starting from Mountsorrel Green, took in Rothley House, White House, Quorn, the Appletree Inn, and back to Mountsorrel Green. Ten men from each company, plus one from a Leicester company, took part. In August 1917, a second battalion of the Leicestershire Volunteer Regiment was raised. This targeted older men, between the ages of forty-one and fifty, who could be useful in the home defence role *in extremis*.

Automobiles were still a relative rarity in 1914, so offers by owners to make their vehicles available for war-related purposes were gratefully received. The Leicester Motor Corps was formed to ferry wounded soldiers from railway station to hospitals in cars, motorcycles and sidecars, and ambulances. Vehicles were made available in towns as part of Air Raid Precautions, either as ambulances or to ferry emergency personnel to incidents.

The Air War: The RFC and the RAF, Airfields, and Aircraft

On Whit Saturday 1916, a Sopwith Snipe single-seater aircraft came into land on Western Park. Leicester had won the race to become the first town to subscribe money for an aircraft for Lord Desborough's Imperial Air Fleet, supplying aircraft to the Dominions' air forces. During the day, some 30,000 (40,000 in some accounts) people came to see their aircraft which, named *Leicester*, was presented to the Canadian High Commissioner. The life of combat aircraft was short and it was to be the fourth replacement that was finally transferred from the Imperial Air Fleet to the Royal Canadian Air Force in 1919.

The only actual raid on a Leicestershire target was that on the evening of 31 January 1916, when a number of bombs were dropped on Loughborough from one or more Zeppelins, killing ten people and injuring others. However, the Zeppelin fleet continued its activities over the Midland counties, and bombs were jettisoned onto Leicestershire fields on the night of 5–6 March. In October, one of a flight of seven airships was seen over Oakham. As late as 19–20 October 1917, an exchange of fire took place in the skies above Leicester between a Zeppelin and a fighter, which landed at Stamford. Although our counties avoided the later bombing raids by fixed-wing aircraft, it was still felt prudent to take defensive measures. From summer 1916, these took the form of Home Defence fighter squadrons of the Royal Flying Corps. Initially based at Castle Bromwich, 38 Squadron moved nearer to the action in autumn 1916. Its new HQ was established outside Melton Mowbray, with its three flights based at Leadenham, Stamford, and Buckminster, all in Lincolnshire, two of them only just over the border. The key factor in the RFC's strategy of attempting to intercept the Zeppelins was to keep their aircraft in the air for as long as possible. To this end, a network of landing grounds was established where aircraft could land to refuel without having to return to base every time they ran low. Night landing grounds used fires to enable pilots to identify them more easily in the darkened countryside. Small detachments of ground crew, with only minimal facilities, manned these landing grounds, some of which, such as Brentingby and Welham, operated for only a short time. Brentingby closed when 38 Squadron's HQ moved to Scalford Road and needed a flying field nearer at hand. Scalford, opposite Sysonby Farm on Melton Mowbray's Nottingham Road, developed into a busy airfield in terms of traffic, but operational aircraft were never based there. These landing grounds were given very few structures, permanent or temporary: at most, a timber hut for the ground crew, although they very often had to make do with tents. There might have been one or more shelters for the aircraft, usually canvas *Bessoneau* hangars. There was always a fuel tank for the immediate refuelling of aircraft being turned around as quickly as possible to continue their patrols, and a brazier for night-time operations. Landing grounds such as Peckleton, subsumed within Desford aerodrome between the wars, and Castle Donington, developed in the Second World War, had futures as airfields, but most have disappeared without trace.

Although the east Midlands were relatively unaffected by the German air raids, the mere threat could often be disruptive. Industrial production and railway operation were both vulnerable to vague alarms. These caused confusion as the railway companies could not risk their passengers' lives by exposing them to air raids, and the consequent suspension of services caused additional disruption to the movement of troops and munitions. The Railway Executive Council (REC) was charged with the co-ordination of the railways' contribution to the war effort, using its telegraph network to report sightings of Zeppelins and to track them across the country, plotting their positions at five-minute intervals. This enabled rail controllers to base decisions on suspending operations, for instance, on precise information rather than on Chinese whispers and hearsay. This information also benefited factories whose managers could gauge the need for stoppages more accurately thus avoiding much otherwise lost production. The whole country was divided into sections for the purposes of this air-raid warning organisation. Our counties overlapped three of these areas: Leicester was in Area 30; Market Harborough in Area 31; and Loughborough in Area 32. Railway staff reported sightings, movements, and progress direct to the REC in London by telegraph. In each area, GPO staff reported by telephone to GHQ Home Forces and to local air defence units. Railway staff received and acted on warnings of approaching Zeppelins and relayed the message on to other areas.

There is nothing in the official records to suggest that Leicester was protected against aerial bombardment by permanently sited anti-aircraft guns, as neighbouring

Coventry, Nottingham, Derby, and Peterborough were, if only minimally. However, on 10 June 1919, as King George V arrived in Leicester to confer city status, the twenty-one-gun royal salute was fired by the guns of an anti-aircraft battery stationed, only temporarily it must be assumed, on the Welford Road Recreation Ground

Munitions

Many factories reacted to the outbreak of war by laying off their workers, but owners soon realised that wars provided commercial opportunities with the added kudos to be gained from demonstrating patriotic endeavour in support of the brave soldiers and sailors in the firing line. The War Office reopened the Asfordby range for proof-firing ordnance, and in 1915, added Army Remount Depots at Leicester and Market Harborough to that already operating at Melton Mowbray since 1902. Those factories making boots and shoes soon found themselves with enormous government orders to fulfil. At one time, 4 million pairs of boots were stood in Leicester's warehouses, representing just 5 per cent of the total produced nationally to meet the country's needs during the war. The hosiery industry too increased production, knitting socks for soldiers. Industries that involved the use of machine tools were quickly inducted into the production of munitions. In Leicester's Belgrave Road, the British United Shoe Machinery Co. made high-angle AA pom-pom guns for use on land and afloat, and the Tramways Depot on Belgrave Gate became a workshop turning out 6-inch shells, including some filled with poison gas.

The Brush Electrical Engineering Company's Falcon Works in Loughborough won contracts to build military aircraft in 1915. Like many such factories with the relevant expertise and experience, licences were issued to manufacture aircraft to the designs of companies well-established in the aeronautical industry. Brush built Short 827 and 184 seaplanes and Avro 504C Scouts for the Royal Naval Air Service (RNAS), and other trainer marques of 504, as well as Maurice Farman S.7 'Longhorn' trainers for the Royal Flying Corps (RFC). A prototype Farman Astral twin-engined bomber for the RNAS was built and tested by Brush, but further trials at Hendon showed it to be unsatisfactory and no more were built. By the end of the war, over 650 aircraft had been completed, but further orders were cancelled as hostilities ceased. Although Brush had a suitable flying field, Loughborough Meadows, adjacent to their works, which was used for flight-testing their machines, finished aircraft were dismantled, crated, and delivered by road.

Hospitals and Welfare

The provision of medical care by the military was subject to the clear organisation of the Royal Army Medical Corps (RAMC). The permanent establishment of the regular army included field ambulances which travelled with their parent formations, setting up casualty clearing stations as close to the front-line as practicable. TF formations had their own such units in parallel, with Leicester being home to one of the North Midland

Melton Mowbray: First World War-period stables at the Defence Animal Centre.

Loughborough: the BRUSH Electrical Engineering Company's Falcon Works turned out hundreds of aircraft for the RNAS and the RFC throughout the war.

Division's three Field Ambulances. The next stop for a casualty was the Clearing Hospital, another element within the RAMC. The North Midland Divisional Clearing Hospital was also based in Leicester, and was deployed to France with the Division. Second-line units were similarly attached to the 59th Division. In order to cope with those casualties for whom repatriation by hospital train and ferry was appropriate, the War Office had set up, again as part of the TF, a network of twenty-three General Hospitals across Britain, staffed by a nucleus of permanent staff. The Northern Area maintained RAMC General Hospitals in Newcastle-upon-Tyne, Leeds, Sheffield, Lincoln, and Leicester. The 5th Northern General Hospital RAMC, TF was located in the old County Lunatic Asylum, built in 1837, near to Victoria Park and convenient for the Midland Railway Station. As soon as war was declared, the CO mobilised his staff and began to recruit all those other people needed for the smooth running of what was ultimately to become a 1,000-plus-bed hospital. Throughout the war, the War Office policy of calling up all available doctors to serve with the troops left Base Hospitals short of trained medical attention, and the civilian population even shorter. Before the war, large numbers of trained nurses had committed to the TF hospitals and were supplemented by the Voluntary Aid Detachments (VADs). These ranged from patriotic volunteers with minimal training to experienced long-term members of the British Red Cross and the St John's Ambulance Association. With over 100 casualties arriving at the Base Hospital only a month into the war, it quickly became apparent that more hospital provision would be needed. The Poor Law hospital at North Evington, opened in 1905, was taken over in March 1915, staffed by TF personnel of the RAMC, and with an initial capacity of 600-plus beds, rising by the end of the war to over 1,000. North Evington also became the regional centre for ophthalmic cases.

In addition to those two main hospitals, Leicester Infirmary and Loughborough General Hospital, many large houses volunteered or were requisitioned as Auxiliary War Hospitals. These included stately homes such as Burley on the Hill (R), Belvoir Castle and Stapleford Park; smaller houses such as Wicklow Lodge in Melton Mowbray, the Cottage Hospital in Ashby-de-la-Zouch, and Billesdon Workhouse. All these were affiliated to the 5th Northern General Hospital that, by the end of the war, controlled over fifty outposts across several counties. Many of these smaller, more domestic hospitals, some of them functioning as convalescent homes, though staffed by VADs, remained under the control of the lady of the house. It became fashionable for such upper-class ladies to volunteer as VADs. The duchess of Rutland was so concerned when her daughter, Lady Diana Manners, volunteered as a VAD that she opened up her London seat, Rutland House in Park Lane, as an Auxiliary War Hospital so she could keep an eye on the head-strong teenager.

Volunteers who might not fancy hospital work gave their time to organisations such as Queen Mary's Needlework Guild. At Tolethorpe Hall (R), Mrs Dove ran a branch of the Guild, which produced 14,000 garments for hospitals and the Red Cross and also co-ordinated a further sixty working parties producing swabs, bandages, caps, and gowns for the hospital depots, which met the needs of the various establishments caring for war wounded. Others provided, and often drove, the vehicles ferrying casualties from the railway station to the hospitals.

Leicester: the Lodge of the 5th General Hospital.

Leicester: North Evington War Hospital had opened in 1905 as a Poor Law hospital. It was taken over by the War Office in March 1915 and staffed by TF personnel of the RAMC.

The 5th Northern and the North Evington hospitals between them treated just short of 75,000 casualties, amazingly losing only 514. Many patients will have returned to their units as fit for duty, and North Evington had a store where up to 2,000 packs, containing soldiers' kit, could be held for reissue. Most of the hospitals' patients were soldiers, but at Brooksby Hall, home of Admiral Sir David Beatty, Lady Beatty provided a convalescent home for recovering sailors. The Grange at Wing (R) was made available for entertaining convalescent soldiers.

The main block of the 5th Northern General Hospital, containing the administration section, surgery, and several wards, is now the Fielding Johnson Building of the University of Leicester. The lodge, stores, and two substantial ward blocks also remain. The main block and several surviving pavilions of the North Evington hospital still form the nucleus of the Leicester University Hospital. Leicester Infirmary appears to be currently (2015) undergoing radical rebuilding. Billesdon Workhouse was demolished in 1935. The military hospital at Glen Parva, a standard design common to many of the Cardwell depots, still stands next to the officers' mess of the old regimental depot.

Prisoner of War Camps

Conditioned to a great extent by post-Second World War films, the popular picture of a POW camp is of huts surrounded by barbed-wire fences with tall guard towers at intervals, equipped with searchlights and machine guns. There were camps that conformed to this image, but the vast majority of First World War POW accommodation was much more domestic. Many POWs had no wish to return to the horrors of the Western Front and were happy to acquiesce with their captors' directions. Britain faced a manpower crisis, so POW labour, especially on the land, but also in the building and mineral extraction industries, was welcomed. POWs tended, therefore, to be parcelled out in small groups to particular workstations, such as Ragdale Hall and Long Clawson Hall, or were put up in central premises, such as the workhouses at Narborough and Loughborough, from which they would be taken out to their places of work each day. Some were organised as 'migratory gangs', on the move constantly, responding to seasonal demands for labour, and accommodated in a network of billets.

Not only were officers not expected to be put to work, but they were expected to attempt escape. Consequently, they were imprisoned in secure camps, two of which lay in Leicestershire. Donington Hall was built in the early 1790s, decorated in the Gothic style. It was a rectangular block with an imposing *porte cochere*, an open central court and a chapel attached to one corner. The inmates enjoyed the luxury of multiple bathrooms and electric light. Timber huts were added alongside the house, possibly to accommodate the officers' servants. The whole site was surrounded by a sequence of daunting obstacles. The innermost was a fence, 9 feet (2.75 m) high with spikes at 8-inch (20-cm) intervals. Next came an electrified wire, about 2 feet 6 inches (75 cm) off the ground, and then a second fence, identical to the first. Finally, there was a barbed-wire entanglement about 3 feet (90 cm) high. The park wall, a ditch, and a stream completed the challenge. Astride the wire fences there were towers, constantly manned by vigilant guards. The L-shaped timber towers stood about 10 feet (3 m) off the ground on cross-braced stilts. They were roofed and each end-section was glazed, giving the sentries some protection against the elements but retaining good visibility. In July 1915, two German officers successfully scaled these obstacles and got away, one of them making it back to Germany via a neutral Dutch boat, the only German to make it home from Britain in either world war. Kegworth Officers' Camp, similarly guarded to Donington Hall, was also the setting for escape attempts. In July 1917, three German officers cut their way through the wire fences, got away from the camp, but were soon recaptured. A large group of twenty-two officers used an escape tunnel in September 1917, but were soon all rounded up.

Donington Hall: a camp for German officer POWs.

7

The Interwar Period, 1919–1939

One element of Lloyd-George's government's welcome for the soldiers, sailors, and airmen returning from the war was his 'Homes for Heroes' slogan. Leicester City Council built 75 per cent of the 12,000 new houses that went up in the city between 1919 and 1939. Typical of this expansion was the Coleman Road estate in North Evington, built from 1919. The period between the wars was characterised by a short boom as the war ended, followed by a long economic slump. The assumption that it would take any defeated belligerent ten years to rearm meant that successive governments used this axiom, dignified as the 'Ten Year Rule', to justify their continuously downward-spiralling defence budgets. The control economy reverted to peacetime habits, and by 1920, the 5th Northern General Hospital, RAMC, had emerged as the core of what would become the University of Leicester. The south-east corner of the former hospital site became the new boys' grammar school, occupying huts that would remain in use for many years, being demolished only in 1965.

By the early 1930s, the country was rearming in anticipation of another major conflict. This involved the construction of new airfields such as Cottesmore (R); the training of pilots at Desford and Braunstone; the modernisation and expansion of the Territorial Army; an acceleration of the development of new technologies such as Whittle's work in jet propulsion at Lutterworth; and the reactivation of existing facilities, including the artillery proofing range at Asfordby. As was soon to become evident, preparations had been in train for some time in Germany. Target maps of our local airfields, communications centres, and industries, generated by *Luftwaffe* aerial reconnaissance, date from long before the official commencement of hostilities.

The Regular Army and the Territorial Army

The Leicestershire Regiment, which had finished the war with twenty-one battalions, was quickly reduced to two regular battalions, with the 1st Battalion reforming in Liverpool in 1919, prior to service in Ireland. The 2nd Battalion served in India until 1923, when it went to the Sudan, then on the Rhine and in Ireland. The 1st Battalion stayed in India from 1927 until 1939, while the 2nd Battalion moved to Palestine in 1936, following some home deployments to Catterick and Aldershot.

In 1920, the Territorial Army was reformed with an establishment, under the auspices of the Leicestershire and Rutland Territorial Association, of the 4th and 5th Battalions of the Leicestershire Regiment, the Leicestershire Yeomanry, and the Leicestershire RHA (now only a single field battery). Support units were reconstituted only temporarily and had already been disbanded in 1922. Despite a brief period early in 1918 training as a putative unit of the Machine-Gun Corps, the Leicestershire Yeomanry, unlike many such units, had retained its identity and, above all, its horses. Although receiving warnings to expect a change of role, along with thirteen other county yeomanry regiments, it was to retain its mounted status through to the outbreak of a fresh conflict in 1939. In fact, a new Leicester Territorial Association Riding School had opened in 1923, in Brentwood Road off Welford Road, with an adjacent field for cavalry drill, encouraging the former Leicestershire RHA to opt out of mechanisation now that suitable facilities for practice manoeuvres with horses were available.

The idea that modern warfare would curtail the usefulness of horsed cavalry should have been a reasonably easy idea to grasp, but two further, apparently unrelated, notions were to come together to influence the future of this new TA. One was a concern that aerial and armoured warfare together would render the infantry redundant; the other was the recognition that Britain was entirely deficient in dedicated air defence units for home deployment. A subsequent review of the TA's function linked the two, suggesting that the TA should assume responsibility for the defence of the nation against aerial bombardment, and that 'surplus' infantry battalions should be converted to AA units in order to fulfil this new role. By 1936, this new policy was being implemented, and the 4th Battalion of the Leicestershire Regiment became the 44th Searchlight Battalion RE, and in 1939, the 44th (The Leicestershire Regiment) Searchlight Regiment RA (TA).

As the probability of war became ever more likely, the need to increase the size of the Army became more and more apparent. One strategy involved the cloning of TA units. The Leicesters' 5th Battalion provided a cadre of experienced officers and NCOs around which a new battalion, the 2/5th, based in Eastern Boulevard in 1939, might be assembled. Apart from the odd RASC unit featuring driver-training in its prospectus, recruitment into the TA had been very difficult during the 1920s and early 1930s. A combination of the renewed threat of war and the establishment of a new Militia, which would conscript young men for six months' compulsory military training at militia camps such as that at Melton Mowbray, ensured that recruitment levels would quickly rise dramatically. In 1920, the Leicestershire RHA had been reduced to 239 Battery, 60th North Midland Field Brigade RFA (TA) with its three sister batteries spread across Lincolnshire and Nottinghamshire. The same cloning process that enabled the Leicestershire Regiment to recreate its lost battalion made it possible for the old RHA to regain single-county regimental status as 115 Field Regiment RA (North Midland) TA, in 1939.

Drill Halls

A lack of dedicated training spaces had hampered the work of the TF before the war and, despite the unpromising financial climate, a start was soon made on rectifying this. New drill halls opened in Lutterworth in 1921, as well as in Hinckley two years later. The new TA units had particular requirements for properly equipped training spaces. A searchlight unit, such as the newly converted 44th Searchlight Battalion, needed a capacious planetarium-like room. It should have a high ceiling, which would allow lights to be played onto a simulated night sky, and tall roller doors for getting the equipment in and out. As the TA recruited technicians from the factories to perform technical tasks in the new mechanised and technological military, then classrooms were needed, along with workshops to house the new vehicles and machinery. Even the footsloggers of the infantry were provided with armoured Bren gun carriers, A/T rifles, and radios, and they needed the space to learn how to use them effectively. New drill halls that offered these facilities were opened in Leicester, with the 44th Battalion being accommodated in purpose-built premises in Ulverscroft Road, which opened in 1936. The next year, the drill hall in Brentwood Road opened for the 5th Battalion Leicestershire Regiment, as well as another new drill hall in Leicester Road, Loughborough. Both the Yeomanry and the artillery remained at the Magazine Square drill hall in Oxford Street, along with the Territorial Association office and club. During 1939, TA anti-aircraft gunners and searchlight operators received training that was partly provided by a consortium of civilian airlines using Braunstone airfield.

Lutterworth's new drill hall opened next door to the Ladywood Works in 1921.

Hinckley drill hall opened in 1923, but it was very similar in style to the local pre-war design.

Leicester: the Ulverscroft Road drill hall was designed as purpose-built premises for the newly converted 44th Searchlight Battalion RE (TA) in 1936.

Leicester: the Brentwood Road drill hall was opened in 1937 for the 5th Battalion, Leicestershire Regiment.

The RAF between the Wars: Rearmament and Reorientation

The RAF had formed on 1 April 1918, but soon after the end of the war, it was struggling for survival in the teeth of budgetary cuts and opposition from the other services. The Royal Navy and the Army still regarded their experience and potency on sea and land to make the existence of an air force irrelevant. The independent bombing force had barely got off the ground, overtaken by the Armistice, and the antics of the fighter aces were largely regarded as a sideshow. Few lessons had been learned from the course of the conflict, and the potential of air power remained unrealised. The defeated Germans were not to be allowed an air force at all, so it was easy to argue that the maintenance of this costly white elephant in Europe was an unnecessary extravagance. The only justification for the RAF might be as an effective and efficient weapon with which to punish unruly tribesmen on India's Northwest Frontier. Ironically, in the early 1920s, France was perceived as a threat, and it was decided to ensure that the RAF maintained parity with the French air force. This meant an expansion that was exploited by Trenchard, the RAF's leader, as a way of establishing an infrastructure that could sustain future developments. The 1925 Plan established bomber airfields in Berkshire and Oxfordshire to the west of London, with a protective ring of fighter airfields around London itself. Just about the time that the defence budgets hit rock bottom, the realisation that conflict with a resurgent Germany was becoming increasingly likely was beginning to take root. Not only was the RAF in poor shape, but most of it was facing in the wrong direction. Any attack from Germany, and any retaliatory action from Britain, would centre on the east of the country. Alongside a programme of rearmament then, it was also necessary to re-orientate to the east. A succession of Schemes (A–M) was implemented by the Air Ministry to expand the RAF and to rationalise the location of airfields and support services. As the growing RAF became both more complex and more specialised, separate Commands—Bomber, Fighter, Coastal, and Training—were established in 1936. A building programme of airfields for new bomber groups had commenced in 1934, and in 1936, work started on the new bomber station at Cottesmore (R). This ambitious programme of construction was far from complete by the outbreak of war, and the Training Command station at North Luffenham, though planned as part of Scheme M, was only finally started in 1940.

Cottesmore's construction at the peak of the Expansion Period ensured that it exhibited all the features of the programme. The imposition of dozens of sprawling airfields across the countryside had excited concern within those groups such as the Council for the Preservation of Rural England (CPRE). Under the guidance of Sir Edwin Lutyens and the Royal Fine Arts Commission, principles for integrating these new airfields, each the size of a large village, into the landscape were formulated. The neo-Georgian architectural style selected for the domestic and technical buildings was intended to echo the polite country houses that dotted the countryside, particularly in East Anglia and the East Midlands. The layout was to be symmetrical, on a grid pattern, for purely aesthetic reasons. The only apparent recognition of the warlike purpose could be seen in the arc of hangars, designed to avoid destruction by a single (exceptionally lucky) stick of bombs. The buildings were all taken from a suite of designs issued by the Air Ministry's resident architect, Mr A. Bullock, FRIBA, so are instantly recognisable from one airfield to another, and easily identifiable by their individual footprints, particularly from the air.

At Cottesmore, now (2016) occupied by Army units, many of the key buildings remain in use eighty years on. The 1936 build included four steel-framed, concrete-skinned, twelve-bay, C-type hangars built to accommodate two squadrons of bombers. They measured 300 feet (92 m) long with a span of 150 feet (46 m) and a height of 35 feet (10.75 m). The enormous, hollow sliding-doors, designed to be filled with gravel in time of war, were so perfectly hung that they could be moved by a single aircraftman, and the roof space was filled with sand to absorb the shock of bombs. The original Watch Office, which lasted until well into the 1950s, was the concrete version of the usual 'Fort' type (207/36) installed on airfields at this time. The Station HQ stood near the guardroom by the main gate. Officers' and sergeants' messes, Institute, accommodation in H-blocks, decontamination centre, and sickbay were all grouped behind the main workshops and stores buildings, armoury and photographic section, pyrotechnics and parachute stores, and MT Section of the technical site. A tall, brick-clad water tower stood at the centre of the Air Ministry Works Department complex containing central-heating boiler, coal, and oil stores. A training area of specialist structures included a bombing teacher, gunnery turret trainer, link trainer, and synthetic navigation building. An estate of married quarters, with a differentiated hierarchy of house designs for officers, warrant officers, NCOs, and aircraftmen, lay on the edge of the site. Generators were housed in solid two-storey structures and sunken bomb stores lay well away from the main buildings. The flying field was still grassed and would not see concrete runways until 1943. The airfield opened in March 1938 with two squadrons of Wellesley and Hampden medium bombers. During the Munich Crisis later that year, these aircraft would be moved to airfields in Kent as part of the general mobilisation and replaced by two reserve squadrons of Blenheims. Chamberlain's 'piece of paper' obviated the need for this manoeuvre, and a year later, when war was finally declared, Cottesmore was still equipped with Hampdens.

By the time North Luffenham was on the drawing board, the production values of the Expansion Period building programme had been much diluted. Even though the C-type hangar had itself been reduced to an austerity version, North Luffenham was nevertheless given two less-robust J-type hangars. These were of similar dimensions to the C-type, but of flimsier construction, with eighteen bays, defined by steel columns supporting arched steel trusses, and recognisable by the bow-string roof. The watch office was the last of the pre-war designs, nicknamed the 'Villa' (5845/39) as its wraparound steel-framed windows were suggestive of the *moderne* residences of the French Riviera. Most of the airfield's other structures, such as the Station HQ, officers' mess, H-blocks, and guardroom are from the Expansion Period plans, on a regular layout; North Luffenham was among the very last airfields to be laid out to a regular pattern as, in future, military airfields would consist of dispersed sites linked by perimeter tracks.

RAF Cottesmore: one of the four twelve-bay, concrete C-type hangars (6045/36). (*Lt-Col. Richard Chesterfield, Kendrew Barracks*)

RAF Cottesmore: the Station HQ (1723/36) (*Lt-Col. Richard Chesterfield, Kendrew Barracks*)

RAF Cottesmore: the Institute or other ranks' dining room (8055-60/38); an almost identical building may be seen at North Luffenham. (*Lt-Col. Richard Chesterfield, Kendrew Barracks*)

RAF North Luffenham's 'Villa-type' watch office (5845/39), with later VCR.

As war grew more likely, further preparations were set in motion. One of these measures was the application of camouflage to minimise the visual impact of the airfield on the landscape when seen from above. Hangars were not only painted with a mottled green effect, but also had nets draped over them to reduce shadows and to break up their sharp outlines. The flying field itself, masquerading as agricultural land, had simulated hedge lines painted across it and, where it did not interfere with flying operations, the grass was left uncut. Roads and perimeter tracks were painted to reduce glare.

Aerodromes and Flying Training

At the same time that the RAF's development as an independent force had been curbed, recreational flying was being promoted as a pastime, and municipal aerodromes were being established. In 1929, Leicestershire Aero Club leased land at Desford for its airfield. A clubhouse, hangar, and rudimentary refuelling facilities were soon set up, and over the next few years, membership climbed to over 900. In 1934, the Aero Club, having been invited to manage Leicester's new municipal aerodrome, moved the few miles to Braunstone. A clubhouse, hangar, flight offices, and fuel pumps were built by En-Tout-Cas of Syston, and the aerodrome opened for business in 1935. The vacant Desford was snapped up by Reid & Sigrist, instrument manufacturers of south-west London, who wanted to run one of the RAF's thirteen Civil Flying Training Schools. A new capacious hangar, 220 by 70 feet (68 by 21 m) was added with lecture rooms. Fire and photographic sections, parachute store, administration block, and bungalows for the trainees all joined a stylish new clubhouse with control tower. Flying training started at the end of 1935 in de Havilland Tiger Moth biplanes. By 1937, the RAF had decided to ensure a supply of trained pilots available for service by creating the RAF Volunteer Reserve (RAFVR), and chose Leicester as one of its ten centres. Local RAFVR HQ was established at The Cedars, 197 London Road, now replaced by blocks of apartments. Reid & Sigrist's civilian flying school then became No. 7 Elementary and Reserve Flying School (7E&RFTS). In 1938, Desford also hosted No. 3 Civilian Air Navigation School, designed to produce qualified observers and navigators for the RAF. This necessitated the construction of more lecture rooms, a mess building, and extra hangars on Peckleton Common. Braunstone continued in business, but lost its main operator in late 1937 and was looking for new users. The Civil Air Guard was set up in 1938 to train pilots, and an initial cohort of fifty was enrolled, commencing their training that October. Although the Air Ministry was lukewarm about using Braunstone, owing to its restricted runways, plans were nevertheless under discussion for setting up No. 58 E & RFTS there, but were overtaken by the outbreak of hostilities. Braunstone then operated as a satellite of No. 7E & RFTS at Desford for the duration.

During the 1930s, the Automobile Association compiled a list of landing grounds available for use by their members. Two of these were in Leicestershire: one was the former First World War field at Brentingby and the other was at Husbands Bosworth, possibly the site later developed by the RAF. When Loughborough also sought to exploit the fashionable flying habit by establishing an aerodrome in 1929, on a site called Bishop's Meadow, next to the racecourse, they consulted the AA. In the event, nothing happened until 1938, when Boulton & Paul, the aircraft manufacturers with plants in Norwich and Wolverhampton, produced plans for a hangar to be used by Loughborough College's Department of Aeronautical Engineering. Work was still underway when war broke out. Previously, the college's airframe instructional workshop had occupied the Premier dancehall in Ashby Road. The RAF School of Physical Training was established at Loughborough in 1939.

Ratcliffe aerodrome opened in 1930 as a private venture, but was so well-equipped with flying aids (especially floodlights) that it was offered as an emergency landing ground to private and official fliers alike. The field had two bowstring roof hangars and a control top on a lattice tower. By early 1939, Taylorcraft from Thurmaston had permission to assemble their aircraft and to carry out flight-testing there, but flying ceased, only temporarily as it turned out, in the September that war broke out.

Ratcliffe on the Wreake was a civilian airfield where Taylorcraft aircraft from Rearsby were tested before 1939. It was a base for the Air Transport Auxiliary in the Second World War. These bowstring-roof hangars housed the Ansons, which retrieved the pilots once they had collected their aircraft from local factories and delivered them to RAF stations across Britain.

Air Defence: Preparing for the Onslaught

One of the lessons to come out of the Home Front experience in the First World War was the way in which the separate elements of air defence were eventually integrated in the London Air Defence Area (LADA). Given the serendipitous nature of the interception of hostile airships and bomber aircraft by the Home Defence squadrons, it was found that adding aircraft spotting to the role of special constables, coupled with dedicated telephone lines for reporting sightings to Army HQ at Horseguards in Whitehall, made for both an effective and efficient way of co-ordinating the defence against bombing. From 1924, the volunteer Observer Corps was re-established in Kent and Sussex with plans to expand across the country, but it was not until 1934 that the decision was taken to include everywhere south of a line drawn between Preston and Middlesbrough. In 1937, nine posts in Leicestershire were established, with Empingham in Rutland added in 1939. A clue to the appearance and durability of these posts can be found in the derogatory way to which these rudimentary garden sheds were referred as 'rabbit hutches'. Posts were sited on high points with good visibility toward the expected direction of approach of enemy aircraft. Sometimes church towers or windmills were used, but most posts were isolated and exposed. Posts in our counties were administered from several Group HQs: Coventry (No. 5 Group), Derby (No. 6 Group), and Bedford (No. 12 Group). Reporting was by telephone where possible, in order to get the information to the No. 12 Group RAF Fighter Command control centre at Watnall in Nottinghamshire as quickly as possible.

As in the previous war, the railways remained vulnerable to bombing raids. Their 1939 financial estimates, approved in May 1939, included several thousand pounds for the provision of emergency control centres in Leicester and in Melton Mowbray. Such centres were either reinforced concrete shelters or converted rolling stock, which could be shunted around to stay out of danger and to keep the railways running. The LMS ensured that duplicate control panels would be available as back-up in the event of damage.

Aircraft Manufacture

In 1936, in Rugby, Frank Whittle began the experiments that would lead to his invention of the jet engine. Soon, these experiments became quite dangerous and it was necessary to find dedicated premises for his company, Power Jets Ltd. He moved into the Ladywood Works in Leicester Road, Lutterworth, in 1938, having won an Air Ministry contract that paid his development costs and enabled him gradually to expand both the workforce and the plant. The outbreak of war then marked an increase in interest. Reid & Sigrist, hitherto a manufacturer of instruments for the aircraft industry, commenced building their own aircraft in 1939 and developed this side of their work throughout the Second World War. Taylorcraft, manufacturers of light Army co-operation aircraft, started up in Crowther's Britannia Works in Thurmaston in 1938, the first aircraft being test flown from Ratcliffe aerodrome.

Lutterworth: Ladywood works was the scene of Frank Whittle's experiments with jet-propulsion.

ARP and Civil Defence Preparations

Leicester, along with many other cities in Britain, took seriously the threat of aerial bombing in a coming conflict. A mainly volunteer civil defence infrastructure was assembled and training initiated. In 1938, blackout procedures were tested, but the bad weather precluded an effective evaluation from the sky. The major concern, however, related to the use of gas on civilian targets. Therefore, gas decontamination squads turned out for the exercises alongside firemen. Thought was also being given to the provision of air-raid shelters and gas decontamination centres, particularly around the county's centres of industry and population.

8

The Second World War, 1939–45

Though filling vital roles in military training and munitions production alongside their traditional agricultural functions, Leicestershire and Rutland suffered less from bombing than did many other centres of population with industrial bases. The landscape was dotted with RAF flying schools, Operational Training Units, and bombing ranges. Aircraft factories were set up in both urban and rural areas, but also operated in almost cottage industry mode, with work parcelled out to small workshops. Other factories turned their hand to the manufacture of essentials, whose importation the U-boat war had curtailed. As the preparations for D-Day gathered pace, airborne troops, training for delivery by glider or parachute, assembled alongside the depots that processed the munitions and equipment they needed. Large quantities of explosives were stored in corrugated-iron shelters alongside the narrow country roads in the build-up to the invasion, together with petrol dumps and stockpiles of vehicles. As the country's war economy consolidated with everyone on the Home Front in some sort of uniform and doing their bit to win the war, it seemed that they were no less involved than those fighting across the seas.

The Deployment of Locally Based Units

At the outbreak of war, the 3rd Battalion of the Leicestershire Regiment was at the Glen Parva depot, but the other two regular battalions were overseas in India and in Palestine respectively. The 1st Battalion remained at Razmak until February 1941, when it was despatched to defend Malaya against the Japanese invasion. Totally unprepared for the Japanese tactics, it suffered heavy losses, finally forming a composite battalion with the 2nd Battalion, East Surrey Regiment, and fighting until the final surrender of Singapore, followed by slave labour on the Burma Railway. The 2nd Battalion left Palestine to fight in the Western Desert campaigns, which included the siege of Tobruk and action against the Vichy French in Syria. After a stay in Ceylon (now Sri Lanka), it formed Nos 17 and 71 Columns of the Chindits for long-range penetration operations in Burma (now Myanmar). Meanwhile, the 8th Battalion, which had been raised as a new service battalion in Leicestershire in 1940, became the basis of a reformed 1st Battalion in May 1942, trained

Leicester: a fire-watchers' post on top of CORAH's Watling Street Mill, which had been taken over by the Admiralty as a Victualling Stores.

in Britain for the D-Day invasion of Normandy; it subsequently fought through Northwest Europe until the end of the war. The 1/5th Battalion fought in the Norwegian campaign in 1940, suffering heavy losses, while its twin, the 2/5th Battalion, went to France with the BEF and was evacuated from Dunkirk. In early 1943, following recovery time in the UK, it landed in Algiers and then fought its way up through Italy, finishing the war in Greece—involved in the struggle to prevent a communist takeover. The 7th Battalion, raised in 1940, served on home defence duties until late 1942, when it went to Burma to carry out operations alongside the 2nd Battalion as Nos 47 and 74 Columns of the Chindits.

The Leicestershire Yeomanry, along with several other Yeomanry regiments, were mobilised as horsed cavalry in 1939, but soon converted into two RA field regiments in 1940. Armoured divisions, alongside their tank and armoured reconnaissance units, also had a component that comprised field, A/T, and AA regiments, with battalions of mechanised infantry, together known as a 'Support Group'. The 153 (Leicester Yeomanry) Field Regiment served in the Guards Support Group from October 1941 and thence in the Guards Armoured Division, initially training for D-Day and then fighting through Northwest Europe until VE Day. Its companion regiment, 154 (Leicester Yeomanry) Field Regiment, went to the Middle East in December 1942 and was then stationed in Persia, India, Syria, Palestine, and Egypt, fighting at El Alamein in XXX Corps Reserve, equipped with twenty-four 25-pounder gun-howitzers. From

March 1944, it was posted to Italy and finished the war in Austria. The 44 Searchlight Regiment spent three years in 32 AA Brigade in the East Midlands, contributing to the defence of Hull, Derby, and Nottingham. In 1942, it was reorganised as 121 (The Leicestershire Regiment) LAA Regiment and served with Montgomery's 21st Army Group in Northwest Europe for the final year of the war.

One way of ensuring a steady supply of manpower to the armed forces was to engage youngsters early in the various military youth organisations. Leicestershire ACF held summer camps at Bitteswell Park, with 1,000 cadets under canvas. As the Home Guard became better equipped and organised, lads were encouraged to join in order to be ahead of the game when they were called up for military service. Some, especially Boy Scouts with bush-craft skills and local knowledge, were even recruited directly into the secret auxiliary units, often graduating from there to the Commandos. The ACF was always in competition with the ATC and pre-entry training for the RAF was organised by J. F. Wolfenden, headmaster of Uppingham School. Courses were held at institutes of higher education, such as Loughborough College, to introduce potential aircrew to service life, and Loughborough also ran summer schools for ATC cadets and their instructors.

Defence against Invasion

The expulsion of the BEF from France in May 1940 was followed by strong expectations of a German invasion. It was the responsibility of General Ironside, GOC Home Forces, to formulate anti-invasion plans and to take steps to ensure that those plans could be implemented with the resources available. While the successful evacuation of over 330,000 troops from the beaches of France had been little short of a miracle, the fact remained that the vast majority of the Army's equipment, artillery, and transport had been destroyed by the enemy or was abandoned during the retreat. Against all the current military doctrine, Ironside was forced to adopt a static defence strategy, based on linear anti-tank obstacles, supplemented by concrete pillboxes and gun emplacements. The coast batteries, minefields, and field defences of his 'Coastal Crust' were intended to delay the first wave of the enemy, making time for the Royal Navy to sail from her northern bases to destroy the enemy transports bringing reinforcements and supplies. A succession of 'stop-lines' based on waterways would further delay any inland advance until the few armoured units, held in reserve, could be brought into action. An enemy landing in either the Wash or the Humber estuary, aiming for the industrial and manufacturing centres of the Midlands, would encounter lines of A/T obstacles on the River Witham in Lincolnshire and then the more serious barrier of the River Trent.

Between Birmingham and the Trent, a number of canals and rivers were suitable for being exploited as stop-lines. These included the Oxford and Coventry canals and the River Tame and River Dove, linked by the Trent through Burton-on-Trent. All along these waterways are the remains of the defences: pillboxes, gun emplacements, and A/T obstacles. However, seventy-five years on, they are fast disappearing. At Marston

Junction, near Bedworth, the Ashby-de-la-Zouch Canal leaves the Coventry Canal and runs north past Hinckley. At least two pillboxes guarded the road and rail crossings in the south-west corner of the town. That at Nutts Lane, covering road and rail crossings, has been demolished, but the one guarding the Coventry Road canal bridge survives in good order. Backing onto the tow path it is a non-standard irregular hexagon with loopholes in three forward faces and two more over a low doorway in the rear wall. All the loops have been prefabricated, probably in one of the centralised workshops, and delivered to site to be incorporated into the structure by the civilian contractor, a local builder, overseen by a Royal Engineer officer. The bulletproof walls, 15 inches (38 cm) thick, consist of poured concrete inside brick formwork, with a 4-inch-thick (10-cm-thick) concrete roof. Most such pillboxes were built during the summer and early autumn of 1940, after which—as the factories turned out increasing numbers of armoured vehicles and artillery—the defensive strategy was able to contemplate a return to the orthodoxy of mobile warfare.

From mid-1940 to the end of 1941, our counties were defended by an assortment of regular and territorial units. The 4th Battalion Cheshire Regiment, for example, later organised as a machine-gun battalion, belonged to what was left of the 1st Infantry Division of I Corps after its return from France, and it was based in Rutland, with its HQ at Burley on the Hill and companies stationed in Melton Mowbray. As new, locally raised battalions, such as the 7th Battalion Leicestershire Regiment, became available, they were drafted into the home defence Lincolnshire Division, responsible for great swathes of the East Midlands. The 7th Leicesters served in 204 Independent

Hinckley (SP407932): a non-standard pillbox guarding a bridge over the canal.

Infantry Brigade from October 1940 until November 1941 before transferring into 205 Independent Infantry Brigade when the Lincolnshire Division had served its purpose and was dissolved. After the German invasion of Russia in the summer of 1941, local defence was devolved more and more to the Home Guard.

From the first day of the war, devastating aerial bombardment was expected hourly, so the nation's meagre AA defences were immediately deployed with searchlights occupying permanent sites, roughly 3 miles (5 km) apart, along fixed lines. These sites were seized on by Ironside's planners as potential strong points to be fortified and held against invading forces under the direction of the commanding officer of the nearest detachment of the local Field Force. Each AA Brigade HQ decreed that these sites should be defended by wire and fieldworks, and that each be given a concrete pillbox as a centre of resistance. Across Leicestershire and Rutland, there are at least a dozen sites where extant pillboxes represent searchlight sites listed in 32 AA Brigade documents (TNA: WO166/7389, 1942). All these pillboxes are examples, built to a standard plan, drawn from a suite of designs issued by the relevant department of the War Office Directorate of Fortifications and Works (DFW3). Type DFW3/22 is a bulletproof, regular hexagon with an entrance flanked by pistol loops in one side and rifle loops in the other five. Although all were completed to the same specification by local contractors supervised by the same RE officers, and all within weeks, if not days, of each other, there are many, albeit minor, variations. At Tilton-on-the-Hill and Stathern, the contractors were able to obtain timber for shuttering, while the several examples around Melton Mowbray all have brick skins left *in situ*. While the type standard has a Y-shaped anti-ricochet wall supporting the roof, as has Exton, most of its neighbours have merely pillars; these are circular at Ketton, square at Melton Spinney, octagonal at Tilton, and cruciform at Landyke Lane. Loopholes are fairly uniformly prefabricated and entrances are low level, but in some examples, they are edged with bull-nose bricks to prevent snagging clothing. At Brooke, the builder appears to have built the pillbox facing in the wrong direction, as it has clearly been turned around with a blocked doorway and two pistol loops in the back wall. Inside each rifle loop is a cantilevered concrete shelf to support the firer's elbow and these can be either rectangular or half-moon-shaped. One group, including those at Tolethorpe and Stretton, have protected tunnel entrances with a sixth rifle loop above. Such variations could signify either inconsistencies caused by rushed construction or evidence of local initiative and flexibility. All these pillboxes were complemented by barbed wire, communication trenches, and weapons pits, so they were not the stand-alone death-traps that their exposed positions on high ground would now suggest.

The Defence of Airfields and other Vulnerable Points

As if invasion from the sea was not a worrying enough prospect, the experience of Rotterdam and the Belgian forts raised the spectre of an airborne invasion, and this fear was to be confirmed by the assault on Crete's airfields by German paratroops in 1941.

Above: Burley (SK865111): a standard type DFW3/22 pillbox guarding the canal crossing.

Right: Sketch plans and elevations of pillboxes in Leicestershire and Rutland.

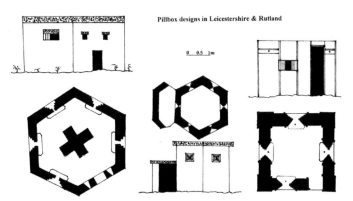

Pillbox designs in Leicestershire & Rutland

0   0.5   1m

Melton Mowbray, Landyke Lane (SK740250)
Type DFW3/22 splinter-proof pillbox
with cruciform anti-ricochet wall

Old Dalby Depot (SK682242)
Hexagonal guard-post with protected
entrance and six loopholes

Ratcliffe on the Wreake (SK623154)
STENT pre-fabricated pillbox
(after William Ward)

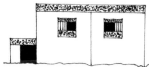

Stretton, searchlight site (SK945153)
Type DFW3/22 splinter-proof pillbox
with tunnel entrance and six loopholes

Hinckley, Coventry Road/Ashby Canal (SP407932)
Brick & concrete, splinter-proof pillbox

The decision to construct defences on Britain's airfields had been taken in the summer of 1940, when General Taylor, head of the War Office Directorate of Fortifications and Works, was invited by the Air Ministry to formulate a policy. Taylor's criteria for the density of defence works and size of garrison related to the importance of individual airfields in repelling invasion forces and their proximity to ports. While none of our counties' airfields belonged in the highest category, it was nevertheless necessary that adequate levels of defence were maintained, so North Luffenham, Cottesmore, Bitteswell, Bottesford, and Saltby all came within Taylor's second category—Class IIa. His specification directed that each would be allocated a garrison of 225 troops, manning a total of fifteen to twenty-four pillboxes with at least one light machine gun for each pillbox. One ring of pillboxes would face inwards onto the landing area with an outer ring facing out toward the field. In an attempt to introduce a mobile element to the defence, each airfield would have three improvised 'armoured' vehicles, usually known as 'Armadillos'. These were flatbed trucks with walls made of gravel-packed boxes with spaces left as loopholes. Open to the sky, they mounted an AALMG, usually a Lewis gun. Supplementing the official garrison, each airfield would organise a force of ground crew and other staff who would be mobilised in the event of an enemy landing. The gaps between pillboxes would be filled by weapons pits and trenches, and open blast shelters doubled as rifle trenches. The defence of the airfield was to be conducted by the garrison commander from a dedicated bunker equipped with a radio for keeping contact with outposts. From 1941, this was a standard Battle HQ to Air Ministry drawing number 11008/41. It consisted of a sunken chamber for a PBX and a room for runners, with a concrete-roofed cupola offering 360-degree observation. Examples survive at Bruntingthorpe, Wymeswold, Market Harborough, and North Luffenham. The tiny number of surviving close-defences pillboxes on our airfields would suggest that many fewer were built than Taylor had recommended. There is a Type DFW3/22 pillbox at Castle Donington and another at Bottesford. An example on the northern perimeter of North Luffenham actually belongs to a searchlight site that pre-dates the airfield's opening. Two prefabricated square Stent pillboxes remain at Ratcliffe-on-Wreake. At Warren Farm, on the edge of Cottesmore airfield, there is a barn that has been loopholed and has had a half-hexagonal pillbox built on the front, entered via a low doorway inside the barn. The three loopholes have monopod mounts for Lewis guns set in the sills. About 50 yards away is a hexagonal pillbox with an open square annexe on one side, containing the mount for an AALMG, which may have had a ground-defence role as well. While this last structure is replicated at airfields across the country, particularly in Bedfordshire, a truly unique defence structure was fashioned at North Luffenham. Here, a rectangular pillbox with four loopholes in three sides was built on to the end of the 25-yard range, which stands at one corner of the airfield perimeter with one end supported on brick piers. The fear of full-fledged airborne invasion, or raids like that carried out by British commandos at Bruneval to secure a German radar set, prompted the Air Ministry to maintain levels of vigilance on airfields right to the end of the war. The RAF Regiment was formed in 1941 specifically to defend airfields, although their role was later to develop along more offensive lines, and No. 92 Group,

RAF Market Harborough (SP718895): a standard airfield Battle HQ (11008/41).

RAF North Luffenham (SK934046): an improvised pillbox on stilts on the corner of the 25-yard range.

Bomber Command Defence School, was set up at Bitteswell in 1943. That summer, US parachutists were dropped on Cottesmore to test the airfield's ground defences, which, having repulsed the invaders, were rated adequate by the umpires.

By this time, reflecting the wider picture that saw a switch from attempts to hold linear defences over to the formation of Defended Localities (DLs), airfield defence moved away from the defended perimeter to strong points, concentrations of field defences, which focused on particularly important or vulnerable areas. These combined barbed wire and anti-personnel mines, weapons pits, and slit trenches with more substantial structures of brick or concrete. They were manned by RAF Regiment personnel, Home Guard detachments, and the crews of AA guns and searchlights.

Other Vulnerable Points included the Central Ordnance Depot at Old Dalby and the Air Force Fuel Depots at Redmile and Stonesby. Old Dalby relied on its position under a hillside as natural camouflage supplemented by paint effects on its sheds. It was also surrounded by guard posts—at least one of which survives. It is hexagonal with square, stepped loopholes in each side, an overhanging concrete roof, and a protected, low-level entrance. Redmile, served by road, rail, and waterway, has a standard DFW3/22 pillbox that overlooks the north bank of the Grantham Canal. Gaddesby was the site of a USAAF ammunition depot, later used to store vehicles. The spigot mortar pedestal (see below) in the centre of the village may have been sited to defend the road to the depot in one direction, and Rearsby airfield in the other.

Old Dalby (SK682242): a guard post at the REME depot.

Local Defence and the Home Guard

By spring 1941, as the Regular Army was being redeployed across the seas, local defence was made very much the responsibility of the Home Guard, supplemented by depot and training units of the army. Raised in the summer of 1940 at a time of acute national crisis, the Home Guard had got by in the early days on a mixture of invention, improvisation, enthusiasm, and adrenaline. By 1941, a great deal of training had been undertaken, weaponry and equipment delivered, and most of the octogenarian dugout admirals and generals, who had first stepped into the breach, had finally retired. Ironside's initial defence plans were quickly modified in the light of improvements in the production of guns and vehicles. The linear defences were largely converted to demolition belts, where bridges were set up with explosive charges to be fired in an emergency, and replaced by centres of resistance. These were known first as 'anti-tank islands' then as 'nodal points' and they usually consisted of all-round defences centred on the junctions or crossing points of important roads, railways, and waterways. All the large towns were automatically included in this designation. By the middle of 1941, a comprehensive Defence Plan had been formulated for each of these nodal points containing details of fixed defences; composition of garrisons; inventories of weaponry; the responsibilities of different organisations; the means of communication, signals, and passwords; aims, actions, methodology, protocols, and procedures; and the circumstances in which emergency measures would be announced and enforced.

Leicester's defence plan reflects the prevailing tactics of the time. Replacing linear defences that, once penetrated, might easily be rolled up—a network of 'defended localities' (DL) was established. These were usually centred on road junctions or rail and river crossings and consisted of both permanent and removable obstructions covered by infantry trenches, bomb posts, and a variety of anti-tank weaponry. A notional defence perimeter—stretching east to west from Humberstone to Braunstone and north to south from Thurmaston to Blaby—linked DLs on every road out of the city. Further DLs were established to block access by rail or waterway. The city was divided into three concentric zones, but it was soon realised that the sheer length of these lines and the densely populated areas militated against a controlled defence based on holding ground. The line of the River Soar and the Grand Union Canal provided a useful barrier, perhaps more psychological than physical, to penetration from the north-east, with all crossing points obstructed. However, given the nature of the terrain, fighting would necessarily have been much more fluid. On the one hand, some Home Guard units had mobile roles anyway, while on the other, the sheer density of the built-up areas could have afforded benefits to tenacious house-to-house defence. Their efforts, combined with similar actions in those outlying villages grouped together as DLs, would have slowed down the enemy's advance and then chipped away at his supply chain, using local knowledge of the ground. Oakham (R), Loughborough, Melton Mowbray, Lutterworth, and Uppingham (R) were all nodal points, surrounded by DLs based largely on roadblocks—fourteen of them in the case of Loughborough. In Lutterworth, the important crossroads (where George Street, Coventry Street and Chapel Street all

Uppingham (SK862998): a loopholed wall on the Leicester road into town.

met) was referred to as a 'hedgehog', with roads obstructed in all directions, forming the centrepiece of a DL. At Uppingham, a loopholed wall still commands the approach into town along the Leicester road and a spigot mortar faced north up the Oakham road.

A typical roadblock consisted of permanent obstructions each side of the carriageway, constricting the width to be blocked at 'Action Stations'. Permanent obstructions could be concrete anti-tank blocks, manufactured on site for the specific purpose, or extemporised versions, such as sewer pipes filled with rubble, overturned vehicles, tree trunks, or anything heavy, bulky, and difficult to shift. Anti-tank blocks, usually 4-foot (1.3-m) cubes, were made of concrete poured into wooden formwork and often reinforced with iron-bars. Smaller tetrahedra, referred to as 'dragons teeth', but officially called 'pimples', and small concrete cylinders that could be rolled into place were also used, along with 'buoys', which were cones on domed bases whose unpredictable motion was reckoned to unsettle tank drivers. The Spanish Civil War had also thrown up ideas such as placing upturned soup plates masquerading as mines in the road, as well as hanging blankets across the road on wires, intended to make tank drivers think twice before proceeding into the unknown. As real mines became available, the soup plates were returned to the emergency feeding stations, whose every utensil was recorded in the Defence Plan. The gap in the middle of the road was furnished with slots into which bent rails, or 'hairpins', stacked for immediate use by the side of the road, could be inserted at the last minute. It was a matter of honour that Home Guards manning roadblocks should allow their own defenders through before slamming the door in the face of the foe. Any vehicle left on the wrong side would be drained of fuel and immobilised. A number of A/T blocks can still be seen around the counties. At Launde Abbey, a collection of over forty small cylinders

Newbold (SK393192): one half of this possibly unique roadblock that was formed of hawsers stretched taut between steel frames embedded in the verge on each side of the road.

has been used to edge a drive. A similar cylinder may be seen at Ratcliffe-on-Wreake, where it may have been recycled as a tie down for light aircraft. Larger A/T blocks appear to have been scattered around Asfordby and another can be seen at Redmile.

A unique example of an unusual design of roadblock can be found at Newbold, near Coleorton, on a bridge that takes the Whitwick to Melbourne road (B587) over a long-disused railway line from Ashby-de-la-Zouch to Derby. The roadblock is composed of steel frames each side of the road, which held taut hawsers at two different heights. Deeply embedded in the ground, each frame is around 5 feet (1.5 m) high and 2 feet (60 cm) wide. The uprights are notched to prevent the hawsers slipping when engaged, and there are sturdy horizontal crosspieces to brace the structures. Adjacent are steel anti-tank rails and, in the woods close by, stands a Home Guard explosives and inflammables store.

The Leicestershire and Rutland Home Guard

By autumn 1940, the Home Guard, with its Zone HQ in the magazine, had coalesced into a coherent force that reflected its defensive priorities. North, South, and West Battalions defended Leicester's periphery, with a Central Battalion made up of twenty-seven separate detachments based on factories, works, and utilities. Additionally, there was a mobile force equipped with several dozen cars and motorcycles based in the stadium on Blackbird Road. Outside Leicester, battalions were centred on Ashby-de-la-Zouch, Charnwood, Loughborough, Market Bosworth, Market Harborough, and Melton Mowbray. A Rutland Battalion had its HQ in Oakham's Penn Street drill hall. After the initial crisis as invasion was expected daily, rationalisation produced an establishment of fourteen battalions, organised into four groups plus the Rutland battalion, a motor reconnaissance battalion based in Leicester, and a GPO battalion with detachments spread across a wider area.

Prior to the arrival of large quantities of Ross and P17 rifles from over the Atlantic, the LDV and then the Home Guard became accustomed to improvising weapons. However, the scarcity of A/T weapons, even up to two years into the war, meant that the wizards of Winston Churchill's Toyshop in Buckinghamshire were kept busy. A whole genre of 'sub-artillery' evolved, initially solely for use by the Home Guard. Major Blacker was later to invent the PIAT, a very effective bazooka-type A/T weapon, and to influence the design of the 'Hedgehog', an anti-submarine mortar that contributed to the Royal Navy's success in the Battle of the Atlantic. He had invented the Blacker Bombard or 29-mm Spigot Mortar in the 1930s, offering it unsuccessfully to an unappreciative Board of Ordnance. Faced with the idea of rampaging German tanks and very little with which to threaten them, his design was resurrected. The spigot mortar projected an A/T bomb weighing 20 lb (9 kg) with an effective range of around 450 yards according to the manual, but an optimal one of under 100 yards. There was also an anti-personnel bomb of 14 lb (6.5 kg), which was reckoned to be effective up to 785 yards. The spigot mortar could be mounted on a portable frame of scaffold-type poles with spade grips or on a permanent, static mounting—officially a 'pedestal', but often referred to as a 'thimble'. A framework of tubular metal, about 3 feet (0.9 m) high, was embedded in a concrete cylinder the size of an oil drum, with just the stainless-steel pintle protruding from its domed top. The pedestal was set in the middle of circular pit, revetted with palings or, better still, brick, with ready-use ammunition lockers set into the sides of the pit. At 'Action Stations', the spigot mortar could be brought out of its dry store to be mounted on one of these prepared positions, usually located in pairs, perhaps 100 yards apart. In late 1941, hundreds of these Blacker Bombards had been distributed, not only to the Home Guard, but also to the RAF Regiment. The advantage of the fixed pedestal was that the crew could have already ranged on the hump of a bridge to catch the underside of a tank as it came into view. The disadvantage was that once it had shot its bolt and been overrun, the weapon was effectively lost. If a crew could keep its nerve, the weapon was extremely accurate, especially by 1942, when many of the inevitable teething troubles had been ironed out. Both mortar and ammunition were usually kept in a dedicated store. Pedestals may still be seen on the Saxby road approaching Melton Mowbray alongside a former railway; in Gaddesby; on a road junction at Rotherby; in Harby; and on the outer earthworks of Oakham Castle. In August 2015, one was being buried under the patio of a house in Main Street, Ratby.

One of the earliest of these sub-artillery weapons was the Northover Projector, a drainpipe mounted on a tripod that fired Self-Igniting Phosphorus (SIP) grenades. In Leicester, like spigot mortars, these projectors were produced in the workshops of the City Transport Department and issued to the Home Guard—two per platoon. The Smith Gun was a 3-inch (75-mm) artillery piece that could be towed behind an Austin-Seven car. In action, one wheel became a turntable and the other became overhead

Above left: Harby (SK753312): spigot mortar pedestal at the entrance to the village; a Home Guard explosives and inflammables store, where the bombs were stored, formerly stood nearby.

Above right: Replica Northover Projector: a Home Guard weapon for firing Self-Igniting Phosphorus (SIP) grenades.

cover. It was attached to a limber, which held the shells. This gun was also issued to the RAF Regiment, and a clue to its reliability may lie in the habit of the RAF MUs storing Smith Gun shells as far away as possible from all other munitions. This circumspection is borne out by the unlucky experience of members of No. 13 Platoon, at Hathern, when shells they were transporting spontaneously exploded.

Many of the obstacles and ruses taught by the Home Guard training staff were intended to halt enemy tanks. A stationary tank, especially if separated from its infantry chaperones, can more easily be permanently immobilised than can a moving one. Sticky bombs, mines on bogies, SIP grenades, AW (Albright & Wilson) bombs, or even crude Molotov Cocktails all had the capacity to immobilise if brought within close range. The Fougasse, several of which were installed alongside Leicestershire roads, had a long history of use, going back to eighteenth-century Malta, where rocks were discharged explosively. The Home Guard version comprised oil drums of petrol and other inflammables set off by a SIP grenade or even electrically. Each of the group of six drums could discharge 45 gallons (200 litres) of flaming liquid over any person or vehicle within a range of 30 yards, burning fiercely for over five minutes. They were often positioned in front of roadblocks as a way of wrong-footing those very infantry who escorted vulnerable tanks.

Viscount Hanworth was a Cambridge mechanical sciences graduate and volunteer pilot who joined the REs and was posted to Nottingham to advise local units on A/T techniques. He invented a range of mines that could be launched from the roadside.

Austin Ruddy describes the torpedo version used in Leicestershire as a quartet of anti-tank mines mounted on a skateboard and fired electrically and remotely as an oblivious enemy tank clattered up to the tree, which acted as the firer's sighting point.

Most of these weapons and materials needed safe and secure storage. Home Guard explosives and inflammables store came in all sorts of designs and materials, but all observed the War Office directive that demanded the regulation two compartments, segregating their volatile contents. Ideally, they were robustly built in brick, with a substantial concrete roof and two solid doors. That at Coleorton conforms to this pattern, as did one at Dunton Bassett, now demolished, while the sunken, now buried, example at Rotherby was probably similar. At Scraptoft is a store that has a door at each end. Until recently, a store, surviving at Harby, was more like a strengthened Anderson shelter, presumably with an internal cross wall. At Great Casterton (R), the store consists of two sections side-by-side, but under one, albeit not very impressive, roof. Apart from these purpose-built structures, the Home Guard used whatever accommodation was available for training and administrative activities: drill halls, such as Coalville or Oakham; village institutes, such as Enderby or Markfield; public houses and hotels, such as Griffydam, Rothley, or Oadby; schools, such as Appleby Magna or Woodhouse Eaves; and private houses, such as at Birstall, Sutton Cheney, or Thurmaston.

The coastal counties of Britain were provided with secret Home Guard units, known as Auxiliary Units or the British Resistance Organisation, which, in the event of an invasion, would go underground, operating in small, self-sufficient cells to disrupt enemy communications. They were expected to survive for just two short weeks. Such units also operated in Worcestershire, which would have become the bolthole for government, royalty, and the BBC, and it appears that Leicestershire also justified the existence of such a force. One feature of these Auxiliary Units was the generosity of their equipment, from Tommy guns to plastic explosives. Beaumanor Hall (see below) was an extremely sensitive site that warranted its own independent Home Guard platoon. Its armoury included Sten and Tommy guns, both light and medium machine guns, all the usual sub-artillery, and even a 2-pounder A/T gun with a truck to tow it. Additionally, Home Guard Shock Sections, or Squads, were formed in Quorn, Rothley, and Barrow-upon-Soar as protection for Beaumanor and, if necessary, to operate as auxiliaries. Guerrilla training was carried out in local woods, and an underground operational base was hidden nearby, possibly at Bull-in-the-Hollow Farm. Realistic training included testing the Home Guard defences of Beaumanor by carrying out night raids, and this also constituted useful preparation for any post-Invasion sabotage role. An elite group of Home Guard guides, trained to aid defending troops through their detailed knowledge of the terrain, already existed openly, but Austin Ruddy has also posited the existence of further Shock Sections in the south of the county but not in Rutland. Many 'old-school' officers disapproved of irregular forces as ungentlemanly, ill-disciplined, and flashy, whose members would have been much better employed stiffening the ranks of conventional units.

Great Casterton (TF002092): the Home Guard store built with separate sections for explosives and inflammables.

Enderby Institute: HQ of 'C' Company, 3rd (West Leicester) Battalion, Home Guard.

Beaumanor Hall: the armoury of this top secret site's resident Home Guard unit.

The Regular Army in Leicestershire and Rutland

A large Victorian house, 'Elmfield' in Stanley Road, Leicester, now a care home, housed the HQ of the East Midland Area, Northern Command, under the District HQ at Bestwood Lodge, outside Nottingham. After the immediate danger of invasion in 1940–41 had passed, there were few regular units in our counties, so the Home Guard took on a wide range of responsibilities. However, the Regular Army maintained a presence throughout the war, retaining the important functions of training, manning many of the AA defences, and the organisation of munitions. The RAOC at Garendon were primed to field a mobile column if required, and the REME at Old Dalby were doubtless similarly wired up.

Training

From early in the war, the Leicestershire Regimental depot at Glen Parva Barracks functioned as an Infantry Training Centre, but after 1941, the number of such establishments was reduced to twenty-five; in 1942, the General Service Corps was set up to provide basic training for all army recruits prior to postings to specialist training units. A Primary Training Centre operated on Leicester Racecourse, from which those recruits bound for infantry regiments would be sent to the nearest ITC, either No. 7 at Lincoln or No. 22 at Warwick. In 1940, the Leicester-based RAOC Training Establishment was moved to Derby, but the next year, the RAOC OCTU in Kettering, Northamptonshire, moved to Leicester, where larger premises were available. Gopsall Hall, near Twycross, housed the REME Radio and Radar Training School; Garats Hay and Beaumanor Hall at Woodhouse Eaves, the War Office Intelligence School No. 6; and Gumley Hall, near Market Harborough, the Special Operations Executive No. 41 Special Training School and Quorn Hall, a RN training establishment. Possibly in connection with the Asfordby heavy artillery proofing range, there was a Royal Artillery establishment for training instructors in Brook Street, Melton Mowbray, either during or soon after the war. A possible candidate for this building is a large, chapel-like complex (now a garage) labelled as 'Depot' on the 1965 OS map. By early 1944, in the run-up to D-Day, Cottesmore and Saltby were operating as US airborne forces bases carrying out preparatory training exercises with both parachute and glider-borne units. There were practice drop zones at Keyham and elsewhere. The Army's rifle range, long established at Six Hills, continued in use, with others at Belvoir, Oakham (R), and Wardley Hill (R). All of these were also used by the Home Guard. Grenade-throwing practice was generally carried out in old quarries or brick-pits, but a purpose-built range was constructed at Ratby, with individual throwing bays and an observation blockhouse. From 1941, there was an Army Bomb Disposal School at Donington Park race circuit.

Leicester: 'Elmfield', in Stanley Road, served as the Army's East Midland Area HQ.

Wardley Hill (SK835014): the robust range building variously described as serving Uppingham School OTC rifle range, and the (later) RAF bombing range.

Depots

A number of important depots were located in rural areas thought unlikely to be bombing targets. The Central Ordnance Depot at Old Dalby was begun in 1939 and opened at the end of 1940. It was planned as a vehicle depot, a satellite of Chilwell outside Nottingham, but its designation was altered to become a storage depot for machinery, spares, and tools. In 1942, it passed to the newly formed Royal Electrical and Mechanical Engineers (REME) as No. 5 Central Workshop, employing nearly 4,000 civilian and military personnel to build, repair, and maintain vehicles, machinery, and equipment. A scheme to decentralise vulnerable supplies from urban storage depots brought signals, artillery, and small arms onto the site. The depot lies alongside the LMS railway line between Melton Mowbray and Nottingham; however, while it was possible to put in a new siding with its own signal box, the depot's steeply sloping site made it impossible for lines to be laid directly into the vast sheds. Therefore, a grid of wide roads services the site. There are six principal sheds with saw-tooth or hipped gabled roofs built as stores. REME added a large workshop for repairs to Bofors AA guns, field bakeries, trucks, etc., and an enormous, hangar-like radar workshop on the top of the hill. There was a guardhouse, PBX, canteen, MT section, HQ building, and fire station, along with assorted Romney, Iris, and Nissen huts.

In 1937, the Air Ministry had commenced a programme to construct reserve fuel depots in order to maintain supplies even when delivery by sea was disrupted by enemy action. By 1943, the RAF and USAAF bomber airfields, especially in the East Midlands, required vast quantities of fuel, which was piped across from Stanlow on the Mersey to Misterton in north Nottinghamshire. From here, a pipeline ran south to Sandy in Bedfordshire, feeding the numerous airfields in East Anglia. The Army fuel depot at Bottesford and the Air Force Reserve Fuel Depot at Redmile both tapped into this supply. Redmile had a capacity of 5,200 tons in eight tanks. In 1943, Stonesby, due south of Redmile, was added to the network with three tanks, but did not open until after the war. Redmile is still a fairly complete working depot. The remains of the installations at Bottesford include Nissen huts, traces of fuel tanks, and signs of the rail tracks that fed the Jerrycan-filling points operated by the RASC and the Pioneer Corps.

Along with fuel, a constant supply of bombs was vital to the air forces' operations. Gaddesby Hall, known to the USAAF as Paske Hall, was loaned as a temporary armaments depot holding 20 kilotons of munitions, in partnership with Great Dalby, but it was later converted to vehicle storage. The manor house at Ashby Folville provided billets and HQ space. In the lead up to the Normandy invasion, much of Leicestershire was turned into one enormous munitions dump. The RAOC, centred on Garendon Park, set up roadside storage sites across large swathes of Leicestershire. Bombs and shells, including chemical weapons, were stored in often open-ended Anderson-type shelters. At Garendon, the RAOC organised a permanent two-storey brick building with a high-ceilinged single-storey annexe that was used as a control room. Painted on one whole wall is a diagrammatic, colour-coded map of Leicestershire, at a scale of 6 inches (15 cm) to 1 mile (1.6 km), displaying the status of all the byways with the types of munitions stored along their verges: phosgene, mustard gas, shells of different types, and

Old Dalby: the sheds of the REME Depot, seen from above, showing how it was built into the hillside in order to provide protection from air attack.

Redmile: the RAF Fuel Depot on the pipeline running from Misterton in Nottinghamshire to Sandy in Bedfordshire, serving the RAF and USAAF bomber bases of East Anglia.

Garendon: the RAOC building, now the Estate Office.

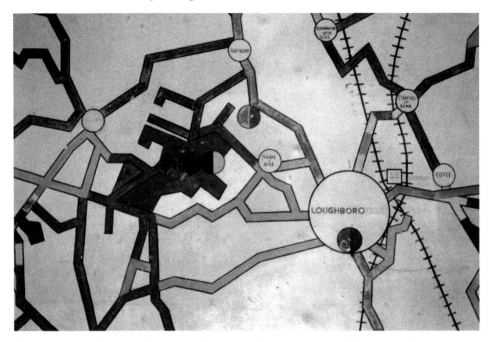

Garendon: part of the map of ordnance dumps which covers one wall of the estate office.

non-chemical munitions. At a number of points, coloured discs appear to denote the signature colours of the RAOC (blue or blue/red/blue), the Pioneer Corps (red/green), and the RASC (yellow/blue). Garendon, Bradgate Park, and Belvoir are particularly prominent, and this may indicate where the heaviest concentrations of materiel were stored in secure parkland. A black line encloses what is clearly a marked-out area taking in Whitwick and Belton in the west; Harby in the north; Anstey, Rotherby, and Melton Mowbray in the south; and Saxby and Belvoir in the east. A southerly extension includes the backroads and villages between Houghton-on-the-Hill and Uppingham (R).

Additional to the original plans for Old Dalby as a vehicle storage facility under COD Chilwell, Castle Donington became a Group HQ for vehicle storage with satellites at Wigston Magna for tank tracks; at New Parks, in Glenfield, where there was a REME Workshop Stores with extensive vehicle storage; and vehicle and motorcycle repair depots at Gopsall, Breedon, and Syston.

Airfields and Aviation

By 1945, there were nineteen airfields serving the needs of the military, one way or another, in our counties, most concerned with training, specifically for either RAF Bomber or Transport Commands. At the start of the war, Desford, with its satellite at Braunstone, together with Ratcliffe-on-the-Wreake had accounted for much basic pilot training through the RAF Elementary Flying Training Schools (EFTS). As the war progressed, more specialised and sophisticated aircraft came into service, necessitating pilots receiving specific training in Operational Training Units (OTU) or later on, when Lancasters and Stirlings appeared, in Heavy Conversion Units (HCU). A significant representation of airborne forces in Leicestershire, prior to the D-Day landings and the operation to secure the bridges over the Rhine, meant that pilots were needed for a range of troop carriers, heavy gliders, and the aircraft that would tow them. Some airfields, such as Bottesford and Saltby, were handed over to IX USAAF Troop Carrier Command in preparation for opening a second front; others, such as North Luffenham and Woolfox Lodge, were scheduled for use by the USAAF, but were not needed; some, like Castle Donington and Bruntingthorpe, were OTUs throughout the war; Ratcliffe and Melton Mowbray were involved in ferrying aircraft to operational bases at home and abroad; Loughborough, Rearsby, and Desford were part of the aircraft manufacturing process; and some, including North Luffenham, Cottesmore, and Woolfox Lodge, also hosted fully operational squadrons at different times. An account of all the counties' airfields appears in Appendix IV. Participation in bombing or leafleting operations formed an important part of the curriculum of the OTUs, so aircrew-in-training faced all the dangers from day one. The Air Transport Auxiliary pilots at Ratcliffe on the Wreake faced entirely different challenges, flying unfamiliar, unarmed aircraft with no radios into strange airfields in all weathers. The pilots of No. 12 Ferry Unit flying overseas out of Melton Mowbray faced even greater potential dangers; in particular, when delivering Spitfires to France in early 1945.

Of the nineteen airfields, only four were operational prior to the war, and of those, only Cottesmore (R) was purpose built as a military airfield. North Luffenham had been designed before the war, and two were extensions of aircraft factories, but the remaining twelve were built to very different production values. Instead of grouping buildings in nice, neat layouts echoing country estates, these new airfields were based on principles of dispersal and invisibility. All the buildings were built of easily sourced materials, using simple construction methods. Hangars clad in steel sheeting on a steel frame were designed to be transportable; structures on the technical, synthetic training, and administrative sites had walls of a single brick's width, hence 'temporary brick' or 'tb'; many of the workshop and stores buildings were Romney huts and accommodation was in Nissen or Ministry of War Production timber huts. The occasional conveniently sited country house might be requisitioned for an officers' mess, but, generally, conditions were Spartan. Tents were not unknown on newly operational airfields where bad weather had delayed completion and living areas were seas of mud. Early in the war, airfields were still being built with grass flying fields and eventually had to be shut down for several months while the triangle of three concrete runways, necessary for the ever-heavier aircraft and all-weather operations, were laid.

The dispersal principle meant that airfields covered enormous tracts of land. The concrete runways, laid in a triangle to ensure that there was always sufficient wind to provide lift, were bordered by a number of discrete sites. The technical site included workshops, a T2 hangar or two, a main stores plus specialist buildings for storing parachutes, dinghies, pyrotechnics, and SAA. The specialist buildings of the synthetic training site included turret trainers, bombing teachers, free gunnery, and navigation trainers. The Station HQ and separate squadron offices, along with a protected

Wymeswold: a typical temporary brick (tb) hut on the technical site; Building 41 was the electrical and instrument workshop in the early 1960s, when Field Aircraft Services were in occupation, and that may well have been its original use.

operations block, occupied the administration site. A further site contained the sickbay, decontamination centre, and morgue. Further out from these were communal sites with accommodation huts, ablutions, dining rooms, and messes for officers and NCOs. Beside the runway was the watch office, accompanied by sheds for fire tenders, night-flying equipment, and fuel tankers. In an often isolated location, a B1 hangar was provided for the onsite repair of damaged aircraft by civilian MAP staff.

Airfields were constructed with particular functions in mind and a range of watch offices was designed to meet their differing needs, but this failed to anticipate the need for flexibility, and an all-purpose model, the 343/43, was ultimately developed. The whole range of watch offices was evident in our counties. Cottesmore's 'Fort' from the Expansion Period, North Luffenham's 'Villa' of 1939, the transitional model at Bottesford and Wymeswold, and an early austerity model at Saltby, demonstrate clearly the shift from a pre-war aesthetic to wartime utility. Inexplicably inappropriate watch offices also appeared, that designed for a night-fighter station at Woolfox Lodge and for a fighter satellite at Castle Donington, but Bitteswell and Nuneaton both got the right towers for OTU satellites. The earliest attempt at a general-purpose watch office was built at Saltby (replacing an earlier model), at Bruntingthorpe, and at Melton Mowbray, where it had an extra lower floor. The final version of this design can be seen at Leicester East and Husbands Bosworth.

Apart from hangars and watch offices from this wartime construction period, there are many other examples of surviving buildings on a number of different sites. Some of the smart huts on the Rosedale Business Park at Bottesford are the original tb ones, recently refurbished. Market Harborough retains a gymnasium and chapel; a parachute store remains at Husbands Bosworth; and an unusual combined turret trainer and bombing teacher (633/42) is located at Woolfox Lodge. Many of Wymeswold's buildings remain, dominated by the Braithwaite water tank on its lattice tower. The most complete, however, is Bruntingthorpe, much of whose technical and synthetic

Bruntingthorpe: the B1 Ministry of Aircraft Production hangar (11776/41), recently refurbished as a conference centre, marketed as 'Hangar '42'.

North Luffenham: three T2 hangars (8254/40), not specifically provided for glider storage, but probably put to that use.

Bottesford, Roseland Business Park: the original watch office forms the basis for this elegant, if imaginative restoration. An original of the type (518/40) survives at Wymeswold.

Leicester East: the standard watch office (343/43) still used by Leicestershire Aero Club.

Market Harborough (SP698886): the Gymnasium/Church (14604/40 and 15424/41) on the Chapel Farm communal site.

Bruntingthorpe: the crew procedure and airmanship hall on the airfield's training site.

training sites survive, with several different gunnery and bombing training buildings and the crew procedure trainer/airmanship hall, plus some tb offices, a tall fabric store, and workshops in Nissen huts.

As more and more airfields were needed, a number of further potential locations were identified but never developed. These included Croft, south of Narborough; Countesthorpe, south of Leicester; Essendine (R), north-east of Stamford; Kilby, south of Great Glen; Foxton Lodge, near Market Harborough; Ragdale, near Six Hills; and Snarestone, north of Twycross. Ragdale was planned as a second satellite of Wymeswold, but because of objections from the Army, who had an established rifle range on the site, it became a bombing range for No. 28 OTU instead. Snarestone was projected as a Fleet Air Arm Advanced Flying Unit to cover 600 acres (240 hectares). As laid out on the ground, most of the projected area of Essendine would actually have been in Lincolnshire. Vehement objections to both Essendine and Snarestone were triggered by the loss to agriculture of so much productive land.

Bombing Training

OTUs and HCUs across our counties used the bombing ranges at Wardley Hill (R), Bosworth Gorse, Ragdale, and Mowsley (R), but operational difficulties plagued these training activities and alternatives were sought. One solution lay with the simulation offered by using infrared targets, and over fifty infrared projectors were installed at selected bombing target sites across Britain. These were invisible to the naked eye, but they were capable of being picked out at bombing height by cameras loaded with photographic film sensitive to infrared light. The sequence was as follows: the bomber makes its approach, the bomb aimer opens the shutter on his camera, he locates the target using his bombsight, he releases the imaginary bomb, he starts timing the fall of the 'bomb' by stopwatch, he estimates the impact moment, and he closes the shutter after the 'bomb' has detonated. The resultant print will have recorded the bomber's approach and the 'bomb's' point of impact in relation to the target, lying in the centre of the photograph, which spans the time between the shutter being opened and closed. This will reveal the accuracy of the bombing and the extent and nature of any error. Projectors were used from August 1939, and some were retained after 1945. At each site, personnel were detailed to check the projector lamps and to replace failed ones. This caused problems on many non-official sites, where these duties could not be monitored, so relocations were common. Infrared projectors were resited from Holwell Ironworks in Melton Mowbray to Nottingham Central telephone exchange in 1943, and from a railway junction at Church Honeybourne, near Evesham, to Leicester telephone exchange in 1944. There are no records of switchboard operators suffering simulated injuries.

While the RAF trained operational aircrew, Loughborough College, in conjunction with Boulton & Paul, contributed to the development of military aviation by teaching aircraft manufacture as a discipline. This took place in the purpose-built workshops on Derby Road, which replaced the Premier dance hall on Ashby Road, previously the airframe instructional workshop. Loughborough also trained aeronautical engineers for the FAA from 1942. The training school for WAAF officers was located in Loughborough. After the bombing of the RAF Officers' Medical Rehabilitation Unit in Torquay (Devon) in 1942, it moved to Loughborough College, remaining there until 1947.

Air Defence

The great fear at the beginning of the war was that the country would be obliterated through aerial bombing, but the resources to prevent this happening were scant. The Observer Corps was mobilised and two new posts were established at Empingham (R) and at Rearsby, but mere observation was not enough if there was insufficient force to deal with the threat. The first major bombing raid on Leicester was in November 1940, when over 100 people were killed and great damage caused to houses, utilities, and factories. There was enormous frustration that little was done to provide defences against such attacks being repeated. The city of Leicester was quick off the mark in setting up a system of emergency feeding under a city feeding officer with a dining officer, supported by the WVS. In the event of an emergency, feeding centres, backed up by a warehouse full of foodstuffs and supplemented by six mobile canteens, stood by for activation on the command: 'Prepare to feed'.

Given the almost total dependence on the railways for moving personnel, food, munitions, and fuel, it was essential that measures were taken to safeguard their control mechanisms. From 1940, Leicester was a district office in the LMS network of emergency telephone links. Before the war, the notion of protected control centres had been raised and budgeted for, and in 1941, such structures came into operation at Leicester and Melton Mowbray, replacing the previous sandbagged improvisations. There were various versions of these control centres, some of which, located in places considered to be particularly vulnerable, had roofs 10 feet (3 m) thick. Both Leicester and Melton Mowbray, however, received B2 versions with roof and walls only 15 inches (37.5 cm) thick. The B2 building measured 40 feet by 20 (12 m by 6 m) and was divided into four main areas. The largest space was the control room with seven desks. The rest of the space was taken up by the generator room, the battery room, and the switch room. The Melton building was of a design which could easily be converted to offices at the end of the war.

Guns, Rockets, and Searchlights

Much of the East Midlands was covered throughout the war by 32 AA Brigade, with its HQ at RAF Hucknall (Nottinghamshire), where liaison with the RAF Fighter Command filter room at Watnall was possible. However, in the early days, there were hardly any AA guns available, so those airfields that had AA defences at all made do with Lewis guns. In June 1940, Cottesmore (R) was defended by sixteen of them, manned by 27 LAA Regiment, and a similar number were based in North Luffenham when it opened. Only in March 1941 did

Leicester receive any HAA guns at all, possibly as a response to the raids of the previous November and the angry local response. Manned by elements of 78 HAA Regiment, they were in four sites—at Thurnby, Enderby, Anstey, and Syston—but they did not stay for long. By now transferred to 136 HAA Regiment, all four sites had been disarmed by June 1942. After completing its training on mobile guns in August 1943, 129 LAA Regiment set up HQ in Braunstone Park, Leicester, with one battery based at the militia camp in Melton Mowbray. The neighbouring 40 AA Brigade, which covered the westerly reaches of East Anglia, occupied the militia camp at Ashwell, outside Oakham, as its new HQ. Unit histories reveal that in February 1944, a HAA battery was moved from Leicester to Grantham, and 396/127 Battery arrived at the Thurnby site (H1) from Great Yarmouth. The next month, HAA batteries were exchanged between Peterborough and Leicester, manning the Enderby site (H3), which was still described as non-operational. The four HAA sites round Leicester were of the standard pattern with octagonal gun pits for the 3.7-inch guns, a command post—that at Thurnby having recently been demolished—and magazines. Accommodated in a veritable village of huts were offices, gun stores, workshops, messes, and living quarters. Each had an attendant searchlight site close by, Barkby Lane for Syston and Stoughton for Thurnby. The British United Shoe Machinery Company in Belgrave Road, Leicester—producing essential parts for Rolls-Royce—and the Power Jets factory at Whetstone were each given AA cover in the form of nine Oerlikon 20-mm cannon mounted up on the factories' flat roofs. They were manned, respectively, by 530 and 532 Home Guard LAA Troops, attached to their local battalions. In early February 1944, AA units were still on the move. One LAA battery was redeployed from Melton Mowbray to Sheringham via the practice camp in Somerset, while another was brought in to relieve the unit defending the Power Jets plant at Whetstone with Bofors guns.

The scarcity of AA guns and the popular fallacy of the barrage had prompted explorations into alternative methods of putting large concentrations of AA projectiles in the way of enemy bombers. One solution lay in the Z-battery, which comprised banks of projectors firing 3-inch UP (Unrotated Projectile) rockets into the air. Projectors were built to fire two rockets and were usually grouped in multiples, thus putting salvoes of rockets—each rocket being the equivalent of a 3.7-inch HAA shell—into the air simultaneously. The 10th Anti-Aircraft Regiment, Home Guard, maintained a troop each in Peterborough (RHQ), Cambridge, and Leicester, each numbered 101 in their local Home Guard organisation: the Leicester troop being officially No. 227 (101 Leicestershire Home Guard) AA Rocket Battery. It was set up in the eastern corner of Victoria Park alongside the A6 road, with vehicular access from Victoria Park Road and its HQ in No. 148a London Road. Their three initial twin (U2P) projectors were upgraded to nine U9Ps, producing a formidable salvo of eighty-one rockets, later increased by two further projectors to fire a salvo of ninety-nine rockets. The larger projectors each had a crew of seven, so each watch comprised over 100 personnel. As all these crews had full-time day jobs, they could only turn out one night in eight, which entailed a large-scale recruitment campaign to produce the required numbers. The battery was mixed, meaning that many tasks, other than gun crew, were carried out by women of the ATS. While the rockets tended to cause extensive damage on the ground and were therefore banned from being

Right: Leicester, 148a London Road: the battery office of the anti-aircraft Z Battery in Victoria Park.

Below: Leicester: plan of the anti-aircraft Z Battery in Victoria Park, manned by 227 (M)/101 Leicestershire 'Z' Rocket AA Battery. (*Austin Ruddy*)

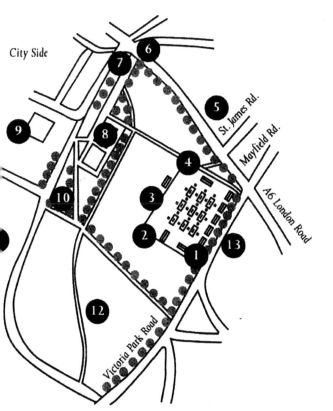

KEY

- U9P (No.4 MK1) Rocket Projector
- • Crew shelters/ammunition store
- Nissen hut
- Tree

1. Entrance Track
2. Close Defence 40mm Bofors gun
3. Perimeter fence
4. Command Post
5. Old Horse Hotel clubroom/battery stores
6. Battery HQ office, 148a London Road
7. Victoria Park main gates
8. Bomb damaged Victoria Park pavilion
9. De Montfort Hall
10. War Memorial
11. Leicester University
12. Wartime Allotments
13. Royal Artillery Personnel house billets

fired over the more built-up parts of Leicester, they would have served their purpose in diverting bomber pilots from their preferred targets simply by the sudden, unexpected detonation of so much explosive. The Z-battery lay within a wire fence, patrolled at night by armed sentries. The nine concrete pads held the launchers, each comprising three rows of three steel launch rails. Between each pair of projectors were crew shelters and ready-use rocket storage. Further rockets were stored in Nissen huts around the perimeter. The battery was protected against low-flying aircraft by a single 40-mm Bofors LAA gun.

The Leicesters' 4th Battalion had been converted into a searchlight regiment, but their patch was enormous and their lights were spread thinly. Early in the war, a belt of searchlight sites was assembled consisting of fixed lines of lights about 3 miles (5 km) apart. Later, the staff experimented with clusters of three. The important thing was to illuminate targets for the guns, but to also allow space for night-fighter aircraft to operate without being shot down by the AA guns. Gradually, additional equipment was gathered—five 90-cm projectors, for instance, being delivered in June 1941 to HQ 42 Searchlight Regiment at Melton Mowbray militia camp. As they were moved around, searchlight sites were very often little more than a few sandbagged platforms for the lights, some slit trenches, a pit (to the design of the eminent archaeologist Sir Mortimer Wheeler), for an AALMG, a diesel generator, and some tents for sleeping.

Single searchlights were emplaced on the sports ground on Wigston Road, Oadby, near the Washbrook, and in Western Park, Leicester. In addition to those lines of sites listed above as being defended by pillboxes, 32 AA Brigade documents listed further searchlight sites at Lutterworth, Walton Lodge, Swinford, and Husbands Bosworth

Fooling the Bombers: Bombing Decoys and Beam Bending

Targets were hidden, dispersed, or camouflaged to avoid presenting themselves too obviously, but enemy bombers were encouraged to set down their bombs in entirely the wrong place, with a number of techniques being successfully employed to that end. From mid-1940, the majority of established pre-war airfields were provided with one or more decoy sites, far enough away to be safe, but close enough to be plausible. There were two types of bombing decoy for airfields: the daylight 'K' site, which used dummy aircraft, and the 'Q' site, which employed lights at night—sometimes the two were combined in a single site. The 'K' site's dummy aircraft, often fabricated in film studios, were appropriate to their parent airfield and were shifted around by a ground crew to give the impression of a working airfield. The night decoy, simulated aircraft movements, and landing lights were operated by the crew from a control blockhouse, built to a standard pattern with a generator and a revolving Chance light on its roof. As the approaching aircraft were heard, the controller waited for a second to ensure that the lights had been observed and then dowsed them. The majority of bombing decoys drew bombs that would otherwise have fallen on real targets, causing casualties and damage. The airfield decoys operated from mid-1940 into autumn 1942. Cottesmore had a 'Q/K' site at Swayfield; Woolfox Lodge had two 'Q' sites at Pickworth and Swinstead; and Bottesford had three 'Q' sites at Tithby, Belvoir, and Foston.

As the bombing offensive switched to urban targets, Special Fires (SF) or 'Starfish' sites were built to simulate the effects of incendiaries and high explosive on built-up areas. Large amounts of combustible material in grid patterns (laced with petrol and oil to produce sudden flare-ups) were placed outside cities and ignited to attract the guiding pathfinder aircraft. Leicester had 'Starfish' sites at Galby, Beeby, Newton Harcourt, and Willoughby Waterless. There appears to have been another at Diseworth protecting the Toton railyards. All these operated for a year from May 1942. These sites then became permanent Starfish sites co-located with specialist QL sites intended to mimic specific targets. Galby simulated a factory using appropriate lighting, some of it as simple as lights in boxes with hinged lids masquerading as closing doors and windows. The other three were presented as marshalling yards with normal yard lighting, but supplemented by glows and sparks, contriving to appear as locomotive furnaces. Beeby, Newton Harcourt, and Willoughby Waterless corresponded respectively to the railway yards at London Road, Knighton Junction, and Wigston. A raid in May 1941, which unaccountably unloaded hundreds of bombs on the Vale of Belvoir, has long been thought to have been the result of a successful operation of the Tithby decoy, but since it remained unlit that particular night, there must have been an alternative explanation for the Luftwaffe's disorientation.

The German 'Lorenz' system of blind landing using a radio beam was familiar to aviation planners, and it was not long before the RAF's boffins suspected that the use of such a beam had been extended to provide a means of homing bombers onto their targets. Once the existence of two intersecting beams had been verified, then a new organisation, No. 80 Wing RAF, was set up to jam or corrupt the beams, which came together near Derby, where Rolls-Royce produced their aero engines. Four distinct German systems were counteracted by techniques codenamed 'Aspirin', 'Bromide', 'Benjamin', and 'Meacon'. Out-stations of 80 Wing, manned 24/7 by specially trained RAF Wireless Mechanics, were scattered across the country, controlled from their Hertfordshire HQ. One of these out-stations, equipped with 'Aspirin', 'Bromide', and 'Benjamin', was located in St Joseph's Field next to St Bernard's Abbey in Charnwood. It is acknowledged that 80 Wing's beam bending was so successful that only one bomb ever hit Rolls-Royce in Derby, and that the bombing of the Vale of Belvoir was most likely evidence of this same ability to disrupt the enemy's guidance system. In St Joseph's Field, the blast walls of the trailer shelter and generator house survive, but the three huts housing the various transmitters have gone. The Charley Heritage Group has thoroughly researched the topic, re-enacted the wartime activity, and produced an interpretative book and video.

On a slight eminence beside a backroad about a mile from RAF Cottesmore, but in line with the main runway, is a cluster of small brick buildings, most of them having half-height blast walls in front of entrances in their side walls. Most are roofless and some are open-fronted, suggesting that trailers carrying technical equipment might have been parked inside. Although there is ambiguity over their age, local knowledge ascribes the installation to the Second World War period—for the purpose of housing portable direction-finding or homing equipment for returning aircraft. Local tradition also suggests that enemy aircraft found it useful for locating their target, which would confirm a wartime provenance. In March 1945, in Operation Gisela, the Luftwaffe

Coalville, St Joseph's Fields: the blast walls of this out-station of RAF 80 Wing, the 'beam-benders', who ran the radio counter-measures operation to foil the Luftwaffe's beam-guided bombers; photographed at a re-enactment event. (*Terry Sheppard and the Charley Heritage Group*)

Cottesmore: one of a group of structures, protected by blast walls and reputed to have housed radio beacons for guiding aircraft back to base.

attacked British airfields. This involved intruders getting in among the bomber stream and carrying out attacks as returning aircraft landed. Two Lancasters from Woolfox Lodge were shot down over Cottesmore, and bombs were dropped on the airfield, damaging gliders and aircraft on the ground.

Intelligence

During the First World War, the 'Y' Service was set up to eavesdrop on the German navy's radio traffic. In the Second World War, there were separate listening networks run by the Navy, MI6, and the RAF. In 1939, the Army established No. 6 War Office Intelligence School and War Office 'Y' Group (WOYG) Strategical Intercept Station at Beaumanor Hall, Woodhouse Eaves, in the depths of Charnwood Forest, with its operational HQ in Quorn. Beaumanor Hall is a large Victorian country house with a stable yard and extensive grounds, ideally situated for such a top-secret operation. Here, upwards of 150 ATS personnel at a time listened in to German Army radio transmissions, which were passed on to Bletchley Park for decoding. The ATS listeners worked in groups of thirty-six in four 'Set Houses', all linked together by underground cables and camouflaged as rural buildings, including a pair of cottages, a stable, and a cart shed. The teleprinter room, served by pneumatic message tubes from the set houses, presented as a cricket pavilion, and the canteen for civilians, who shared some of the ATS duties, was disguised as greenhouses. Later, a fifth set house was added after the need for camouflage had disappeared. A row of timber huts provided administration space. The stable yard accommodated the workshop, the aerial and rigging store, the barrack store, and access to the 'air-raid sheltr [*sic*]', command post, and first aid post, all still signposted after seventy years. Attached to the canteen is the Home Guard Armoury, used to store the array of weaponry described above. The ATS personnel were billeted in houses in Barrow upon Soar and Quorn. Brand Hill, in Woodhouse Eaves, was an ATS camp, and Garats Hay, a nineteenth-century house in Woodhouse Eaves, supplemented by Nissen huts, became an ATS barracks. Fearon Hall, Loughborough, was used for ATS Special Operator Advanced Training.

The BBC maintained 'H' Transmitters at the university in Leicester and at the Swain Street workhouse. The BBC were involved in a number of clandestine wartime activities: gaining intelligence by listening in to foreign-language radio transmissions; transmitting coded messages to SOE agents and resistance groups; providing homing signals for RAF aircraft returning from raids; and organising dispersed studio space for emergency backup transmission facilities.

Gumley Hall, near Market Harborough, housed a SOE operational training school (STS 41). Trainee agents used the lake and the woods around the hall and the Old Rectory for exercises, while work on developing and adapting their specialist equipment was carried on in the Hall's outhouses. Although the house was never lived in again after the war, and was demolished in 1964, the stable block with its prominent tower survives.

Beaumanor Hall: the teleprinter hut was camouflaged as a cricket pavilion.

Beaumanor Hall: Operational Hut 'H' was disguised as farm cottages.

Gumley Hall: the stables are all that remain of the house, used by SOE as a training school.

Preparations for D-Day and Beyond

As preparations for the opening of a Second Front gathered pace, the East Midlands became an assembly area for significant elements of the airborne forces, which would secure the flanks of the Normandy bridgehead on the eve of D-Day. The US Army's 82nd Airborne Division had landed in Belfast in mid-December 1943, and by February 1944, it had established its HQ in Leicester's Braunstone Park, with its constituent units in camps in the surrounding area. US Army regiments were the equivalent of British Army brigades. The 82nd Division's two Parachute Infantry Regiments—the 504th and the 505th—were based at Shady Lane, Evington, and Quorndon respectively, with the 325th Glider Infantry Regiment at Scraptoft, and the 319th Glider Assault Regiment at Lubenham. The 80th A/T Battalion occupied a camp at Oadby, while a number of logistical units were based nearby, including ordnance depot and ordnance munitions companies at Melton Mowbray. The Divisional HQ shared Braunstone Park with the 60th US Army Field Hospital and the 892nd Signal Depot Company. All these units were in hutted camps, which subsequently became POW camps, homes for displaced persons, and then temporary homes for local residents suffering from the acute post-war housing shortage.

Prior to the airborne operations to capture the Rhine bridges, British units were also billeted in our counties. The 4th Parachute Brigade, with its HQ at Knossington Grange (R), consisted of the 10th, 11th, and 156th Battalions of the Parachute Regiment, either raised from scratch or formed from established infantry regiments. The 10th Battalion was centred on the villages of Somerby, Thorpe Satchville, Burrough on the Hill, and Twyford. Staveley Lodge in Melton Mowbray was the HQ of 156th Battalion, with its four companies spread between Newport Lodge, Scalford Hall, and The Spinney. The 11th Battalion was also billeted in and around the town. Uppingham was home to support services, with the two troops of 4th Parachute Squadron RE at Glaston House and neighbouring Bisbrooke Hall, and 133 Parachute Field Ambulance just outside Oakham at Barleythorpe Hall (R). The Army also requisitioned Wicklow Lodge in Melton Mowbray.

Against the opposition of the Air Ministry, which feared an erosion of its bomber fleet and pilots, a force of aircraft dedicated to airborne operations was eventually assembled. No. 38 Group came first, followed by No. 46 Group, each consisting of nine squadrons that were equipped with Stirlings, Albemarles, and Halifaxes. The standard British glider was the Horsa, which typically carried loads of ten men or a Jeep and trailer. The American Waco, known in Britain as the Hadrian, could be broken down for transportation but had a smaller payload. When the larger Hamilcar, designed to carry the Tetrarch light tank, came on stream, a Heavy Glider Conversion Unit was formed at North Luffenham to train the pilots. Operating as part of these two airborne groups were squadrons flying Stirlings out of Leicester East, as well as units based at Saltby and Melton Mowbray.

Melton Mowbray, Staveley Lodge: the base for HQ Company, 156 Battalion, Parachute Regiment.

Aircraft Production

During the war, Leicestershire saw an explosion of aircraft manufacture from those firms such as Power Jets, Reid & Sigrist, Taylorcraft, and Boulton & Paul, who were already established in the field; from firms such as Brush, who picked up where they had left off in 1918; and from firms such as Armstrong Whitworth Aircraft (AWA) and Vickers-Armstrongs, which both dispersed production to new sites and integrated local firms into the aircraft manufacturing process. From 1943, AWA replicated their Lancaster bomber assembly line at Baginton, near Coventry, in a purpose-built hangar complex on the southern edge of Bitteswell airfield. As Vickers-Armstrongs' Castle Bromwich became vulnerable to bombing attacks, a network of small factories was established in Leicester, Hinckley, Coalville, and Whitwick to produce undercarriages for Spitfires. A Spitfire assembly line was set up in Reid & Sigrist's new hangars at Desford, completing a thousand aircraft by the end of the war. Owing to the unsuitability of Lutterworth's Ladywood Works, a brand-new factory was built for Sir Frank Whittle's Power Jets company at Whetstone, opening in 1943. Flight-testing took place at Bitteswell and, later, at Bruntingthorpe as well. Brush, in Loughborough, assembled de Havilland Dominies, test flying them from a grass field north-west of the town; Taylorcraft, at Rearsby, produced their own Auster air observation post aircraft. Much effort went into the Civilian Repair Organisation workshops, which returned damaged aircraft to service. Airwork in Loughborough specialised in Douglas DB-7s, both the Havoc night-fighter version and the Boston bomber. Reid & Sigrist at Desford took in Boulton-Paul Defiants and Mitchell bombers, while Taylorcraft at Rearsby looked after Hawker Hurricanes among other aircraft. Both Brush and Airwork in Loughborough repaired Lancaster wing sections. Boulton & Paul assembled Horsa gliders in their King Street works in Melton Mowbray.

Desford: the Over Blister hangar on the Civilian Repair Organisation site.

Loughborough: the BRUSH flight test hangar in Swingbridge Road.

Rearsby: the interior of one of Taylorcraft's hangars where Austers were assembled.

Munitions Production

Leicestershire had two government establishments that were important elements in the drive to produce munitions. The Royal Ordnance Factory (ROF) National Filling Factory No. 10 on Melton Road, Queniborough, was begun in 1941, managed by Unilevers, with production commencing the next year. It was intended to produce explosive ordnance, specifically detonators and fuses. ROFs were composed of specialist buildings categorised into ten groups. At Queniborough, buildings from Groups 8, 9, and 10 were present. Groups 8 and 9 were designed for the filling of shells and grenades with high explosive, as well as their secure storage. Group 10 included all the infrastructure of workshops and proofing ranges. The factory covered the entire area of what is now East Goscote, and it comprised dozens of robust structures, designed to withstand explosions. Many were surrounded by earth traverses and blast walls. The workforce, the majority of them female, were recruited locally or lived in hostel accommodation nearby. The Asfordby proofing range had been closed in 1918, but it reopened in 1938. It was an out-station of Woolwich Arsenal and used for proof-firing artillery. The extent of the range, alongside the disused Melton to Nottingham railway line, can still be seen in aerial views.

Many of those factories not already involved in manufacturing aircraft or vehicle components, or other essential supplies for the war effort, were converted into arms manufacturing plants. Leicester's Co-op Shoe factory in Knighton Fields Road East was licensed to produce Bren guns. Several other local firms, including the British United Shoe Machinery Company of Belgrave Road, Leicester, made parts for the Mark IV SMLE rifle, the standard infantry weapon across Britain and the Empire.

Our counties made a significant contribution to production on the agricultural front. Land Army hostels were spread across the area, with examples on Uppingham Road, Billesdon, and in Lyddington. Produce was stored in purpose-built facilities such as the Ministry of Food Storage Depot at Shepshed and the Coldstore in Loughborough. Local War Agricultural Committees oversaw the working of farms and could direct what crops would be sown and determine the arable–livestock ratio, with the power to take over those farms deemed to be underperforming or being run by uncooperative farmers.

Collateral Damage

The effects of enemy air raids, while devastating to the victims, was minor compared to that suffered in other parts of the country, but there were other long-term effects of the war, and the causes of damage were not confined to enemy action. The military occupation of the two mid-eighteenth-century stately homes of Garendon Hall and Gopsall Park caused so much damage that neither ever returned to family occupation and both were subsequently demolished after the war—in 1964 and 1951 respectively. Edmondthorpe Hall was also burnt out in 1943 during its occupation by the military, and Gumley Hall was never reoccupied, being demolished in 1964. Of slightly lesser gravity was the demolition of Billesdon's First World War memorial by a Canadian tank that fell off its transporter, but it was replaced by the War Office. Owing to its proximity to Nuneaton's approaches, the spire of Stoke Golding church was reduced by 60 feet (18.5 m) and the numbered stones put into store. In August 1947, the spire was restored to its former height by the Air Ministry.

Hospitals and Welfare

As in the previous war, the established hospitals were supplemented by a dozen or so Convalescent Homes or Auxiliary Hospitals run by the Red Cross. These occupied country houses such as Burley on the Hill (R) and Stapleford Park. Working parties of volunteers, co-ordinated by sub-depots of the Leicester and Leicestershire Hospital Supply Depot such as that at Quorn House, produced packs of medical supplies for use wherever they were needed. The RAF ran a Medical Rehabilitation Centre in Loughborough. Keythorpe Hall, Tugby, and Preston Hall (R), near Uppingham, were 'Flak Shacks' where USAAF aircrew were sent for the occasional spell of rest and recuperation as a response to combat stress incurred a long way from home. They were under the command of military personnel, but staffed by generally female American Red Cross volunteers.

POW Camps

Early in the war, provision for holding POWs could be improvised, pressing such buildings as Shepshed's Old Liberal Club or Edmondthorpe Hall into service, but as the war progressed and the advantage swung in favour of the Allies, the need for camps gradually increased. By 1944, many of those camps, such as Quorndon, Stoughton, and Scraptoft, vacated by their previous US Army occupants, were adapted as POW camps, as were some communal sites on airfields where operations were running down. Few traces now remain as the mainly temporary buildings have decayed or been demolished and the pair of Nissen huts remaining at Garendon Park may represent the most significant survival.

9

The Cold War and its Aftermath, 1945–2015

Unlike in 1918, it took a long time after 1945 to dismantle the war economy, and the continuation of austerity and central government control into the 1950s probably contributed to the fall of the Atlee Government. As airfields and Army camps were filled with displaced persons and refugees, the armed services shed their hostilities-only personnel and scrapped vast amounts of arms and equipment. The gliders—assembled by Boulton & Paul in Melton Mowbray—that had been so precious in 1944, were now being chopped up down the road at Market Harborough. Husbands Bosworth RAF camp was in use by Polish refugees from 1946, and still housed around 500 in 1950. Melton Mowbray was home to a resettlement unit for Polish airmen. Paradoxically, Britain's armed forces, which had mobilised nearly 5 million personnel by the end of the war, were rapidly discovering staffing shortfalls. Conscription in the form of National Service, intensive recruitment into the Reserve Forces, and the need to remedy workaday skills shortages accompanied Britain's entry into the Atomic Age.

Military Aviation in the Post-War Period

While many of their personnel had been demobilised, the majority of their airfields deactivated, and vast numbers of their aircraft scrapped, the RAF still entered the supersonic age equipped with aircraft that were world leaders. In 1946, the Whetstone works of Sir Frank Whittle's Power Jets (Research & Development) Ltd, the School of Gas Turbine Technology in Lutterworth's Ladywood works, and the testing facilities at Bruntingthorpe were nationalised as the National Gas Turbine Establishment. The major product of Whittle's pioneering work was the aero engine, which was perfected by Rolls-Royce as the Derwent and the Welland and installed in the Gloster Meteor. Under new management, the flight-testing operations were moved to Bitteswell. From 1949, Armstrong Whitworth Aircraft (AWA) was assembling Meteors at Bitteswell in two extensive hangar complexes. Nearly 1,200 Meteors had been produced there by 1954, including twenty aircraft for the Danish Air Force. In 1952, production of the Hawker Sea Hawk, a carrier-borne fighter-bomber powered by a Rolls-Royce Nene jet engine, was transferred to AWA at Bitteswell. By 1959, several hundred of the different versions of this aircraft had been supplied to the FAA, the RAF, and the air forces of India, the Netherlands, and West Germany. Another of Hawker's fighters, the Hunter, was in great demand in the mid-1950s, and AWA provided an assembly line at Bitteswell, producing several hundred between 1953 and 1957. However, the Hunter was so successful that hundreds returned for refurbishment, modification, or conversion until 1981, and significant numbers were exported to the many countries that deployed this popular and long-lived aircraft. The Gloster Javelin, a delta-wing jet fighter armed with Firestreak air-to-air missiles, was another ground-breaking aircraft produced in quantity by AWA at Bitteswell. As well as these fighters, many of Avro's Vulcan V-bombers were brought here to be overhauled or modified, right up until 1981. The military version of the AWA Argosy transport aircraft was supplied to the RAF and to USAF freight contractors between 1959 and 1964. Other significant aircraft, such as the Harrier and Sea-Harrier jump-jet and the Buccaneer, came to Bitteswell for attention. In the three years from 1979, the factory also assembled forty Hawk advanced jet-trainers—the aircraft used by the Red Arrows RAF display team.

The RAF in the Cold War

While the aviation industry was producing cutting-edge designs, very few of them were seen in our local skies; flying from most of the wartime airfields ceased shortly after 1945, with only a handful remaining active. North Luffenham was one airfield that maintained some continuity. Its heavy glider conversion unit had been succeeded by an operational conversion unit (OCU) of Transport Command that, in June 1948,

Whetstone: the administration building of Whittle's new Power Jets works.

found itself on the front-line of the Cold War; its complement of Dakotas became the spearhead of the Berlin Airlift. By the end of the first month, No. 240 OCU had carried over 3,000 tons of freight into the city, flying over 1,000 sorties, and continuing to supply beleaguered Berlin for over a year. A resumption of training must have seemed rather tame after the excitement and danger of confrontation with the Russians.

Wymeswold was closed for several years but reopened in 1949 for a fighter squadron of the RAuxAF, initially flying Mark XXII Spitfires, but then becoming the first such unit to fly Meteor jets and then Hawker Hunters. Until its final closure in 1957, a number of regular fighter squadrons were based at Wymeswold, and Rolls-Royce's test-bed fleet moved in for the whole of 1955 while new runways were laid at Hucknall (Nottinghamshire). For several months in 1951, North Luffenham hosted mandatory refresher courses for RAuxAF pilots flying Harvard trainers and then Vampire and Meteor jet fighters. Later that same year, the airfield was handed over to the RCAF, who brought in a fighter wing of three Sabre-equipped squadrons, which stayed for three years prior to new deployments in France and West Germany.

The 1950s was the era of Britain as an 'unsinkable aircraft carrier'. The American Strategic Air Command (SAC) stationed squadrons of heavy bombers here in order to be within practicable range for dropping atomic bombs on Russia. Bruntingthorpe was one of those bases handed over to the USAF in 1957. As the SAC deployment policy, known as 'Reflex Alert', was formulated, it eventually became home to a dozen B-47 Stratojets that were rotated on a weekly basis. This was, in effect, a dispersal system using a spread of bases, each holding a small number of aircraft. In 1959, the French withdrawal from NATO meant that the USAF was forced into a reshuffle. A detachment of RB-66 Destroyer tactical reconnaissance aircraft, from Alconbury (Cambridgeshire), moved into Bruntingthorpe in1960, displacing the SAC units. After the Americans left in 1962, the RAF maintained the base as an unmanned dispersal for Wittering's (Cambridgeshire) V-bombers, with only very occasional use during the deployment exercises, which involved Harriers operating from forward positions.

The decade after the end of the war saw Cottesmore as home to training units, but in 1954, a new role for the airfield was emerging when new occupants, in the form of four squadrons of Canberra jet bombers, arrived. By the next year, they had all moved on as the station closed for the preparations necessary to accommodate V-bombers. Throughout 1958, two squadrons of Handley-Page Victor bombers assembled and remained at Cottesmore until 1964, in the meantime updating to Victor B.2s. After that, three squadrons of Vulcans stayed until they were redeployed to Cyprus in 1969.

By 1962, the V-bombers constituted Britain's primary nuclear deterrent force and were distributed around nine or ten airfields, each of which was equipped with Operational Readiness Platforms for the four aircraft that were permanently on fifteen-minute notice to fly. Additionally, there were five airfields with comparable facilities acting as dispersal fields, and a further twenty-two airfields, of which Bruntingthorpe was one, with facilities for two aircraft. In this way, the V-bomber force was spread far and wide between Leuchars and Macrihanish in the north; Valley and St Mawgans in the west; Manston and Boscombe Down in the south; and Stansted and Coltishall in the east. Such dispersal ensured that some aircraft might be expected to survive a first strike and would be able to carry out retaliatory strikes on military targets and the enemy's cities. This widely held knowledge was the basis for the deterrence embodied in the notion of Mutually Assured Destruction (MAD).

Cottesmore was one of those airfields with its own secure atomic weapons storage. The V-bombers initially carried Britain's first atomic weapon, Blue Danube, which was a cumbersome package requiring large aircraft—the Victor, Valiant, and Vulcan—to deliver it. It was superseded in 1961, however, by Red Beard, weighing in at just one-fifth of the weight of Blue Danube, and which could be carried in smaller aircraft such as the Canberra or the Buccaneer. Although only a tenth of the weight of Blue Danube, the WE-177 was ten times more powerful and remained in service until 1998.

In 1969, the Canberras returned to Cottesmore, and the world's very first jet bomber conversion unit (231 OCU) was formed alongside an operational Electronic Counter-Measures (ECM) squadron, whose task it was to find ways of fooling the opposition's air defence systems. In 1976, the airfield entered a period of disuse until, in 1978, a new project began a fresh phase in Cottesmore's career. The Tri-National Tornado Training Establishment (TTTE) opened for business in January 1981, with pilots from Britain, Italy, and West Germany, later joined for a short period by Saudi aircrew.

Airfield Development in the Cold War

Changes in the function of individual airfields and the enhanced performance of aircraft combined to necessitate more sophisticated facilities on the ground. One major change concerned runways. Larger and faster jet aircraft, such as the USAFE B-47s and B-52s and the British V-bombers, all needed longer and more robust runways. It was not only runways that needed expansion; in order to maintain all-weather operating, taxiways and dispersals had to be laid in concrete. Wymeswold's runway was extended in 1952 with Operational Readiness Platforms added to each end. Additionally, a wide expanse of concrete was laid in front of two of the hangars as an Aircraft Servicing Platform. In 1955, the main runway at Cottesmore was lengthened to 3,000 yards and, two years later, a 3,400-yard-long runway was laid at Bruntingthorpe. In 1978, concrete hard-standings to hold twenty-eight Tornados were laid at Cottesmore. Often, new buildings were also needed. At Bruntingthorpe, a Wimpey steel-framed and steel-clad hangar, for the B-47 Stratojets, was built. It measures 320 by 160 feet (97.5 by 48.6 m). Cottesmore's old 'Fort'-type watch office was totally obsolete by the early 1950s, so a new one was built to the latest pattern—the Vertical Split Control type (2548c/55)—but North Luffenham retains its original 1940-pattern tower. A certain amount of recycling also occurred, with two hangars from Desford going to Tollerton (Nottinghamshire) and the VCR from Nuneaton's watch office ending up at Duxford. Totally different structures were needed when the Aviation Medicine Training Centre came to North Luffenham from Upwood (Cambridgeshire) in 1964, requiring decompression chambers and a 60-foot-high (18.5-m-high) ejection training tower.

Bruntingthorpe: the USAF Wimpey hangar was built to accommodate the B-47 Stratojet.

RAF Cottesmore's post-war Vertical Split Control-type (*2548c/55*) watch office. (*Lt-Col. Richard Chesterfield, Kendrew Barracks*)

Thor IRBMs

In order to compensate for a perceived missile gap, which could have rendered the SAC and RAF bomber forces vulnerable to a Russian first strike, the US pumped large amounts of money into defence projects to develop missiles. Until a viable Intercontinental Ballistic Missile (ICBM) became available, the Thor Intermediate Range Ballistic Missile (IRBM) would be deployed as an interim measure. As Thor's limited range precluded its use against prime Russian targets from US soil, the British Government agreed to station it down the eastern side of England, under what passed for dual GB/US control. Four main stations, including North Luffenham, were selected, each of which had four subsidiary sites. Those controlled by North Luffenham were Melton Mowbray; Harrington and Polebrook in Northamptonshire; and Folkingham in Lincolnshire, all former RAF airfields. Thor was a rocket whose motor was powered by liquid fuel, a mixture of kerosene and the decidedly unstable liquid oxygen (LOX).

RAF North Luffenham: the Thor missile inspection building.

RAF North Luffenham: the concrete blast walls and the remains of the launcher erector mounting on one of the three Thor launch emplacements/platforms.

RAF Melton Mowbray: one of the three long-range theodolite buildings on the Thor site.

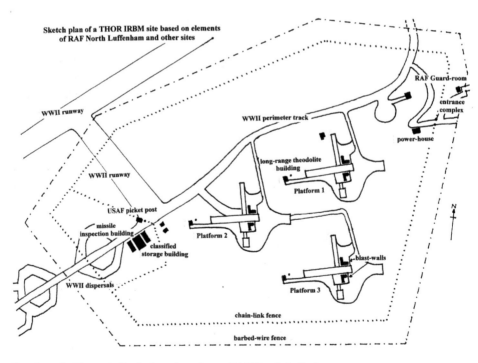

Site plan of a Thor missile site based on that at RAF North Luffenham.

Each site held three rockets, stored on trailers with canvas covers. They were launched from concrete pads with L-shaped concrete blast walls, serviced by ducts that carried electricity and rocket fuel. The rocket was hoisted into a vertical position, fuelled, and fired, its route controlled by an inertial guidance system set by short- and long-range theodolites on site. The three pads, a servicing building, storage for the warheads, and the two fuels were all contained within a flood-lit compound, guarded by RAF and USAF personnel and surrounded by double security fences. Thor was 65 feet (20 m) long, with a diameter of 8 feet (2.5 m); it could deliver a 1.4-megaton warhead up to a distance of 1,500 miles (2,400 km). As a stop-gap—and an unsatisfactory one at that—Thor was only in place from the end of 1959 for under four years. North Luffenham was the last to close down in August 1963, when the missiles were airlifted back to the USA.

The Regular Army and the TA

The Leicestershire Regiment, which had finished the war with eight battalions, was shortly reduced to two regular battalions; however, it was rewarded for its war service, which was reflected in its twenty-three battle honours and the 'Royal' prefix in 1946. Yet those two battalions were further reduced to one just two years later. Service in small wars and insurgencies in Korea (where it took significant casualties), Cyprus, Brunei, and Aden was interspersed with duties in Germany, Malta, and Bahrein. The early 1960s saw the shift from one or two battalion-strength county regiments to larger infantry regiments organised on a regional basis. The first step was to group county regiments into regionally based brigades. In 1960, the Leicesters' regimental depot at Glen Parva became the training centre for the Foresters' Brigade. The subsequent amalgamation in 1965 of ten regiments in the eastern counties resulted in the Leicesters becoming the 4th Battalion of the Royal Anglian Regiment. In 1975, this 4th Battalion was disbanded, and the Leicestershire tag was transferred to 'B' Company, 2nd Battalion. In the meantime, the three TA battalions of the Anglians had been reduced to just one, whose 'C' Company is currently linked to Leicestershire and Northamptonshire. Since then, the 2nd Battalion has served in Bosnia, Sierra Leone, Iraq, and Afghanistan. After a spell in Cyprus, it came home to take up residence in Kendrew Barracks, the former RAF Cottesmore, in 2012. In 2014, the TA was renamed the Army Reserve, and 'C' Company, 3rd Battalion, is currently based at Ulverscroft Road, Leicester.

The Leicestershire Yeomanry finished the war as 153 and 154 Field Regiments RA (TA). The duplicate regiment was disbanded, but 153 Field Regiment finally rejoined the cavalry as Hussars equipped with Comet tanks. They were then reconfigured into a self-propelled A/T regiment, retaining armoured vehicles, but in 1957, they amalgamated with the Derbyshire Yeomanry. There followed a long spell as infantry in the Worcestershire and Sherwood Foresters Regiment and then in the Royal Anglians. In 1985, they were once again restored to the armoured corps as 'B' Squadron of the Royal Yeomanry, enjoying an affiliation with the 9/12th Royal Lancers, whose then home HQ was Leicester. After further changes, they now (2015) constitute 'E' (Leicestershire

& Derbyshire) Squadron of the Royal Yeomanry, based in what remains of the former Glen Parva Barracks in Wigston. The Royal Yeomanry, with HQ in Fulham, and six squadrons spread across the Thames Valley and the Midlands, is a reconnaissance regiment equipped with armoured Land Rovers. Glen Parva Barracks had remained home to the RAPC until 1997.

In 1946, the RAVC merged with the Army Remount Service and in 1948 moved to Melton Mowbray, taking over what had been a remount depot. Now a Joint Services establishment, dealing with dogs and horses, it is known as the Defence Animal Centre (DAC). Its buildings range from the traditional red-brick stable blocks of the original nineteenth-century stud farm to the state-of-the-art kennels and veterinary facilities. Riding instructors from the Household Cavalry and the RHA are trained there in the new indoor riding school using the complement of resident horses. Tired from the demands of ceremonial activities in London, horses come to the DAC for a bit of rest and recreation on the lush meadows. Farriers learn their trade in a dedicated school with blacksmiths' forges. Dogs and their handlers are trained for the whole range of tasks to which canine noses, teeth, and barks can be applied. At the centre of the site are the new administrative block and gymnasium, only yards from stables dating from the First World War. A dog-training outpost operates across the road from the former Old Dalby REME depot.

In 1998, the RAF vacated North Luffenham and it shortly became St George's Barracks. Its first occupants were the Royal Fusiliers, who, on their deployment to Germany in 2003, were succeeded by the Kings' Own Border Regiment, which stayed

Melton Mowbray: the Indoor Riding School at the Defence Animal Centre.

until its absorption into the new Duke of Lancaster's Regiment in 20
Regiment RA, whose batteries were rotated through postings to mar
defences of the Falklands and as part of Operation Herrick in Afghanist
St Georges is now home to 2nd Medical Regiment RAMC and 1st Militar y . . -
Dog Regiment RAVC. The 2nd Medical Regiment has Army Reserve squadrons at Hull
and in Leicester, where 222 Medical Squadron is based at the Brentwood Road centre.
The 1st Military Working Dog Regiment, recently returned to Britain from Germany,
also has both regular and reserve elements. The only other Army Reserve unit currently
resident in Leicestershire is 203 Squadron of 158 Transport Regiment RLC, based in
Loughborough with its RHQ in Peterborough.

Air Defence

In 1945, there remained a perceived need for a gun-based AA system reliant on radar
for the early detection of targets and the instant and accurate direction of fire from
electrically operated guns. This was the immensely expensive and short-lived ROTOR
system. However, it quickly became apparent that modern aircraft would be long
gone before the guns could engage them. Those existing TA AA units, which were not
deemed part of the field force, were gradually combined and absorbed into other units.
In 1955, AA Command was disbanded, and by 1961, all the local AA units were gone.

The Bloodhound Surface-to-Air Guided Weapon (SAGW) System

A solution to the problem of engaging supersonic jet aircraft was sought in missile
technology. From 1947, research was undertaken to develop an AA rocket, and the result
was 'Red Shoes', which became the army's Thunderbird, and 'Red Duster', which entered
service with the RAF as Bloodhound. Given the impossibility of defending cities against
the threat of lone aircraft each capable of obliterating their targets with a single bomb, the
decision was taken to focus on the east coast. Hence, the Bloodhound missile sites were
located specifically to protect the twenty Thor sites and the V-bomber bases from attack
by Russian bombers, as well as to destroy enemy aircraft before they could approach their
urban, industrial, or strategic military targets. The sites, eleven of them on existing airfields,
stretched from Yorkshire to Suffolk and included Woolfox Lodge (R). The network was
controlled from four Tactical Control Centres, one of which was at North Luffenham.

The Bloodhound site, typified by Woolfox Lodge (which survives in an almost
complete form alongside the A1), consisted of two sets of eight missile launchers
mounted on hard-standings served by tarmac roads, with adjacent arming shed,
Nissen-like refuelling building, and launch control buildings. Near the entrance to
the site, with its guardroom, is the gabled, double-pile missile assembly building and
the station HQ. The Type 83 illuminating radar, with a range of 55 miles (88 km) was
mounted on a raised platform atop a lattice-work tower to the rear of the launchers.

RAF Woolfox Lodge,: the Bloodhound surface-to-air guided weapon site; in the foreground is the Works Services Building with beyond it the launch control building for the southern section of sixteen missiles; in the distance is a second launch control building for the northern section.

The Bloodhound missile was propelled by four booster rocket motors and then by the two main ramjet engines, which fired after four seconds, taking the missile, guided by the radar, to its target at twice the speed of sound, up to a range of 50 miles (80 km). Detonation by proximity fuse released a cluster of steel rods that caused the target aircraft to crash

The Tactical Control Centre at North Luffenham, controlling missile sites at Woolfox Lodge and Warboys (Cambridgeshire), comprises a large two- to three-storey building, which housed the weapons control team feeding data to the missile sites. Quite close by is the plinth for the Type 83 Orange Yeoman radar. It is a four-storey cuboid block with a semi-octagonal end section where the radar was mounted and a high beam at the opposite end for winching heavy equipment into place. Bloodhound sites enjoyed roughly the same lifespan as Thor sites, between late 1958 and late 1964. Bloodhound II operated for longer (until 1988), but on only three sites in Norfolk and Lincolnshire. North Luffenham, as St George's Barracks is still closely associated with the Rapier, ground-to-air missile system. Beside one of the 1940 J-type hangars is a dome-shaped Air Defence Tactical Training Theatre (ADT3), and the hangars are used for maintenance.

RAF North Luffenham: the radar plinth for the Type 82 'Orange Yeoman' radar. The array consisted of a horizontal transmitter aerial 45 feet (13.7 m) across, with an octagonal dish-shaped receiver aerial standing upright on top of it.

A Bloodhound Surface to air-guided weapon, photographed at Misson, Nottinghamshire.

A Rapier surface-to-air missile; introduced in 1971, it remains Britain's primary anti-aircraft weapon; photographed at St George's Barracks, North Luffenham.

The Royal Observer Corps

The ROC had finished the war working from a wide variety of structures, ranging from the standard-issue 'rabbit-hutch' to ambitious brick towers with viewing platforms, as at Stoke Golding; when it was reformed in 1946, this situation continued. After five years, it was decided that purpose-built posts should be provided, and Messrs Orlit were commissioned to design a prefabricated concrete structure that could sit at ground-level (Orlit A) or be raised up on stilts (Orlit B)—400 had been supplied by 1955. One or two pre-Orlit brick-built posts, including that at Coleorton, had previously been provided. The same problems of spotting and identifying fast-moving aircraft, which signalled the end of AA Command, however, also forced a change of role for the ROC. Finding this new role proved relatively easy; the threat of nuclear war revealed a need to monitor the source, presence, intensity, and spread of nuclear fallout. The ROC, stationed across Britain in over 1,500 posts linked by telephone or radio to regional controls, were ideally suited to this task. The ROC went back to Orlit to design a protected post, this time to be sunk underground, a concrete box, measuring roughly 20 feet (6 m) by 8 feet (2.5 m) by 8 feet (2.5 m). Access was through a trapdoor, leading via steel rungs down a 14-foot-deep (4.5-m-deep) shaft. The three-man crew was equipped with instruments that would record the ground zero of a nuclear blast and data relating to fallout. On the surface, all that can be seen is the entry hatch, a ventilator, and the tops of the bomb power indicator and the fixed survey meter probe. There was a reduction in the number of active posts in 1968, but the survivors were manned until stand-down in 1991. Good examples of underground posts' surface features can be seen at Cold Overton (R), Harby, Billesdon, and elsewhere.

Intelligence

After the end of the war, Beaumanor Hall continued as the War Office Intelligence School and Strategical Intercept Station for the 'Y' Group (WOYG). The GCHQ Intercept School transferred from Benhall, Cheltenham, as the Royal Signals Centre at Woodhouse Eaves, officially referred to as Loughborough. Garats Hay remained a barracks and some 900 ATS personnel worked at Beaumanor Hall. A few minor changes were made to the Hall's outbuildings. In 1948, a new MT Section, since converted into the sports hall, was built behind the stable yard, and the former Civilian Canteen, now the Outdoor Learning Centre, became the Operations Block. Garats Hay was relinquished by the military only in 1998, the old house and outbuildings becoming private housing, while the Army's Sixth Form College moved from Welbeck (Nottinghamshire) to occupy new buildings on the barracks site.

Throughout the Cold War, there was a need for personnel to be trained to listen in to foreign radio transmissions, particularly those coming out of Russia and China. From 1964 until 1997, RAF North Luffenham was one of several locations that served as satellites of the Joint Services School of Linguists, providing tuition in mainly Russian,

Right: Coleorton (SK387164): an early brick example of a post-war ROC aircraft-spotting post.

Below: Harby: an underground ROC post for recording nuclear blasts and tracking the spread of radiation. It was entered through a hatch on top of the cube-shaped structure in the foreground.

Beaumanor Hall continued as the War Office 'Y' Group centre throughout the Cold War.

Polish, and Mandarin, up to interpreter standard. The unit's official name was the Communications Analysis Training School.

Depots

The former airfield at Market Harborough served as a depot for Army vehicles from 1951 until 1961, when plans for conversion to a high-security prison were drawn up. Old Dalby, which had finished the war with a workforce of nearly 4,000, made up of equal numbers of military and civilian personnel, also retained the labour of 200 POWs into 1947. Despite absorbing both the stock and the operations of other similar sites, the functions of both REME and RAOC gradually contracted over the next fifty years, particularly affected towards the end of that period, by the peace dividend, and gradually handed operations over to civilian MOD staff. The site is now an extensive industrial estate and business park, housing firms such as Toyota.

Defending against Nuclear War

Throughout the Cold War (1945–1990), the British Government purported to subscribe to the delusion that life could continue after a nuclear strike. Complex plans were made

Old Dalby REME Depot: the guard house.

for the emergency decentralisation of government offices, and the population was fed completely misleading information in pamphlets, with such titles as 'Protect and Survive'. As late as the mid-1980s, the Thatcher Government was persisting in urging local authorities to build nuclear bunkers by offering generous subsidies.

The Government set up a network of Regional Seats of Government (RSG) where regional commissioners would rule under martial law. Our counties would be run from RSG3 in Nottingham, but in the 1970s, this one centre was felt to be inadequate for such a scattered and populous region and two sub-RSGs were added. Although it was a surface structure, the Ministry Cold Store in Loughborough was judged to be of sufficient solidity to do the job. It contained control rooms, command posts, and administrative offices for the Commissioner and his staff, for the judiciary, the military, and the emergency services, and for civil servants from the departments of food, health, transport, agriculture, and fuel supplies. Government scientific advisers and officials from the Central Office of Information guided the Commissioner on what policies would be adopted, and studios were provided for the BBC to broadcast information, directives, and advice to anyone who might still be out there. Large areas were given over to generators and switch gear, and the balance was taken up the communal living space for the lucky 200 who staffed the place, having abandoned their families to the mushroom cloud and the nuclear winter. Loughborough's bunker was demolished *c.* 1997.

Local authorities were expected to replicate these bunkers, staffing them with a similar spread of organisers at a local level with coverage of the day-to-day issues of public health, emergency feeding, public order, communications, and public utilities. Most county bunkers expected to carry a complement of about eighty staff. Until 1968, a Civil Defence (CD) organisation existed, generally based on the ARP of the Second World War, heavily dependent on the voluntary organisations such as the WRVS and the Red Cross and St John's Ambulance axis. In Leicester, the CD HQ was at 50 Belvoir Street. In 1968, the new Leicestershire County Hall opened at Glenfield with a radiation-proof bunker in its basement. Charnwood District Council built its bunker under an extension to its Loughborough offices *c.* 1990, and Melton Council included a similar facility in its Nottingham Road offices around the same time. Rutland has never had anything beyond an emergency communications room in its Oakham offices, and it continues to share emergency planning functions with Leicestershire.

Public utilities also provided protected structures for their controls. At Saxby, near the now-disused rail line, is a large hangar-like structure that was the emergency stores for the National Grid's Region 3, holding all the equipment and materials necessary for restoring power after a nuclear attack. It is currently a secure self store, resplendent in a bright blue and yellow paint scheme. The Ministry of Agriculture, Fishery and Food (MAFF) established grain silos and depots to store non-perishable foodstuffs. A number of such depots were built in our counties and that at 47 Station Road, Castle Donington, now another self store, survives, easily recognised by its standard design of triple gabled sheds with clerestory roofs, but identified on the 1965 25-inch OS map as an anonymous 'depot'.

Melton Mowbray: the 1980s council offices on Nottingham Road, with a nuclear bunker in its basement.

Saxby: the National Grid emergency supplies bunker next to a former railway station.

Castle Donington: the Cold War MAFF emergency depot.

Emergency Communications Systems

The British Telecom microwave tower network, epitomised by the GPO Tower in London's Tottenham Court Road, constituted the Government's primary emergency communications link. Completed during the early 1960s, this national system was designed both to transmit warnings of a nuclear attack across the country and issue orders to those areas that might have survived the first strike. Copt Oak near Coalville was a key point on the main 'BACKBONE' line, which ran up from Stokenchurch, west of London, all the way to Edinburgh. From Copt Oak, spurs linked westwards to the Birmingham GPO Tower via Twycross and to a subordinate eastern line via Oakham Radio Relay Station to Morborne Hill near Peterborough. This network of microwave towers was chosen to avoid the use of cables, which could be destroyed by bombing. The towers were also located away from the urban centres that would inevitably represent targets for atomic weapons. Their cover was the transmission of the new 625-line television.

Copt Hill microwave tower was part of the 'Backbone' military communications network.

Alongside the microwave towers, the Home Office established a communication system using UHF Radio, based on its own network of towers, including two in Leicestershire at Bardon Hill at 912 feet (280 m)—the highest point in the county—and at Glebe Farm, Skeffington. The purpose of these was to allow the Home Office to keep abreast of internal security issues; to direct the operations of the police, fire service and Civil Defence organisations; to disseminate information from the ROC/UKWMO; and to provide support for military signals. From a later period, there is a Marconi UNITER communications bunker on North Luffenham airfield next to the redundant Bloodhound tactical control building.

The Second World War had seen dozens of protected railway control centres built all over the country. While a couple of new ones were built at the start of the Cold War, the new policy was for mobile centres that could be deployed wherever they were needed, accommodated in four-carriage trains. One coach held the control and communications equipment; another was the office coach fitted out with desks and teleprinters; the third coach contained stores and a mess room for the crew; and the last coach carried the generator and telephone battery. One of these trains was located in each railway region, and it was planned that the London Midland one would be stabled at Market Harborough.

While civilians would be told to stay put and discouraged from travelling, there would be no outright prohibition issued. However, given that fuel stocks available to the public would be immediately curtailed, no one would be going very far. In addition, there was a network of designated essential service routes that would be sealed off by the TA. Just as the declaration of martial law would require troops to shoot looters, it also allowed troops to open fire on unauthorised vehicles. Those roads denied to the general public were the obvious ones: the A47, linking the A5 to the A1 (passing through Uppingham, Leicester, and Hinckley), and the A46 Fosse Way (passing through Leicester). The M1 also formed a section of the Military Road Route System, codenamed 'BAT', running between London and Hull via Leeds and the A1 was a key section in the route from Folkestone to Edinburgh, codenamed 'STAG'.

While the thaw following the end of the Cold War may have caused a relaxation of tension and a reduction in levels of military establishments, the less predictable threat of terrorist action has given greater prominence to the gathering of ELOINT and SIGINT. An awareness of this continuing possibility of terrorist attack is reflected in the security measures in force at the few remaining overtly military sites in our counties. Entry to military premises is regulated by the presence of armed guards, but the only other visible barrier consists of wire fences and the ubiquitous Yarnold sangar.

Pre-Conquest Fortifications

Prehistoric Camps, Forts, and Linear Earthworks

Appleby Magna (SK329089): triple-ditched Iron-age enclosure
Belton Moat: possible small circular Iron Age camp (SK451200)
Billesdon: Life Hill univallate hill-fort (SK722049)
Breedon on the Hill: The Bulwarks (SK405233) univallate fort
Bringhurst: medieval church occupies Iron Age enclosure (TL841922)
Burrough Walls Camp (SK761119): from 400 BC
Croxton Kerrial: King Lud's Entrenchments, possible Bronze Age boundary ditches between
    Leicestershire and Lincolnshire (SK860280-865280)
Lockington: site south-east of Dunster Barn (SK478306)
Market Overton: church occupies a rectangular banked enclosure (SK885164)
Ratby, Bury Camp: rectangular earthwork (SK498057)
Ridlington (R) (SK846026): probable Iron Age fort
Tipton-on-the-Hill, Robin-a-Tiptoe (SK774043): possible unfinished hillfort
Woodhouse, Beacon Hill Camp (SK512147): probable Bronze Age hillfort

Roman Forts and Fortified Settlements

Great Casterton: (TF002091) first-century fort followed by defended town
Leicester (Ratae): Legionary fortress and walled town
Tripontium: fort on Watling Street (SP532795)
Witherley (Manduessudum): fort on Watling Street (c.SP325967)
Wigston Parva: fort on Watling Street (SP464894)

Saxon Towers

Leicester, St Nicholas: central tower of late eleventh century
Market Overton (R), St Peter & St Paul: indications of former Saxon belfry

Castles and other Medieval Fortifications

Earthwork Castles

Note: doubtful or unconfirmed examples in italics

Beaumont Chase (R), Castle Hill: motte	SK850005
Belvoir: motte and bailey, pre-1088	SK820337
Burley (R), Alstoe Mount: motte and bailey	SK894120
Castle Donington: motte	SK448276
Desford: probable mill-mound	*SK482029*
Earl Shilton, Castle Yard	SP470982
Essendine (R): ringwork and bailey	TF049128
Garthorpe: possible motte or mill mound	*SK834208*
Gilmorton: motte and bailey	SP570879
Groby: motte and bailey	SK524076
Gumley: a landscape feature	*SP679899*
Hallaton: motte and bailey	SP780967
Hinckley, Castle Hill	SP428938
Hungarton, Monk's Grave: motte	SK681049
Ingarsby: motte	SK681049
Kibworth Harcourt: motte	SP681945
Launde: probable mill mound	*SK790047*
Leicester: motte pre-1100	SK583041
Melton Mowbray: probable mill mound	*SK748188*
Mountsorrel: motte	SK585149
North Luffenham, Morcott Spinney: possible motte	*SK928023*
Oakham (R): Saxon burh and post-1075 motte	SK861089
Pilton (R): landscape feature	*SK928023*
Ravenstone: suggested site for castle	SK411131
Sauvey: motte and bailey	SK787053
Sapcote, Toot Hill	SP486933
Scraptoft, The Mount: landscape feature	*SK654059*
Shackerstone: motte and bailey	SK375069
Shawell/Catthorpe: motte south of church	SP541796
Whitwick: motte	SK436162
Woodhead (R): ringwork and bailey	SK996116

Stone Castles

Ashby-de-la-Zouch: strong house of 1350s with great tower added in 1474
Bagworth: licensed in 1474, referred to as 'castle' in 1373; moat at SK454086
Belvoir: shell wall and keep
Castle Donington: large motte with walls and towers
Kirby Muxloe: unfinished moated brick castle of 1480
Leicester: stone hall, defences and ancillary buildings added in twelfth century
Mountsorrel: stone buildings added to motte
Oakham: hall and stone defences added to earlier royal castle 1190–1200
Sapcote: stone structures uncovered
Sauvey: rebuilt in stone by King John
Whitwick: licensed in 1321
Woodhead Castle (R): probable quadrangular castle with towers and gatehouse

Later Castles, Fortified Manor Houses, Moated Sites, and Tudor Strong Houses

Appleby, Moat House: medieval moated manor house
Ashby Parva: moat at SP524884
Aylestone Hall: timber-framed hall on stone plinth
Bardon Hall: fifteenth-century moat around later house, SK462122
Birds Nest: moated site (Battersbee Road) SK552059
Bradgate House: fifteenth-century palatial manor house
Burton-on-the-Wolds: moated grange of Garendon Abbey
Donington-le-Heath: moated stone house of *c.* 1280
Evington, The Hollow (or Piggy's Hollow): late-thirteenth or early fourteenth century moated manor
Flitteris: hunting lodge built 1373, Flitteris Park Farm, SK820078
Garthorpe: thirteenth-century stone house, SK832209
Groby Old Hall: brick towers of late fifteenth century
Hemington Hall: fragments of thirteenth-century house, rebuilt sixteenth century
Horsepool Grange: moat at SK470101
Ingarsby Old Hall: moated grange of Leicester Abbey from 1352
Kirkby Mallory, Kirkby Moats: SK454018
Knaptoft, Hall Farm: brick manor house with stone gatehouse, SP625894
Lubenham, The Old Hall: moated site, SP709870
Lydington, Bede House: palace of bishops of Lincoln, licensed in 1336
Misterton: moats at SP557842
Nevill Holt: stone manor house by 1302, much enlarged from sixteenth century
North Luffenham: moated house destroyed in Civil War, SK928033
Pinwall: moat at SK304005
Potters Marston Hall: late-fifteenth-century granite east wing of house
Ratby, Old Hays Farm: moated site with later house
Ratcliffe Culley: moat at SP328995
Ryhall, Green Dragon Inn: thirteenth-century manor house vaulted undercroft
Seagrave: earthworks at Hall Farm may indicate previous existence of a fortified house, SK621174
Sheepy, New House Grange: moated with early Tudor tithe barn, SK318023
Staunton Harold: fifteenth-century embattled manor house built after 1423
Stoke Golding, The Moats: SP397969
Thorpe Arnold: earthworks of possible fortified house, SW of church, SK769200
Thurlaston, New Hall (Park Farm): moated site with fragments of walls, SK506003
Tilton-on-the-Hill: moated site with robber trenches of stone house, SK745052

Tolethorpe Hall: post-1316 house rebuilt from fifteenth century
Whissendine 1: moated site with manor house at SK8350143
Whissendine 2: moated site of manor at SK839151

Ecclesiastical Fortifications

Anstey, Beaumont Leys: Preceptory of Knights Templar, SK565093
Bradley and Charley Priories: earthworks delineate the line of the precinct walls
Dalby Preceptory: established by 1206, absorbed Heather, Rothley & Swinford Rothley Preceptory, SK577122,
Leicester: St Mary's Augustinian Abbey with precinct walls and gatehouse
Wellsborough: Temple Hall Farm at SK362025, Temple Mill Farm at SK355035 and Temple Farm at SK360036, all suggestive of properties of the Knights Templar.

Civil War Fortresses

Ashby-de-la-Zouch	SK361166
Bagworth House	SK454086
Belvoir Castle	SK820337
Bradgate Park	SK534102
Burley on the Hill (R)	SK885102
Coleorton Hall	SK392173
Hemington Hall	SK465277
Kirkby Bellars Hall	SK715175
Leicester Castle	SK585040
Leicester City Walls	
Melton Mowbray town	
North Luffenham (R)	SK928033

The Army in the Nineteenth and Twentieth Centuries

Pre-First World War Barracks and Army Camps

Leicester, Three-troop Cavalry Barracks planned 1794, not built
Leicester, Glen Parva, barracks built as Leicestershire regimental depot, *c.* 1880
Leicester, Newarke, Magazine Gate, Militia Barracks 1850s
Loughborough, Sparrow Hill, Cavalry Barracks built 1840

First World War Barracks and Army Camps

Leicester, Glen Parva Barracks, Leicestershire regimental depot
Melton Mowbray, army remount station in former stud farm
Melton Mowbray, Wicklow Lodge stables requisitioned by Yeomanry
Wing, Brocklebank, stables housing army remounts

First World War Recruitment and Training

Groby rifle range, SK526077
Leicester, Granby Halls/Empress Ice Rink: Junior Training Corps & VTC drills
Leicester, Southgate Street (now redeveloped) and Market Street: Royal Navy recruiting offices
Leicester Town Hall: recruiting office
Melton Mowbray drill hall: recruiting office
Ragdale/Sixhills: army rifle range
Whitwick, High Tor Farm: summer camp for Leicestershire Regiment, TF

Second World War Barracks and Army Camps

Ashwell Camp (R): used by RE & RASC, 1940, then US airborne forces 1943–4
Barleythorpe Hall (R): 133 Parachute Field Ambulance, 1944
Beaumanor Hall and adjacent Garats Hay: requisitioned by War Office 1939, for War Office 'Y' Service Group and Intelligence School
Bisbrooke Hall (R): billets for a troop of 4th Parachute Squadron, RE, 1942–5
Braunstone Park: HQ US 82 Airborne Division, 1944
Burley on the Hill Rectory (R): tented camp for 4 Battalion Cheshire Regiment, 1940

Burrough on the Hill: billets for 10th Battalion, Parachute Regiment, 1943–4

Charley: Army camps

Coleorton Hall: Army camp

Cottesmore House (R): US 92nd Parachute Maintenance Company (Riggers), 1944

Earl Shilton: public buildings requisitioned 1940 for army occupation

Evington, Shady Lane: camp for 504th Parachute Infantry, 82nd US Airborne Division

Glaston House (R): billets for a troop of 4th Parachute Squadron, RE, 1942–5

Garendon Park (demolished 1964): occupied by RAOC

Glen Parva Barracks: depot of Leicestershire Regiment, and ITC until 1941

Gumley Hall (demolished 1964): SOE Operational School, STS 41

Kirby Mallory: Royal Army Pay Corps camp, SK456007

Knossington Grange (R): HQ 4th Parachute Brigade, 1st Airborne Division

Leicester, 'Elmfield', Stanley Road: HQ East Midland Area, Northern Command

Leicester, Aylestone Road cricket ground: US Army Pioneer Corps and NFS

Leicester, RAOC Training Establishment 1940, then on to Derby

Leicester, RAOC OCTU, 1941, expanded (from Kettering)

Long Whatton: Army camp, SK488225

Lubenham, Papillon Hall: camp for US Army 319th Glider Assault Regiment

Melton Mowbray, Brook Street: training for RA heavy artillery instructors

Melton Mowbray: militia camp, 1939, then for AA units

Melton Mowbray, Newport Lodge: 'B' & 'C' Companies 156 Battalion Parachute Regiment

Melton Mowbray, The Spinney: Support Company 156 Battalion Parachute Regiment, 1944

Melton Mowbray, Staveley Lodge: HQ Company 156 Battalion Parachute Regiment, 1944

Melton Mowbray, Scalford Hall: 'A' Company 156 Battalion Parachute Regiment, 1944

Melton Mowbray: billets for 11th Battalion, Parachute Regiment

Melton Mowbray, Wicklow Lodge: requisitioned by the Army

North Luffenham: militia camp, 1939

Oadby Racecourse: British Army Primary Training Centre, 1942–5

Oadby Racecourse: camp for 80th A/T Battalion, 82nd US Airborne Division, 1944

Old Dalby: RAOC then REME Depot

Quorn, Wood Lane Camp: Royal Pioneer Corps, 1940–1

Quorn, Wood Lane Camp: 505th Parachute Infantry, 82nd US Airborne Division, 1943–4

Quorn, Manor House, Tennis Pavilion: RAOC detachment, 1942

Scraptoft: camp for 325th Glider Infantry Regiment, 82nd US Airborne Division, 1943

Somerby: billets for 10th Battalion, Parachute Regiment, 1943–4

Swithland Camp: civilian evacuees from Leicester, SK535124

Thorpe Satchville: billets for 10th Battalion, Parachute Regiment, 1943–4

Twycross, Gopsall Hall (demolished 1951): REME radio and radar training school

Twyford: billets for 10th Battalion, Parachute Regiment, 1943–4

Uppingham (R): HQ 4th Parachute Squadron, RE

Uppingham (R): Southwell (Church) Rooms requisitioned by Army

Post-Second World War Barracks and Army Camps

Beaumanor Hall: Intelligence Corps, 1945 to late 1950s

Cottesmore (R): Kendrew Barracks, post-RAF use from 2012

Garats Hay: Intelligence Corps and ATS, 1945–1998

Melton Mowbray: Defence Animal Centre (DAC), opened 1948

North Luffenham (R): St George's Barracks, post-RAF use from 1998

Military Airfields and other Aviation-related Sites

Notes:
i. USAAF designated Station Number in brackets
ii. Air Ministry design numbers in italic; number after '/' denotes year of issue—e.g. *343*/43 is design number 343 in (19)43

Bitteswell

Opened in June 1941 as a satellite of Bramcote (Warwickshire), home to No. 18 OTU, training Polish aircrew on Wellington bombers. By the end of the year, the field had become unusable and flying ceased for over a year while three concrete runways were laid. At the same time, hangars were constructed for the manufacture of Avro Lancaster bombers by Armstrong Whitworth Aircraft Ltd, whose Coventry works were vulnerable to enemy bombing. The opportunity was also taken to establish a ground defence school for airmen from 92 Group to supplement the newly formed RAF Regiment's airfield defence squadrons. With the new runways complete, flying was resumed as a satellite of Bruntingthorpe, training on Wellingtons under No. 29 OTU, recently moved from North Luffenham. Bitteswell then reverted to Bramcote, by now part of Transport Command, training Dakota crews of No. 105 OTU as glider tows. The RAF finally quit the airfield in 1947, but flying continued for the testing of engines for Power Jets, soon to be subsumed into the National Gas Turbine Establishment for Armstrong Siddeley Motors and for Rolls-Royce under the control of the Ministry of Supply and subject to the Official Secrets Act. Liquid fuel rocket motors were trialled in the early 1950s. Construction of aircraft by Armstrong Whitworth continued—turning out the Sea Hawk, Meteors, Hunters, Javelins, Hawk jet trainers, and Argosy freighters—many hundreds, all told, terminating in 1982. The bomber airfield had one T2 hangar and one B1; the watch office was that allocated to bomber or OTU satellites (*13726*/41); the technical site was temporary buildings, and there was accommodation for 1175 RAF and 103 WAAF personnel. Aircraft manufacture was carried out in four single hangars and a double on the 'Old Site' next to the A5, and in one double and one triple aircraft sheds on the northern 'New Site'. The site now lies under the Magna Park distribution centre.

Blaby Wharf

This was a salvage site for crashed aircraft from late 1940, operated by No. 65 Maintenance Unit. Prior to its requisition, it had been a civilian transport contractor's yard so many of the buildings were simply made over to their new use. Two Blister hangars were added, the last of which was in process of disintegration in July 2015. It ceased RAF working in 1945 and reverted to industrial use.

Blaston

Blaston (SP830963) was a First World War night landing ground, which was succeeded by Welham in 1916.

Bottesford

Bottesford (Station 481) opened in late 1941 in 5 Group RAF Bomber Command with 207 Squadron, affiliated to the City of Leicester through the Municipal Liaison Scheme, flying Manchester bombers. A succession of bomber squadrons flying Stirlings and Lancasters operated raids against targets in France, Germany, and Italy, with pauses when the flying surface required attention. By late 1943, the station was transferred to the IXth Troop Carrier Command of the US IXth AAF, perfecting the use of Skytrains to tow Horsa troop-carrying gliders. The units moved to southern airfields to prepare for their D-Day missions. The Americans were replaced by a Heavy Conversion Unit equipped with Lancasters, some of which were fitted with Gee-H, a blind-bombing radar. Flying ceased in late 1945, but until 1960, the station was used for the storage and disposal of redundant munitions by 93 MU first and then 92 MU. The airfield was built with one B1 and two T2 hangars for normal operations; four T2s were added to equip the airfield as a Base Major Maintenance Section, with four more for glider storage. The *518/40* watch office has been beautifully refurbished in a *moderne* style, the centrepiece of Roseland Business Park, retaining many original wartime buildings.

Braunstone

Operated as a civilian aerodrome from early 1935. Plans to establish RAF No. 58 E & RFTS were cancelled in 1939, but it became a satellite of No. 7 EFTS at Desford in 1940, flying Tiger Moths. Three Blister hangars were added to the existing hangars and clubhouse. Only in 1947 was the airfield derequisitioned and its proximity to an expanding Leicester precluded any further flying. It is now an industrial estate.

Bretingby

Bretingby (SK784184) was a First World War night landing ground, succeeded by Scalford in late 1916. It was listed by the AA in the 1930s as 'Melton Mowbray' (SK782182) with a maximum run of 600 yards.

Bruntingthorpe

Bruntingthorpe opened in late 1942 by No. 29 OTU, flying Wellingtons and using the bombing range at Wardley Hill (R). Training was also carried out here to develop fighter techniques for escorting bombers. During 1943, abnormally hot weather caused parts of the concrete runways to break up. Towards the end of the war, 11 Aircrew Holding Unit dealt with demobilising RAF personnel, and Power Jets carried out some trials work. In 1953, the airfield was allocated to the USAF SAC. A 3,400-yard-long (3.1-km-long) runway and a Wimpey-type hangar were built for their B-47 bombers and RB-66 Destroyer reconnaissance aircraft, but operations ceased in 1962. Since then, the site has been used for vehicle testing and storage and as an industrial estate. An aviation museum occupies part of the site, which has also been home to the last airworthy Vulcan—now, sadly, permanently grounded. The wartime airfield had one B1 and four T2s, with a *12779/41* watch office. Refurbished as a conference and exhibition centre, the B1 hangar has been renamed 'Hangar 42'. The watch office and speech broadcast building survive, along with at least one T2 hangar and much of the technical and synthetic training sites continue in industrial use.

Buckminster

Buckminster was an airfield used by Home Defence fighter squadrons, initially under the control of Melton Mowbray, from 1916–18, and latterly an Aircraft Acceptance Park. The village lies in Leicestershire with the airfield in Lincolnshire.

Burton-on-the-Wolds

Burton-on-the-Wolds (SK609213) was a First World War day and night landing ground.

Castle Donington

Castle Donington (SK449256) was established in late 1916 as a day and night landing ground, but was downgraded to a day landing ground in 1917. A satellite of Wymeswold opened here on 1 January 1943, flying Wellingtons of No. 28 OTU, replaced by No. 108 (Transport) OTU in 4 Group RAF Transport Command equipped with Dakotas. The RAF left in late 1946, leaving the airfield abandoned for the next two decades. East Midlands Airport opened in 1965. The wartime airfield at first operated with no hangars, but one B1 and one T2 were subsequently built. The watch office, unaccountably, was a type designed for fighter satellites (*12096*/41). The T2 survives as Hangar 31, with an imported post-1965 half-height T2 next to it.

Cottesmore

Cottesmore (R) (Station 489) opened in 1938 as a two-squadron bomber station. By the outbreak of war, it was in 5 Group RAF Bomber Command flying Hampdens, but it soon transferred to 6 (Training) Group as No. 14 OTU, operating until August 1943, when Wimpeys moved in to lay concrete runways and to add a T2 hangar. In October 1943, the IXth Troop Carrier Command of the US IXth AAF arrived using Skytrains as tow planes for Hadrian (Waco) gliders. Officers were accommodated in the requisitioned Cottesmore Hall. HQ IXth Troop Carrier Command moved to St Vincents in nearby Grantham before Christmas. On D-Day, Cottesmore aircraft successfully dropped two battalions of parachutists with artillery support on to their Normandy target. Further airborne operations included Market Garden and Varsity. After the war, the airfield operated flying training units with Mosquitos and Harvards, and by 1954, Canberra jets, in the world's first jet bomber conversion unit. After a fleeting occupation by Valiants, in 1958, the 'V' Bombers arrived to take up permanent residence at a completely revamped airfield, now with Class 1 status, with a 3,000-yard runway, concrete hard-standings, a Vertical Split Control type tower (*2548c*/55), an enhanced technical site, and atomic weapon storage. The Victors practised three-minute scrambles from their H-shaped dispersals and Operational Readiness Platforms, but in 1964, they were exchanged for the Vulcans, which stayed until 1976. More changes, including 10 acres (4 hectares) of Aircraft Servicing Platforms, were required prior to the station's new role flying Tornados and training pilots from West Germany and Italy. Soon after the Tornados redeployed to Marham in Norfolk, Cottesmore was handed over to the Army as Kendrew Barracks.

Desford (Peckleton)

Desford operated as Peckelton (qv) from late 1916 as a day and night landing ground, but it was downgraded to a day landing ground in 1917. It was restarted in 1929 as a flying club, and opened in 1935 as the ninth of thirteen Civil Flying Training schools, becoming No. 7 E & RFTS using Tiger Moths, and with a parallel course for observers and gunners, until 1939. It then became No. 7 EFTS with a satellite at Braunstone. The school had been run by Reid & Sigrist, who, in 1939, brought aircraft construction to Desford as well as a Civilian Repair Organisation (CRO) working on RAF aircraft. Blister hangars were erected for the school's aircraft, and large sheds, including a Bellman hangar, were built on both sides of the airfield, supplementing the two existing pre-war hangars for the aircraft factory. The assembly of Spitfires was dispersed from Castle Bromwich and Reid & Sigrist produced some 200 at Desford as well as building their own range of single and twin-engined trainers. The largest of the factory sheds on the south of the airfield still stand as part of the Caterpillar construction plant factory. Across the road lies the CRO site with an Over Blister hangar, a T2, and four joined Super Robins hangars forming a third large workshop area. After the war, No. 7 Reserve Flying School stayed until 1953.

Husbands Bosworth

Husbands Bosworth was listed as a landing ground by the AA in the 1930s, but with no details. A new bomber airfield opened in summer 1942 as a satellite of No. 14 OTU at Market Harborough, flying Wellingtons, then a base for No. 85 OTU. Bombing practice was carried out on Mowsley range, which was equipped with lights for night bombing. Training of parachute troops from the US 82nd Airborne Division dropping from Skytrains was carried out in preparation for Market Garden. While flying ceased in June 1945, a number of personnel units occupied the huts. The four T2s were sold to Vickers-Armstrongs for re-erection elsewhere. The watch office (343/43), parachute store, and other tb buildings survive.

Keythorpe Hall

Keythorpe Hall (Station 566) near Tugby (SK767003), dating from 1843, served as a USAAF aircrew rest and recuperation centre or 'Flak Shack', designated 'K' 93rd Station Complement Squadron, and run by the American Red Cross with places for thirty NCOs.

Leicester

Leicester (Station 527) US VIIIth AAF and US Tactical AF, Quartermaster Stores.

Leicester East

Leicester East eventually, after three false starts, gained some operational units in November 1943, when two squadrons of Stirlings moved in temporarily, followed by a third squadron that carried out glider tow training and made drops for SOE. In April 1944, training began on Dakotas of No. 107 OTU, practising dropping parachute troops, carrying out supply drops, and towing gliders. Men of the US 82nd Airborne Division were involved in these exercises and RASC personnel were trained as airborne despatchers. After the war, the station was placed in care and maintenance, and in 1950, the Leicestershire Aero Club took over. One of the original T2 hangars survives; the watch office (343/43) as Club HQ; karting is run from a SAA store.

Loughborough

Loughborough was home, in the First World War, to the Brush Electrical Engineering Company, which built large numbers of aircraft for the RNAS, carrying out flight tests on them on Loughborough Meadows (SK542212). Loughborough College's Department of Aeronautical Engineering, hitherto using the premier ballroom on Ashby Road to store air frames in 1936, acquired a site on which Boulton & Paul built a hangar, an engine test building, and an aircraft assembly workshop. On the outbreak of war, the Ministry of Aircraft Production allocated the site to Airwork for the modification of Douglas Bostons and Havocs. Towards the end of the war, Airwork and Brush Falcon Works both repaired Lancasters, with Brush additionally building Dominies. Activity tailed off until, in 1951, the lease expired. All the others have gone, but the Brush hangar in Swingbridge Road (SK528210) survives.

Loughborough College

Loughborough College's RAF School of Physical Training with a Royal Naval Air Training Section was opened in 1939. The WAAF officers' training school was present from 1940, and the RAF Officers' Medical Rehabilitation Unit from 1942–7.

Market Harborough

Market Harborough (locally Lubenham) opened in August 1943, with No. 14 OTU from Cottesmore flying Wellingtons, Ansons, and Oxfords. It took over Husbands Bosworth as its satellite. Training also included bomber defence tactics using old Tomahawks and Hurricanes. At the end of the war, the airfield carried out storage and disposal functions into 1947. Following ten years as an Army vehicle depot, the site was earmarked as HM Prison Gartree in 1961.

There were four T2 hangars and one B1, and a watch office (*343/43*). At Chapel Farm, parts of a communal site with a gymnasium and chapel and a sergeants' mess survive.

Melton Mowbray

Melton Mowbray was a landing ground for 38 (Home Defence) Squadron in the First World War. Covering 60 acres (24 hectares) on a site opposite Sysonby Farm and close to the Squadron HQ on Scalford Road, it was heavily used 1916–18. In August 1943, a new airfield south of the town opened under 44 Group RAF Transport Command. Resident units included Nos 304, 306, and 307 Ferry Training Units, 1943–4, followed in November 1944 by No. 12 Ferry Unit, delivering aircraft overseas, and part of No. 107 OTU from Leicester East, training glider tows. Horsa gliders were assembled by Boulton & Paul in their King Street plant. In the early 1960s, a Thor IRBM site was built, but by 1964, the RAF had gone. There were four T2 hangars and an unusual watch office with its third floor underpinning an otherwise normal *12779/41* tower. A few BCF huts and concrete blast walls remain from the Thor era, but, otherwise, there is very little remaining. Also at Melton Mowbray was US VIIIth AAF Station 520, an Air Force Service Command ordnance, and transport depot.

North Luffenham

North Luffenham was planned before war broke out, but it was not started by Laings until 1940, opening on 1 January 1941 with sixty pupils of No. 17 EFTS learning on Tiger Moth biplanes. By July, two squadrons of Hampdens were carrying out bombing operations against targets, mainly in Germany and France, using Woolfox Lodge as a satellite airfield. In April 1942, No. 29 OTU flying Wellingtons arrived. A year later, flying was interrupted while concrete runways were laid, resuming in March 1944, when gliding became the station's focus with the Heavy Glider Conversion Unit (HGCU) moving in. While the airfield was out of action, MAP had operated from new B1 and T2 hangars, working on Hamilcar gliders. Soon, Albemarles took the place of Whitleys, and training continued with the establishment of a Glider Instructors School and co-operation with USAAF glider tows from Cottesmore. At the end of 1944, a Heavy (Bomber) Conversion Unit moved in with mainly Lancasters, succeeded in 1946 by No. 21 HGCU. The jet age arrived with Canadian Sabres and Meteor interceptors. North Luffenham was selected as a base for Thor IRBMs and a Bloodhound SAGW Tactical Control Centre. By 1964, all these missile systems had gone and the station became home to such diverse units as the Joint Services School of Linguists, the Aviation Medicine Training Centre, and an Explosive Ordnance Disposal (EOD) unit. The station is now occupied by the Army as St George's Barracks, occupied currently (2015) by EOD, medical, and working dog regiments. The transitional J-type hangars and the 'Villa' watch office (*5845/39*) remain, with all three wartime and one post-war T2s, but the B1 has gone. The radar plinth, the Bloodhound Tactical Control Centre, and elements of the Thor site, including the three launch emplacements, are also extant.

Nuneaton

Nuneaton (locally Lindley) opened in August 1943 with No. 105 OTU flying Wellingtons. As part of 44 Group RAF Transport Command, the unit also flew Dakotas and hosted US Army Grasshopper Air Observation Posts. From 1946, the airfield became a testing ground for the Motor Industry Research Association (MIRA). The watch office, designed for OTU satellites (*13726/41*) survives, minus its VCR; the single T2 hangar contains MIRA's wind tunnels.

Peckleton

Peckleton (SK479022) operated as a First World War day landing ground from 1916–17, on a site later subsumed by Desford aerodrome.

Preston Hall

Preston Hall (Station 565), near Uppingham (R) (SK870027), is thought to have been a USAAF aircrew rest and recuperation centre or 'Flak Shack', although it is listed merely as 'Air Service Command' in USAAF schedules.

Queniborough

Queniborough (SK656114) was a First World War day and night landing ground in 1916–7.

Ratcliffe

Ratcliffe started as a private aerodrome in 1930, with a licence for Avro 504s and light aircraft. The provision of night flying equipment, floodlights, and navigational aids made it ideal for an RAF emergency landing ground and for flight-testing Taylorcraft aircraft. In 1940, the airfield became the home of No. 6 Ferry Pilot Pool of the Air Transport Auxiliary (ATA), serving most of the Midlands' aircraft factories and RAF MUs. After the war, club flying resumed until 1950. The two pre-war Belfast truss hangars survive, but the large wartime MAP hangar was dismantled in 1945.

Ratcliffe Hall

Ratcliffe Hall (SK628144) provided open house for the ferry pilots' brief off-duty hours throughout the war.

Rearsby

Rearsby started as the County Flying Club Ltd in 1937, and by 1939, it was participating in the Civil Air Guard scheme, with Tiger Moths supplied from Desford. Taylorcraft had been using the airfield, but lacking new orders, they were happy to be given a contract—initially for repairing Hurricanes. Hangars were erected and the flying field expanded. Through the war years, hundreds of varied aircraft were repaired by the CRO. An initial order for 100 Taylorcraft AOPs was placed by the Army in 1941. Better-known as the Auster, over 1,500 of them had been built by 1945 and others were repaired. Production of Austers, Beagles, and other derivatives continued after the war for both military and civilian customers until 1964. The sheds on Gaddesby Lane now form part of a business park.

Saltby

Saltby (Station 538) opened in 1941 as a satellite of Cottesmore, with No. 14 OTU flying Hampdens then Wellingtons off the grass airfield. In August 1943, the OTU moved to Husbands Bosworth while concrete runways were laid. The airfield was surrounded by woodland, which gave cover to the buildings. While the runways were building, gliders were stored in the new hangars, and on the station's completion, it was handed over to the US IXth AAF Troop Carrier Command flying Dakotas to tow the Horsas already on site, along with C-47 and C-53s troop carriers, in preparation for D-Day and the later Arnhem operation. The RAF returned in March 1945, overseeing conversion training of aircrew and operations by their own and US transport units. The airfield closed to flying, but maintained a storage role until 1955. It is now used for gliding, but few signs of wartime use remain. An early model watch office (*15975*/40) for bomber satellites was replaced by the later all-purpose type (*12779*/41), but both have gone. The official list records the one B1 and two T2 hangars, which were standard for bomber satellites, but aerial photographs from 1947 show an additional pair of T2s built for glider storage.

Scalford

This site (SK744216) was close to 38 (HD) Squadron's HQ and was the biggest and busiest of the First World War day and night landing grounds, taking over from Brentingby in 1916.

Welham

Welham (SP770933) was a landing ground used briefly during 1916.

Woolfox Lodge

Woolfox Lodge opened as a satellite of Cottesmore in December 1940, with elements of No. 14 OTU flying Hampdens; they were later replaced by operational units from North Luffenham in August 1941. From mid-1942, a number of training units flew from here until October, when the airfield was closed for refurbishment. Concrete runways were laid and one B1 and four T2 hangars were built, with accommodation for 1,300 personnel. Conversion units and operational squadrons flying Stirlings with GEE-H radars alternated over the months, bombing and minelaying, with a Lancaster Finishing School and two Heavy Conversion Units in residence during 1944 and 1945. Two dedicated hangars on site held gliders prior to major airborne operations. From July 1945, it became an Equipment Dispersal Depot run by 259 MU. From 1960-4, a Bloodhound SAGW squadron was based here. The airfield was sold in 1966. The watch office designed for night fighter stations (*4532/3/43*) remains along with many of the buildings of the Bloodhound site, including the large missile-assembly sheds.

Wymeswold

Wymeswold opened in May 1942 as home to No. 28 OTU, who flew Wellingtons initially before converting to a wide range of aircraft. From October 1944, it switched to No. 108 OTU of RAF Transport Command, with Dakotas, which stayed until 1947 when the station closed. Five years later, it reopened for use by auxiliary fighter squadrons—the first to fly jets. Finally closing in 1957, the airfield is an industrial estate. The watch office (*518/40*) survives along with several of the hangars, originally a B1 and four T2s, and many of the technical, synthetic training, and administrative structures.

US IXth AAF Troop Carrier Command Deployment 1943-5

HQ US IXth AAF Troop Carrier Command, Cottesmore* then Grantham Lodge, St Vincents, Grantham.

US IXth AAF Troop Carrier Command Pathfinder School, Cottesmore*

HQ 50th Troop Carrier Wing and Advanced Air Depot, Bottesford* with Groups based at Bottesford*, Leicester East*, Fulbeck, Langar, and Balderton.

HQ 52nd Troop Carrier Wing, Cottesmore*, then to Exton Hall* with Groups based at Cottesmore*, Saltby*, Folkingham and Barkston Heath.

North Luffenham* scheduled as expected HQ of a third Troop Carrier Wing, with Groups to be based at North Luffenham*, Wakerley (known as Spanhoe), Woolfox Lodge*, and North Witham, but none taken up by USAAF.

Note: Leicestershire or Rutland locations marked (*)

Bombing Ranges

Bosworth Gorse, Mowsley (R), Ragdale, and Wardley Hill (R)

Aircraft Manufacture 1939-45

Bitteswell: Armstrong Whitworth aircraft factory (two sites) plus flight-testing
Bitteswell: flight-testing for Power Jets Ltd
Bruntingthorpe: Power Jets Ltd testing Meteors, 1945
Coalville, Owen Street: Cascelloid Ltd, No. 10 Factory, Spitfire production
Desford: Reid & Sigrist, built Boulton Paul Defiants and Mitchell bombers
Desford: Reid & Sigrist, No. 8 Factory, Spitfire production (Vickers-Armstrongs)
Hinckley, Rugby Street: H. Flude & Co., Nos 11 & 11a Factories, Spitfire production
Leicester, Percy Road, Aylestone Park: Parmeko Ltd, electrical parts for MAP
Leicester, Blackbird Road: AS Yates Ltd (Omega), No. 22 Factory, Spitfire production
Leicester, Blackbird Road: AS Yates Ltd, No. 23 Factory, Spitfire production
Leicester, Briton Road: Bus Depot, workshop for Lancaster components
Leicester, Percy Road, Aylestone Park: Parmeko Ltd, electrical parts for MAP
Leicester, Western Boulevard: Old Skating Rink, No. 21 Factory, Spitfire production
Leicester: Freeman, Hardy & Willis, & D. Henderson & Sons, Lancaster components
Leicester, Watling Street: Paynes Garage, No. 12 Factory, Spitfire production

Leicester, Weymouth Street: Alfred Davies Ltd, No. 17 Factory, Spitfire production

Loughborough: Brush Falcon Coachworks, de Havilland Dominies, parts for Lancasters, and sub-contract work from Derby LMS workshops, repairing Hampdens

Loughborough, Derby Road: Airwork, repairs and modifications to Bostons and Havocs

Loughborough, Ashby Road: Premier Dance Hall, airframe instructional workshop

Loughborough, Derby Road: Boulton & Paul and Loughborough College, workshops for teaching aircraft manufacture, 1940

Loughborough, Derby Road: Loughborough College, FAA aeronautical engineer training, 1942–5

Lutterworth, Leicester Road: Ladywood Works, Power Jets Foundry (Whittle)

Melton Mowbray, Boulton Paul works on King Street: assembled Horsa gliders

Melton Mowbray: Airwork and Douglas

Rearsby: Taylorcraft repair unit for Tiger Moths & Hurricanes then building Austers in AOP role, 1941–5

Whetstone, Cambridge Road: Power Jets Foundry (Whittle) from Lutterworth 1942

Whitwick: Searles Elastic Web Manufacturers, No. 34 Factory, Spitfire production

Drill Halls, TA and Army Reserve Centres

Note: || denotes extant buildings.

Ashby-de-la- Zouch
1. Church Street, The Armoury: in use 1891.
2. Range Road, |Drill Hall|, *c.* 1914, in use up to early 1950s; hall, indoor range, and offices fronted by semi-detached houses, one of which may have been the orderly room; sash windows with bars on appear original; art rooms for High School.

In 1914, base for 'A' Company, 5th Battalion, Leicestershire Regiment.

Coalville
Ashby Road, |Drill Hall|; E-plan two-storey front block with lateral hall behind; attached house (No. 32) at west end; garage to rear; in commercial use.

In 1914, drill station for 'A' Company, 5th Battalion, Leicestershire Regiment, and for North Midland ASC, Mounted Brigade Transport & Supply column.

Hinckley
1. Stockwell Head, HQ of 'L' Company, 1st Volunteer Battalion.
2. Brunel Road, |Drill Hall|, 1923, two-storey front block with hall behind.

In 1914, drill station 'D' Squadron Leicestershire Yeomanry, and base for 'D' Company 5th Battalion, Leicestershire Regiment.

Leicester
1. Newarke, |Magazine Gateway|, fifteenth-century gatehouse added to in 1859 to create an armoury for the Militia, with further additions in 1894 for a drill hall for the Rifle Volunteers; the barracks extended around a parade square, but in 1966, all but the gatehouse was demolished for a new road. In 1914, the Magazine Square was given as the base for RHA and the ASC.
2. Market Square, |Corn Exchange|, built 1850–5; in use by Rifle Volunteers during 1860s, with drills taking place in the marketplace.
3. 48 Lincoln Street, orderly room of Yeomanry Cavalry, 1891.
4. Oxford Street; some of the premises of Magazine Square, opened onto Oxford Street, which is given as the 1914 base for 4th Battalion, Leicestershire Regiment, and the Divisional Field Ambulance.
5. Saffron Road, |Glen Parva Barracks|, *c.* 1880 depot for Leicestershire Regiment; buildings remaining include officers' mess, barrack block, QM stores, guardroom, hospital block, etc.; current Army Reserve & ACF presence.

6. Brentwood Road, 1923, Territorial Association Riding School and practice field.
7. Brentwood Road, 1937, |ARC|, (RAMC); three- to four-storey front block and garaging, etc.; Tigers' badge over main door and possible riding school to rear.
8. Ulverscroft Road, 1935, |ARC| (Royal Anglians); two-storey blocks wrapped around lateral hall, plus large yard and garages; a Tigers' XVIIth Foot badge over door; built for 44 Searchlight Regiment, RE, TA, formerly the 4th Battalion, Leicestershire Regiment.
9. Blackbird Road,1930s, ex-|TAC|; two- to three-storey central block surrounded by yard, with extensive workshops, garages, explosives/inflammables stores, etc.; now City Council works & housing department; also two pairs of staff houses.

In 1914, HQ Leicestershire Yeomanry; HQ North Midland Mounted Brigade; Battery and Ammunition Column, Leicestershire RHA; HQ and 'A' Company 4th Battalion, Leicestershire Regiment; North Midland Mounted Brigade ASC Transport and Supply Column; HQ North Midland Divisional ASC Transport and Supply Column; 2nd North Midland Divisional Field Ambulance RAMC; General and Clearing Hospitals RAMC.

Loughborough
1. Granby Street/Market Place, drill hall, in use 1891, demolished *c.* 1990 for carpark; traces of boundary walls remain.
2. Leicester Road, |ARC|, 1937, in current use (RLC); main block with hall to rear, and staff house.

In 1914, base 'C' Squadron Leicestershire Yeomanry; HQ & 'H' Company 5th Battalion, Leicestershire Regiment

Lutterworth
Leicester Road, |Drill Hall|, possibly pre-1914; hall and two-storey house/office/stores dated 1921; now in commercial use.

In 1914, base for 'D' Squadron, Leicestershire Yeomanry.

Market Harborough
1. High Street base in use 1891 (perhaps Corn Exchange) for 1st Volunteer Battalion, Leicestershire Regiment.
2. Coventry Road, Drill Hall, in use from 1909, demolished 1990s for housing; now Yeomanry Court, and ACF hut.

In 1914, drill station D Squadron Leicestershire Yeomanry; base for 'E' Company Leicestershire Regiment; and drill station for North Midland ASC Divisional Transport and Supply Column.

Melton Mowbray
1. Nottingham Street, |Corn Exchange|, in use 1891 by 'C' Company, 1st Volunteer Battalion, Leicestershire Regiment.
2. Asfordby Road, |Drill Hall|, 1914 date-stone over main door; imposing front block with hall behind and garages to both sides.

In 1914, base for 'A' Squadron Leicestershire Yeomanry, and 'C' Company, 5th Battalion, Leicestershire Regiment.

Mountsorrel
Main Street, |Drill Hall|, built 1901 (plaque) by Mountsorrel Granite Co. as offices, three-storey block, now house, and social club; hall, now workshop; built of granite with upper parts in brick, now used by haulage company;

In 1914, drill station 'C' Squadron, Leicestershire Yeomanry, and base for 'F' Company, 5th Battalion, Leicestershire Regiment.

Oakham (R)

1. Catmos Street, |Drill Hall| and |Riding School| of Rutland Yeomanry Cavalry of 1790s; two-storey stone-built quarters, 'Catmos Cottage'; riding school, stables with accommodation over; later hall and out-buildings.
2. Penn Street, |Drill Hall|, likely date of 1914; two-storey front block, hall behind with garages.
3. Oakham School Cadet Corps |Armoury| originally in the old Gaol, now the school's art studios; now in purpose-built |Cadet Centre|.

In 1914, drill station for 'A' Squadron, Leicestershire Yeomanry, and base for 'B' Company, 5th Battalion, Leicestershire Regiment.

Shepshed

Kings Road, |Drill Hall|, dated 1914 over main door; two two-storey blocks and garage alongside, front onto the street; now in commercial/industrial use.

In 1914, base for 'G' Company, 5th Battalion, Leicestershire Regiment.

Uppingham (R)

No dedicated building, but the School's |Memorial Hall|, with later CCF Armoury built onto side, may have served from 1905.

In 1914, drill stations for 'A' Squadron, Leicestershire Yeomanry, and 'B' Company, 5th Battalion, Leicestershire Regiment.

Other locations of TF drill stations in Leicestershire and Rutland (R): Anstey, Barrowden (R), Bisbrooke (R), Bottesford, Cottesmore (R), Fleckney, Harby, Ibstock, Ketton (R), Kibworth, Market Bosworth, Rearsby, Syston, Whitwick, Woodhouse Eaves, Whissendine (R), and Wymondham.

Extant Fixed Defences of the Second World War

Airfield Defences

Bottesford: DFW3/22 pillbox	SK809405
Bruntingthorpe: 11008/41 Battle HQ	SP298895
Castle Donington: DFW3/22 pillbox	SK445264
Cottesmore (R): fortified barn with half-pillbox	SK899146
Cottesmore (R): pillbox with LAA annexe	SK900147
Market Harborough: 11008/41 Battle HQ	SP718895
North Luffenham (R): 11008/41 Battle HQ (demolished)	SK946043
North Luffenham (R): pillbox built into range	SK934046
Ratcliffe on the Wreake: Stent prefabricated pillbox	SK628152
Ratcliffe on the Wreake: Stent prefabricated pillbox	SK623154
Wymeswold: 11008/41 Battle HQ	SK592229

Defended Searchlight Sites

Asfordby Mine (Welby): DFW3/22 pillbox	SK722215
Brickfield Farm (Freeby): DFW3/22 pillbox	SK792154
Brooke (R): DFW3/22 pillbox	SK843053
Croxton Lodge (Knipton): DFW3/22 pillbox	SK819300
Edith Weston (North Luffenham) (R): DFW3/22 pillbox	SK941055
Exton (R): DFW3/22 pillbox	SK919103
Ketton (R): DFW3/22 pillbox	SK992059
Landyke Lane (Melton): DFW3/22 pillbox	SK740250
Manton (Hambleton) (R): DFW3/22 pillbox	SK896052
Morcott (R): DFW3/22 pillbox	SK922002
Stathern Hill: DFW3/22 pillbox	SK775305
Stretton (Greetham) (R): DFW3/22 pillbox	SK945153
Thorpe Arnold (Melton Spinney): DFW3/22 pillbox	SK767206
Tixover (Barrowden) (R): DFW3/22 pillbox	SK960011
Tolethorpe (Little Casterton) (R): DFW3/22 pillbox	TF017109
Whissendine (R): DFW3/22 pillbox	SK835148
Withcote: DFW3/22 pillbox	SK788058

Vulnerable Points

Ashwell (Burley): DFW3/22 pillbox	SK865111
Dalby: guard post	SK681235
Gaddesby: spigot mortar pedestal	SK688129
Great Casterton: Home Guard store	TF002092
Harby: spigot mortar pedestal	SK753312
Hinckley: non-standard pillbox	SP407932
Melton Mowbray: spigot mortar pedestal	SK773192
Newbold: frame and hawser roadblock	SK393192
Newbold: A/T rails and Home Guard store	SK393192
Oakham (R): spigot mortar pedestal	SK863090
Ratby: spigot mortar pedestal	SK513060
Redmile: DFW3/22 pillbox	SK790354
Rotherby: spigot mortar pedestal and store	SK681165
Scraptoft: Home Guard store	SK651063
Uppingham (R): loopholed wall	SP862998
Whissendine (R): DFW3/22 pillbox	SK840151

Premises used by the Leicestershire and Rutland Home Guard

Note: different locations and unit designations reflect changes over time.

Appleby Magna, The Grammar School: HQ 'D' Company, 11 (Ashby) Battalion
Asfordby, Holwell Works: HQ 'D' Company, 6 (Quorn) Battalion
Asfordby, Main Street, Dowson's: HQ 'A' Company, 6 (Quorn) Battalion
Ashby-de-la-Zouch, Drill Hall: HQ 11 (Ashby) Battalion
Ashby-de-la-Zouch, 20 Wood Street: HQ 'B' Company, 11 (Ashby) Battalion
Barrow-on-Soar, Strancliffe House Eastern Company: Charnwood Battalion, 1940
Barrow-on-Soar, J. Ellis & Sons: HQ 'C' Company, 10 (Charnwood) Battalion
Beaumanor, Hangingstone Quarry: rifle range
Beaumont Leys: HQ 'D' Company, 1 (North Leicester) Battalion, 1941–4
Beaumont Leys: rifle range
Belvoir Castle, Estate Offices: HQ 'A' Company, 5 (Belvoir) Battalion
Billesdon, The White Hart: HQ 'D' Company, 7 (Market Harborough) Battalion
Birstall Golf Club: HQ 'A' Company, North Leicester Battalion, 1940
Birstall, The Grange: HQ 'A' Company, 1 (North Leicester) Battalion, 1941–4
Blaby, 13 Cork Lane, Glenhills: HQ 'C' Company, South Leicester Battalion, 1940
Blaby, 42 Enderby Road: HQ 'C' Company, 2 (South Leicester) Battalion, 1941–4
Bradgate Park: battle-training area
Breedon on the Hill, Three Horseshoes: HQ No. 3 Company, Ashby Battalion, 1940
Coalville, Drill Hall: HQ 'G' Company, 11 (Ashby) Battalion
Coalville, High Street, Tower Chambers: HQ 'E' Company, 11 (Ashby) Battalion
Coalville, Owen Street: HQ 'F' Company, 11 (Ashby) Battalion
Desford, RAF station: HQ 'F' Company, 8 (Market Bosworth) Battalion
Donington Park race circuit: Army Bomb Disposal School, 1941
Donisthorpe Colliery: HQ 'A' Company, 11 (Ashby) Battalion
Earl Shilton, Hinckley Road, Hollydene: HQ 'D' Company, 8 (Market Bosworth) Battalion
Enderby, The Institute: HQ 'C' Company, 3 (West Leicester) Battalion, 1941–4
Glenfield, Station Park: grenade range in former quarry
Glen Parva, 13 Cork Lane: HQ 'C' Company, 2 (South Leicester) Battalion
Griffydam, Wagon & Horses: HQ 'C' Company, 11 (Ashby) Battalion
Groby, The Barn, Stamford Arms: HQ 'D' Company, 3 (W Leicester) Battalion
Hinckley, Bond Street, Old Cottages: HQ Company, 8 (Market Bosworth) Battalion
Hinckley, Conservative Club: HQ 'A' Company, 8 (Market Bosworth) Battalion
Hinckley, Brunel Road, Drill Hall: HQ 8 (Market Bosworth) Battalion
Hoton, The Old Parsonage: HQ 'B' Company, 10 (Charnwood) Battalion

Ibstock, 119 High Street: HQ 'C' Company, Market Bosworth Battalion, 1940
Ibstock, Reform Road: TOC H Rooms, HQ 'C' Company, 8 (Market Bosworth) Battalion
Kegworth, The Manor House: HQ 'A' Company, 10 (Charnwood) Battalion
Keyham, The Old Hall: HQ 'C' Company, 6 (Quorn) Battalion
Kibworth Beauchamp, St Wilfrid's Church and Grey House: company bases, 1940
Kibworth: rifle range
Kirby, Golf Club House: HQ 'A' Company, West Leicester Battalion, 1940
Kirby Muxloe, Woodlands: HQ 'A' Company, 3 (West Leicester) Battalion, 1941–4
Leicester, Aylestone Road cricket ground: NFS depot
Leicester, Belgrave Gate, Tramway Office: HQ Company, 4 (Central Leicester) Battalion
Leicester, Blackbird Road, Stadium: HQ, 'A' and 'B' Companies, Mobile Unit, 1940
Leicester, Canning Street: later HQ 12 (Motor Reconnaissance) Battalion
Leicester, Corporation Road, Abbey Pumping Station: HQ 'A' Company (Central Leicester)
    Battalion
Leicester, 25 de Montfort Street: HQ 1 (North Leicester) Battalion, 1941–4
Leicester, East Park Road, St Barnabas School: HQ 'D' Company, 4 (Central Leicester) Battalion
Leicester, Evington Valley Road, Partridge Wilson & Co.: HQ 'C' Company, 4 Battalion
Leicester, Friar Lane: County ARP HQ
Leicester, Friday Street: ZAA Battery training centre
Leicester Golf Club: HQ 'C' Company, 1 (North Leicester) Battalion, 1941–4
Leicester, 51 Grafton Place: HQ 12 (Motor Reconnaissance) Battalion
Leicester, 28 Great Central Street: HQ 'B' Company, 4 (Central Leicester) Battalion
Leicester, Head Post Office: HQ 'A' Company, 13 (25 GPO) Battalion
Leicester, 410 Hinckley Road: HQ 'B' Company, 3 (West Leicester) Battalion, 1941
Leicester, Hinckley Road, Westcotes School: HQ 'E' Company, 3 (W Leicester) Battalion, 1941–4
Leicester, Highcross Street: railway club, indoor 0.22-inch rifle range
Leicester, Humberston Lido: HQ 1 Battalion and armoury
Leicester, London Road, Old Horse Hotel: 101 (227M) ZAA Battery Stores
Leicester, 148a London Road: 101 (227M) ZAA Battery office
Leicester, 66 London Road: HQ 'B' Company, 13 (25 GPO) Battalion
Leicester, The Magazine: Zone HQ and HQ 4 (Central Leicester) Battalion
Leicester, 19 Magazine Square: HQ 3 (West Leicester) Battalion, 1941–4
Leicester, Narborough Road, Lockheed Brake Co.: HQ 'F' Company, 3 (West Leicester) Battalion,
    1941–4
Leicester, Regent Road, Wyggeston Girls' School: HQ 'F' Company, 4 (Central Leicester) Battalion
Leicester, Western Park Pavilion: HQ 'B' Company, West Leicester Battalion, 1940
Leicester, University College: HQ 'A' Company, 2 (South Leicester) Battalion, 1941
Loughborough, BRUSH Works: HQ 'D' Company, Loughborough Battalion, 1940
Loughborough, Corporation Gas Works: HQ 'E' Company 9 (Loughborough) Battalion
Loughborough, Drill Hall: HQ 9 (Loughborough) Battalion
Loughborough, Electricity Works: HQ 'E' Company, Loughborough Battalion, 1940
Loughborough, Emmanuel Hall: HQ and 'A' Companies, 9 (Loughborough) Battalion
Loughborough, Old Drill Hall: Granby Street, HQ & 'B' Companies, 9 (Loughborough) Battalion
Loughborough, Morris' South Works: HQ 'D' Company, 9 (Loughborough) Battalion
Loughborough, Town Hall: HQ Loughborough Battalion, 1940
Loughborough, 59 Woodgate: HQ 'A' Company, Loughborough Battalion, 1940
Lutterworth, Staging Camp: HQ Lutterworth Company, Market Harborough Battalion, 1940
Lutterworth, Bank Street, Bray & Bray: HQ 'B' Company, 7(Market Harborough) Battalion
Market Harborough, 2 St Mary's Road: HQ 7 (Market Harborough) Battalion
Market Harborough, 33 St Mary's Road: HQ 'A' Company, 7 (Market Harborough) Battalion
Market Harborough, 44 High Street: HQ Market Harborough Battalion, 1940
Market Harborough, Symington's Factory: Company HQ, Market Harborough Battalion, 1940

Markfield, Memorial & Miners' Welfare Hall: HQ 18 Platoon, 3 Battalion, 1940

Melton Mowbray, Bank Chambers: HQ No. 6 Company, Melton Mowbray Battalion, 1940

Melton Mowbray, 31 Nottingham Street: HQ 5 (Belvoir) Battalion

Melton Mowbray, Remount Depot: HQ 6 (Quorn) Battalion

Melton Mowbray, Sandy Lane, 'Gartree': HQ 'E' Company, 6 (Quorn) Battalion

Melton Mowbray, Wymondham House: HQ No. 2 Company, Melton Mowbray Battalion, 1940

Mountsorrel Drill Hall: HQ Charnwood Battalion, 1940

Narbrough, Empirestone Hall: HQ 'C' Company, 3 (West Leicester) Battalion, 1940

Oadby, 31 Grosvenor Crescent: HQ 'D' Company, South Leicester Battalion, 1940

Oadby, London Road, Midland Bank: HQ 'D' Company, 2 (South Leicester) Battalion, 1941

Oadby, The White Hotel: HQ 2 (South Leicester) Battalion, 1941–4

Oakham, Penn Street, Drill Hall: Zone HQ and HQ 1 Battalion Rutland Home Guard

Old Dalby, Tiptree Cottage: HQ No. 3 Company, Melton Mowbray Battalion, 1940

Quorn, Leicester Road, 'Sunnyside': Garrison HQ, as per Quorn Defence Plan, 1942

Quorn, LNER Station, porters' room: Battle HQ, as per Quorn Defence Plan, 1942

Quorn, The Grange: HQ Western Company, Charnwood Battalion, 1940

Ragdale Hall: HQ No. 4 Company, Melton Mowbray Battalion, 1940

Ratby, Martinshaw Wood: purpose-built grenade range

Rothley, The Coppice: HQ 10 (Charnwood) Battalion

Rothley, The Temple: HQ 'D' Company, 10 (Charnwood) Battalion

Shepshed, Belton Road, 'Haunted Castle': HQ 'B' Company, Loughborough Battalion, 1940

Six Hills: army rifle range (SK663211)

Slawston, Othorpe House: HQ 'E' Company, 7 (Market Harborough) Battalion

Snarestone, Globe Inn: HQ No. 4 Company, Ashby-de-la-Zouch Battalion, 1940

South Wigston, Canal Street, Orson Wright's: HQ 'B' Company, 2 (South Leicester) Battalion

Sutton Cheney, Old Vicarage: HQ 'B' Company, 8 (Market Bosworth) Battalion

Sysonby Lodge: HQ 'C' Company, 5 (Belvoir) Battalion

Thurmaston, Manor House: HQ 'B' Company, 1 (North Leicester) Battalion, 1941–4

Thurnby, The Lodge: HQ No. 7 Company, Melton Mowbray Battalion, 1940

Tur Langton, Langton House: HQ East Norton Company, Market Harborough Battalion, 1940

Tur Langton, The Paddocks: HQ 'C' Company, 7 (Market Harborough) Battalion

Twyford: HQ 'B' Company, 6 (Quorn) Battalion

Whitwick Monastery: Home Guard training camp

Wigston, 139 Station Road: HQ 'B' Company, South Leicester Battalion, 1940

Woodhouse Eaves, The Schools: HQ 'E' Company, 10 (Charnwood) Battalion

Woodhouse Eaves, 'Maplehurst': HQ Forest Company, Charnwood Battalion, 1940

Intelligence and Communications

Second World War

Barrow-on-Soar: 'The Lodge', 'Southfields', 'The Mount', and 'Soar House', all billets for War Office 'Y' Group ATS operators.
Beaumanor Hall: No. 6 War Office Intelligence School
Beaumanor Hall: base for War Office 'Y' Group (WOYG) from 1939
Garats Hay: house plus Nissen huts used as barracks for Army 'Y' Service personnel
Gumley Hall: SOE Operational School (STS 41)
Leicester, University: BBC 'H' Transmitter for emergency broadcasts
Leicester, Swain Street Workhouse: BBC 'H' Transmitter for emergency broadcasts
Loughborough, Fearon Hall: 'Y' Service Special Operator Advanced ATS training
Oaks in Charnwood, St Joseph's Field (SK464163): outstation of RAF No. 80 (Signals) Wing, officially listed as Coalville
Quorn: War Office 'Y' Group HQ
Quorn, Old Bulls Head: 'The Towers', 'The Hurst', 'Rose Cottage', 'May Cottage', all billets for War Office 'Y' Group ATS operators
Woodhouse Eaves: 'Brand Hill', camp for War Office 'Y' Group ATS operators

Post-Second World War

Beaumanor Hall and Garats Hay: Intelligence Corps barracks, 1945 to late 1980s
Copt Oak: microwave tower 'Backbone' (SK484128)
Oakham: microwave relay tower 'Backbone' (SK830089)
Twycross: microwave tower 'Backbone' (SK303081)
Bardon Hill: Home Office 'Hilltop' radio station (SK460132)
Skeffington: Glebe Farm, Home Office 'Hilltop' radio station (SK739035)
North Luffenham: foreign language intercept courses for RAF and RN personnel

Air Defence

HAA Sites (with associated Searchlight Sites)

Anstey (H5), SK563068

Syston (H6), SK625103

Enderby (H3), SP552999

Thurnby (H1), SK645027

Searchlight Sites (32 AA Brigade)

Lutterworth, SP551854

Swinford, SP572794

Walton Lodge, SP600852

Husbands Bosworth, SP645850

Saltby airfield was HQ for the group containing Stretton, Stathern, and Thorpe Arnold

Leicester's sites included Wigston Road (Oadby), Thurmaston, and Western Park.

Royal Observer Corps Posts

Known to have been *destroyed* or extant ||

Billesdon:	1. opened 1948 at SK717023
	|2.| resite 1959 at SK716022
Birstall:	1. open 1937 at SK599097
	2. resite 1943 at 585084
	3. resite 1953 at 590107
|Bottesford|:	open 1953 at SK813396
|Buckminster|:	open 1949 at SK873224
Cold Overton/*Whissendine*/*Langham*:	1. open 1949 at *Langham* SK833122
	2. resite to *Whissendine* at SK842147
	|3.| resite to Cold Overton at SK806097
|Coleorton|:	open 1954 at SK387164
Empingham (R):	open 1939 at *SK946095*
Fleckney:	1. open 1937 at *SP641937*
	2. resite at *SP638932*
|Harby|:	open 1948 at SK754306
Hathern/Shepshed:	1. open 1937 at Shepshed SK437194
	2. resite at Hathern SP495218
Lutterworth:	1. open 1937 at SP535848

	2. resite 1953 at SP520855
Markfield:	1. open 1937 at SK485097
	2. resite 1940 at SK487103
	|3.| resite 1961 at SK500092
|Melton Mowbray|:	1. open 1948 at *SK750206*
	2. resite 1954 at SK742214
Rearsby:	open 1940 at SK663138
Stoke Golding:	open 1937 at *SP398968*;
Thurlaston/Croft:	1. open 1937 at Thurlaston SP489990
	2. renamed Croft 1953
Twycross:	open 1937 at *SK329061*
Uppingham (R):	open 1949 at *SK856992*
Wymeswold:	open 1937 at SK616236

Bloodhound Mark 1 Surface-to-Air Guided Missiles, 1960–63

RAF North Luffenham (Tactical Control Centre)
RAF Woolfox Lodge (SAGW site for sixteen missiles)

Munitions Production and Depots

First World War

Asfordby: proofing range, 1918

Leicester: Army Remount Depot, 1915

Leicester, Belgrave Road: British United Shoe Machinery Co.—high-angle AA 1 and 2-pounder pom-poms

Leicester, Belgrave Gate: Tramways Depot made 6-inch shells (including gas shells)

Loughborough: Brush Coachworks Ltd and Electrical Engineering Company built aircraft

Market Harborough: Army Remount Depot, 1915

Melton Mowbray: Army Remount Depot, 1915

Second World War

Asfordby: proofing range reopened 1938–45 and 1969–71

Blaby Wharf: RAF No. 65 Maintenance Unit

Bottesford: No. 17 RASC Petrol Depot

Essendine: Park Farm, RAF ammunition park

Gaddesby Hall: (Depot 0-690/Station 520) temporary USAAF bomb dump/truck depot

Great Dalby: USAAF Main Ammunition Storage Depot, 1943

Garendon Hall: No. 15 Base ASD (Army) also accommodated RAF explosives

Leicester, Glenfield, New Parks: No. 8 AFV and No. 36 Reserve Vehicle Depots

Leicester: IL Berridge & Co. Ltd, parts for Lee-Enfield rifles

Leicester, Belgrave Road: British United Shoe Machinery Co., Lee-Enfield rifle parts

Leicester, Knighton Fields Road East: Co-op Shoe factory licensed for Bren guns

Leicester, Stoughton Street: Taylor, Taylor & Hobson made optical equipment for gun- and bomb-sights

Leicester, Vulcan Road: Gimson & Co. made parts for Lee-Enfield rifles

Leicester: General Presswork & Stampings made parts for Lee-Enfield rifles

Leicester: North Bridge Engineering made parts for Lee-Enfield rifles

Leicester, St Margarets: Corah Works, Admiralty Victualling Stores

Leicester, Ulverscroft Road: Army salvage depot

Leicester: US Army central Quartermasters Stores depot

Loughborough: Ministry of Food Coldstore

Old Dalby: vehicle depot from 1939, REME from 1942

Queniborough: Royal Ordnance Factory, National Filling Factory No. 10

Redmile: Army and RAF fuel depots either side of canal

Saxelbye Park: No. 15 ASD (Army) sub-site stored small arms ammunition for RAF

Shepshed: Ministry of Food Storage Depot

Stonesby: RAF Fuel Depot, opened after the war had ended

Waltham on the Wolds: military hut storage

Cold War Installations

Leicester Civil Defence HQ, 1951–68, 50 Belvoir Street
Loughborough, Sub-RHQ 3.2 Government bunker

Local Authority Bunkers

Leicestershire County Hall, Glenfield; former Melton District Council offices, Nottingham Road, Melton Mowbray; Charnwood District Council offices, Loughborough.

MAFF Depots

336H and J: New Street, Earl Shilton
336K: Little Glen Road, Glen Parva
336M: Humberstone Lane, Thurmaston, Leicester
336P: New Unit 70, 10 Romany Way, Market Harborough
Memory Lane, Belgrave Gate, Leicester
47 Station Road, Castle Donington

APPENDIX XII

Hospitals

First World War

(affiliated to 5th Northern General Hospital, RAMC, TF, Leicester)

Ashby-de-la-Zouch Cottage Hospital
Belvoir Castle
Billesdon, Workhouse (demolished 1935)
Brooksby Hall
Burley-on-the-Hill
Charnwood Forest VAD Hospital
Coalville VAD Hospital
Dalby Hall
Desford Hall VAD Hospital
Foremark Hall
Gilroes Hospital, Leicester
Glen Parva Barracks, military hospital at regimental depot
Hambleton Hall
Knighton House VAD Hospital
Leicester, Newarke: office, 5th Northern General Hospital RAMC
Leicester, Victoria Road, 5th Northern General Hospital
Leicester, Frith Home of Recovery
Leicester, Gwendolen Road: North Evington War Hospital
Leicester Royal Infirmary
Leicester, Swain Street Auxiliary Hospital in part of Workhouse
Loughborough General Hospital
Lutterworth VAD Hospital
Manton Grange
Market Harborough VAD Hospital
Melton Mowbray, Wicklow Lodge Hospital
Stapleford Park
Tolethorpe Hall, Queen Mary's Needlework Guild, working parties for hospital depot
Ullesthorpe Court, VAD Hospital
Wing, The Grange, hospitality for convalescent soldiers
Wistow Hall

Second World War

Billesdon, Rolleston Hall Red Cross Convalescent Home/Auxiliary Hospital
Brooksby Hall, Red Cross Convalescent Home/Auxiliary Hospital
Burley-on-the-Hill, Red Cross hospital
Dingley Hall, Red Cross Convalescent Home/Auxiliary Hospital
Hambleton Hall, Convalescent Home
Langton Hall, Red Cross Convalescent Home/Auxiliary Hospital
Loughborough, RAF Medical Rehabilitation Centre
Lowesby Hall, Red Cross Convalescent Home/Auxiliary Hospital
Oadby, The Yews Red Cross Convalescent Home/Auxiliary Hospital
Peatling Hall, Red Cross Convalescent Home/Auxiliary Hospital
Quorn House, sub-Depot of Leicester & Leicestershire Hospital Supply Depot
Stapleford Park, Red Cross Convalescent Home/Auxiliary Hospital

Prisoner of War Camps

First World War

Ashby-de-la-Zouch, Queen's Head Hotel
Castle Donington, German Officers Camp
Glenfield
Hinckley
Houghton-on-the-Hill
Illston-on-the-Hill
Kegworth Officers' Camp
Leicester, 5th Northern General and North Evington Hospitals
Long Clawson Hall
Loughborough, The Workhouse
Market Harborough, No. 2 Depot
Market Harborough, Haughton Lodge
Melton Mowbray, Croxton Park
Melton Mowbray, Thorpe Satchville
Narborough, The Workhouse
Normanton Hall
North Kilworth, The Hawthorns
Ragdale Hall
Wymondham

Second World War

No. 94 Billesdon, Gaultby Road (now Billesdon Woodland Pool)
Edmondthorpe Hall
No. 28 Garendon Park
No. 590 Hathern Camp, Pear Tree Lane
No. 616 Leicester, Barkby Lane Camp
No. 167, Leicester, Stoughton, Shady Lane Camp
No. 28 Loughborough, Knighthorpe Camp
No. 49 Market Harborough, Farndon Road Camp
No. 613 Melton Mowbray, Old Dalby Lane
Old Dalby Central Ordnance Depot, working parties
Nos 9 and 183 Wood Lane, Quorndon for Italian and later German POWs
No. 4 Scraptoft Camp
No. 152 Shepshed, Old Liberal Club

Bibliography

Books

Aberg, F. A., *Medieval Moated Sites* (York: CBA Research Report 17, 1978)

Beazley, B., *Wartime Leicester* (Leicester: Leicester Mercury, 2004)

Bennett, M., *Lord Loughborough, Ashby-de la Zouch, and the English Civil War* (Ashby: Ashby-de-la-Zouch Museum, 1984)

Bonser, R., *Aviation in Leicestershire and Rutland* (Hinckley: Midland Publishing, 2001)

Bowyer, M., *Action Stations 6: Cotswolds & Central Midlands* (Wellingborough: Patrick Stephens, 1983)

Brown, A. E., (ed.) *Roman Small Towns in Eastern England and Beyond* (Oxford: Oxbow, 1995)

Brown, R. A., Colvin, H.M., & Taylor, A.J., *The History of the King's Works Volume II The Middle Ages* (London: HMSO, 1963)

Brownlow, J., *Melton Mowbray Queen of the Shires* (Wymondham: Sycamore Press, 1980)

Buckley, R., and Lucas, J., *Leicester Town Defences, Excavations 1958–74* (Leicester: Leicestershire Museums Service, 1987)

Cantor, L., *The Mediaeval Castles of Leicestershire* (Leicester: Transactions of the Leicestershire Archaeological & Historical Society 53, 1978)

Cartwright, T. C., *Birds Eye Wartime Leicestershire 1939-1945* (Wigston: TCC Publications, 2002)

Clough, T., *The Riding School of the Rutland Fencible Cavalry* (Oakham: Rutland Local History and Record Society, Rutland Record No. 15, 1995)

Cocroft, W., and Thomas R., *Cold War, Building for Nuclear Confrontation 1946–89* (Swindon: English Heritage, 2003)

Cornwall, J. (ed.), *Tudor Rutland, the County Community under Henry VIII* (Oakham: Rutland Local History and Record Society, 1980)

Courtney, P., and Courtney, Y., *A Siege Examined: The Civil War Archaeology of Leicester* (London: Post Mediaeval Archaeology 26, 1992)

Creighton, O., *Castles and Landscapes* (London: Equinox, 2002); *Early Castles in the Mediaeval Landscape of Rutland* (Leicester: Transactions of the Leicestershire Archaeological & Historical Society 73, 1999); *Early Leicestershire Castles: Archaeology and Landscape History* (Leicester: Transactions of the Leicestershire Archaeological & Historical Soc. 71, 1997); *The Mediaeval Castles of Rutland* (Oakham: Rutland Local History and Record Society, Rutland Record No. 20, 2000)

Crisp, G., *The Supply of Explosives and Ammunition to the RAF in WW2* (Thetford: Airfield Research Group, Airfield Review No. 124, 2009)

Delve, K., *The Military Airfields of Britain: East Midlands* (Ramsbury: Crowood, 2008)

Forsyth, M., *The History of Bradgate* (Leicester: The Bradgate Park Trust, 1974)

Francis, P., *Airfield Defences* (Ware: ARP, AiX-ARG, 2010); *British Military Airfield Architecture* (Yeovil: Patrick Stephens, 1996)

Francis, P., and Crisp, G., *Military Command and Control Organisation* (Swindon: English Heritage, 2008) in Compact Disc format.

Francis, P., Bellamy, P., and Crisp, G., *20th Century Air-Raid Precautions Railway Control Centres* (Ware: Airfield Research Group, 2014) in Compact Disc format.

Goodall, J., *The English Castle 1066–1650* (Newhaven (CT) and London: Yale, 2011)

Hollings, J., *The History of Leicester during the Great Civil War* (Leicester: 1840)

Jones, D., *Summer of Blood, The Peasants' Revolt of 1381* (London: Harpers, 2009)

Kenyon, J. R., *Early Artillery Fortifications in England and Wales: A Preliminary Survey and Reappraisal* (London: Archaeological Journal 138, 1981); *Castles, Town Defences & Artillery Fortifications in the United Kingdom & Ireland: A Bibliography 1945–2006* (Donington: Shaun Tyas, 2008)

Kenyon, K., *Excavations at Breedon on the Hill, 1946* (Leicester: Transactions of the Leicestershire Archaeological & Historical Society 41, 1950)

King, D. J. C., and Alcock, L., *Ringworks of England and Wales* in Taylor, A. J., (ed.) *Chateau Gaillard lll*, 1966 (Chichester: Phillimore, 1969)

Liddiard, R., *Castles in Context* (Macclesfield: Windgather, 2005)

Liddle, P., *Roman Small Towns of Leicestershire* in Brown, A. E., *Roman Small Towns in Eastern England and Beyond*

McCamley, N., *Cold War Secret Nuclear Bunkers* (Barnsley: Pen & Sword, 2002)

McGlynn, S., *Blood Cries Afar: The Forgotten Invasion of England 1216* (Stroud: The History Press, 2011)

Millward, R., *A History of Leicestershire and Rutland* (Chichester: Phillimore, 1985)

Mitchell, R. G., *Provisional List of Moated Sites in Leicestershire* (Leicester: Transactions of the Leicestershire Archaeological & Historical Society 50, 1974–5)

Osborne, M., *20th Century Defences in Britain: The East Midlands* (Market Deeping: Concrete Publications, 2003); *Always Ready: The Drill Halls of Britain's Volunteer Forces* (Leigh-on-Sea: Caliver Books, 2006); *Defending Britain* (Stroud: Tempus, 2004); *Pillboxes in Britain and Ireland* (Stroud: Tempus, 2008); *Sieges and Fortifications of the Civil Wars in Britain* (Leigh-on-Sea: Caliver Books, 2004)

Peers, Sir C., *Kirby Muxloe Castle* (London: HMSO, 1957)

Richardson, M., *Leicester in the Great War* (Barnsley: Pen & Sword, 2014); *The Tigers: 6th, 7th, 8th and 9th (Service) Battalions of the Leicestershire Regiment* (Barnsley: Pen & Sword, 2000)

Ruddy, A. J., *To the Last Round: the Leicestershire and Rutland Home Guard 1940–1945* (Derby: Breedon Books, 2007)

Sheppard, T., *Battling The Beams* (Coalville: Charley Heritage Group, 2014)

Sherwood, R., *The Civil War in the Midlands 1642–1651* (Stroud: Alan Sutton, 1992)

Stocker, D., *England's Landscape: the East Midlands* (London: Collins/EH, 2006)

Taylor, C. C., *Fieldwork in Medieval Archaeology* (London: Harper/Collins 1974); *Moated Sites: Their Definition, Form and Classification* (in Aberg, above)

Thomas, J., and Taylor, J., *Burrough Hill, Leicestershire* (York: British Archaeology 133, CBA, 2013)

Thompson, J., *Leicester Castle* (Leicester: Crossley and Clarke, 1859)

Todd, M., *The Roman Fort at Great Casterton, Rutland* (Nottingham: University of Nottingham, 1968)

Williams, D., *Fortified Manor Houses* (Leicester: Transactions of the Leicestershire Archaeological & Historical Society 50, 1974–5)

Wilshere, J. and Green, S., *The Siege of Leicester: 1645* (Leicester: Chamberlain Music & Books, 1984)

Websites

Airfield Research Group: *www.airfieldresearchgroup.org.uk*
Castle Study Group: *www.castlestudiesgroup.org.uk*
Fortress Study Group: *www.fsgfort.com*
Pillbox Study Group: *www.pillbox-study-group.org.uk*

Subterranea Britannica: *www.subbrit.org.uk*

Harrington Carpetbagger Aviation Museum (list of twentieth-century sites used for military purposes): *www.harringtonmuseum.org.uk/wp-content/uploads/2017/03/premises-sites-etc-within-30-miles-of-harrington-museum*

Other Sources

Hillier, K., personal communication regarding The Mount House, Ashby, 1992

Nichols, N., unpublished list of First World War POW camps

Quorn Village Museum Item No. 1123, *VTC Walking Contest*

Sapcote excavation, 1958 (Transactions of the Leicestershire Archaeological & Historical Society, XXXVI, 1960)

Index